JERUSALEM FROM SOUTHERN SLOPE OF MT. OF OLIVES
LOOKING ACROSS THE KEDRON VALLEY — Matson Photo Service.

THE GOSPEL OF JOHN

Vol. I

Other books in the
BIBLE STUDY TEXTBOOK SERIES

SACRED HISTORY AND GEOGRAPHY
ACTS MADE ACTUAL
ROMANS REALIZED
THE CHURCH IN THE BIBLE
HELPS FROM HEBREWS
THE GLORIOUS CHURCH IN EPHESIANS

BIBLE STUDY TEXTBOOK

THE
GOSPEL OF JOHN, VOL. I

by
PAUL T. BUTLER

A NEW
Commentary
Workbook
Teaching Manual

1961

PROPERTY OF
THE CHURCH ON THE WAY

College Press, Joplin, Missouri

Copyright 1961

Paul T. Butler

LITHOPRINTED IN THE UNITED STATES OF AMERICA BY
CUSHING - MALLOY, INC., ANN ARBOR, MICHIGAN, 1961

THIS VOLUME IS DEDICATED

to

My Lord Jesus Christ Who bought me and

sought me,

to

My beloved Christian father and mother

Drew and Lois,

to

My devoted and cherished wife,

Gale Jynne,

and to

My loving children,

Sherry and Mark

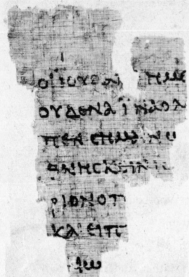
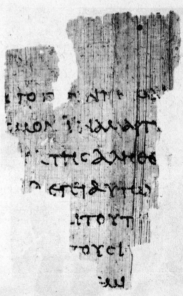

Courtesy of the John Rylands Library,
Manchester, England

This is the Rylands Greek Papyrus 457. It is not two fragments but this picture shows both sides of one fragment. At the present time this is the oldest known manuscript fragment of John's Gospel and is dated about 100-150 A.D. The fragment shows portions of John 18:31-33 and 18:37-38.

TABLE OF CONTENTS

Page

THE GOSPEL OF JOHN

Preface

For nearly nineteen centuries the Gospel according to John has been a tremendous source of testimony for converting the world. This wonderful Gospel has also been a storehouse of strength for the church of Christ. For almost the same length of time innumerable commentaries, translations, and critiques have been written concerning the fourth Gospel.

We entered this work humbly, aware of the great responsibility incumbent upon any who propose to teach God's Word to others (Jas. 3:1ff). We are also humbled when we consider the illustrious and scholarly company with whom we presume to associate ourselves by producing this work on the Gospel of John. In the early years of the Church such distinguished men as Origen wrote commentaries on this particular book. Later scholars have since given equally reputable works on this Gospel. We herewith acknowledge especial indebtedness to B. F. Wescott (who spent 25-30 years in this field), A. T. Robertson, William Hendriksen, R. C. H. Lenski, R. C. Foster, and the many others listed in the Bibliography.

We have not endeavored in this commentary to give to the church another technical, linguistical, and highly critical work. Our aim is to present a book that can be used by Sunday school teacher, preacher, student and layman alike. For those who desire a more technical treatise of the subject, we suggest the works of the aforementioned commentators and those enumerated in the Bibliography.

As excellent as these great works are, however, there are yet new discoveries that need to be incorporated into new commentaries on John. Manuscript discoveries, papyri finds and the recent *Dead Sea Scrolls* have been made available to this generation and were not, of course, available when Wescott, Lenski and others published their works.

We have embodied special studies ("The Kingdom", "Jesus as a Controversialist," etc.), maps, diagrams, outlines and photographs which we hope will both inform and inspire the reader to further study concerning the fourth Gospel.

Grateful acknowledgement is made of the assistance and inspiration of Professors Don DeWelt, Seth Wilson, and Woodrow Phillips, of Ozark Bible College, as they have contributed toward making this commentary possible.

The author further acknowledges with gratitude, the indispensable technical assistance of Mrs. Woodrow (Marjorie) Phillips.

INTRODUCTION

John the Apostle, the writer of the fourth Gospel, has been called "the apostle of love." This is indeed an appropriate title, for John, in both his Gospel and his epistles, dwells extensively and almost exclusively on the love of God as revealed through His Son, Jesus Christ. Clement of Alexandria (190-200 A.D.) said John knew that the other Gospel writers had given the historical data of Christ's life and he (John) was "urged by his friends and inspired by the Spirit" to "compose a *spiritual* gospel."

John's Gospel lends itself to both the profound and the plain. He expounds upon the deepest recesses of the infinite Mind in the simplest language. Although John omits even as much as almost a year's ministry at one place in his record (the period between John 5:47 and 6:1), his account is still the most successively chronological of the four gospels.

Form criticism will not be dealt with in this work. Separate volumes have been written on this subject alone. Neither shall we dwell at length with other introductory material. Our purpose would be defeated by an extended thesis on introductory problems. Furthermore, there are many excellent compositions now available on the precursory problems of John's gospel. A few are mentioned here for reference: *New Testament Commentary,* "the Gospel of John," pp. 3-66, by Wm. Hendriksen; *An Introduction to the Life of Christ* by R. C. Foster; *The Gospel According to John,* pp. 9-195, by B. F. Wescott; not to mention works by Godet, Dodd and Bernard.

WRITER: John, the apostle, the son of Zebedee, brother of James. Usually, two lines of evidence are presented to substantiate the authorship of John the apostle — internal and external.

   a. *Internal evidence:*

     1. The author of this Gospel was a Jew. This is evident by his familiarity with Jewish customs, i.e., weddings, funerals, etc., and with the feasts of the Jews (2:1-10; 11:38, 44; 19:40; 6:4; 13:1; 7:2; 10:22). He was a Jew of Palestine, for he knew the topography of Palestine as only

THE GOSPEL OF JOHN

one who had lived there all his life could know it (1:28, 3:23; 4:11; 5:2; 11:18, etc.)

2. The writer of the fourth Gospel was an eyewitness. He was very observant: he saw that Jesus was tired when He sat by the well in Sychar (4:6); he observed that it was even the *right* ear of Malchus which Peter slashed off (18:10). He was one of the Twelve. This is definitely shown by the fact that he was in the upper room at that last fateful Passover (13:23). His very intimate knowledge would indicate that the writer of this account was one of the "inner circle" three — James, Peter or John. Peter is distinguished by the author by name; James had suffered martyrdom long before the writing of this account; this leaves us unable to escape the conclusion that John, "the disciple whom Jesus loved, who also leaned on his breast at supper," was the writer of this fourth Gospel (cf. 21:20 and 21:4).

b. *External evidence:*

1. There are passages from the earliest writings of the Church Fathers which clearly indicate a knowledge of John's Gospel: Clement of Rome (96 A.D.), the Shepherd of Hermas (100 A.D.), the *Didache* (110 A.D.), *The Epistle of Barnabas* (130 A.D.), and a few others.

2. There is incontrovertible evidence from other writers closely connected with the apostolic age as to the authorship of John. Tatian (170 A.D.), a pupil of Justin Martyr, included John in his *Harmony* of the Gospels. Irenaeus (185 A.D.), who was a pupil of Polycarp — who was in turn a direct disciple of John — reports that John, the disciple who lay upon the Lord's breast, published the fourth Gospel while he was in Ephesus of Asia Minor.

3. Even the heretics and unbelievers attest to the authorship of John the Apostle. Tatian became a heretic after the death of his teacher Justin Martyr. Celsus (178 A.D.), the Clementine *Homilies* (160 A.D.), even Marcion, the Gnostic, quotes from it (130 A.D.) *If these heretics could have established that this Gospel was non-apostolic, they would certainly have done so!*

4. The Muratorian fragment, an incomplete list of New Testament books (180-200 A.D.) gives testimony to the fact that John, one of the disciples, was the author of the fourth Gospel.

12

THE GOSPEL OF JOHN

BY WAY OF EXPLANATION: The peculiar form which this commentary takes needs a brief explanation. Since this book is designed for use in the home as well as in the classroom, certain features have been incorporated which are foreign to other commentaries.

a. *Text:* The American Standard Version. This remains, in the opinion of most scholars, the best translation available today. We recommend, however, that the student not be enslaved by one translation. Compare as many versions as are available.

b. *Queries:* Designed to excite the intellect of the reader to immediate curiosity. The mind must be actively interested as information is being received, else the mind will not retain or grow.

c. *Paraphrase:* A rendering of the literal sense of the text. We have used the Greek text (Nestle) compared with numerous translations and versions at our disposal in an effort to translate the original text into the modern idiom.

15

THE GOSPEL OF JOHN

d. *Summary:* We have endeavored here to put   the reader the kernel, or the heart of the text. One of the basic rules for interpretation of any book, Bible or otherwise, is to seek to understand what the *author* intends to say.

e. *Comment:* An amplification of the text. Our exegesis is aimed not only at understanding the text, but also toward application to life wherever possible.

f. *Quiz:* Questions on the text as amplified by the Comments with a view toward letting the reader test himself as to knowledge of the text gained. These questions also serve as a future aid for one who desires to use this book to teach the fourth Gospel.

g. *Additional features:* At the end of each chapter, one or more *expository sermon outlines* will be found for the chapter as a whole or parts of the chapter. The *maps* and outline of the life of Christ are included as one of the best means to memorize a chronological life of Christ. Of course, some of the places on this series of maps must remain arbitrary. In order to facilitate memorization, however, we have conjecturally located certain places incident to the travels of Jesus in Palestine. Included at appropriate intervals are *special studies* to aid the student's grasp of this wonderful Gospel "according to John."

We now commend you to a serious and prayerful study of the Word of Life as revealed in the fourth Gospel. Our prayer is that you may gain higher experiences in faith and eventually eternal life through your committment to Him.

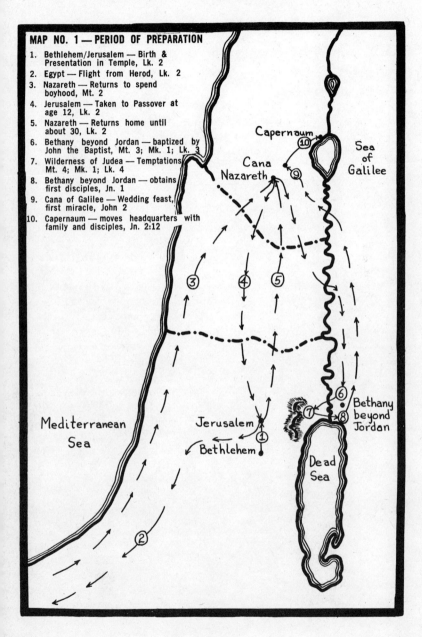

MAP NO. 1 — PERIOD OF PREPARATION

1. Bethlehem/Jerusalem — Birth & Presentation in Temple, Lk. 2
2. Egypt — Flight from Herod, Lk. 2
3. Nazareth — Returns to spend boyhood, Mt. 2
4. Jerusalem — Taken to Passover at age 12, Lk. 2
5. Nazareth — Returns home until about 30, Lk. 2
6. Bethany beyond Jordan — baptized by John the Baptist, Mt. 3; Mk. 1; Lk. 3
7. Wilderness of Judea — Temptations, Mt. 4; Mk. 1; Lk. 4
8. Bethany beyond Jordan — obtains first disciples, Jn. 1
9. Cana of Galilee — Wedding feast, first miracle, John 2
10. Capernaum — moves headquarters with family and disciples, Jn. 2:12

Capernaum

Cana
Nazareth

Sea
of
Galilee

Mediterranean
Sea

Jerusalem

Bethlehem

Bethany
beyond
Jordan

Dead
Sea

CHAPTER ONE

The first eighteen verses of the Gospel according to John contain an abridgment of what John intends to record in detail in the body of his Gospel. First he describes the pre-existent nature of the Word with the Father. Then he briefly relates how the Word became flesh and manifested Himself among men. Some men hated and rejected Him, while others loved and accepted Him. We shall outline the Prologue thus:

I The Prologue, 1:1-18, an abridged history of the earthly ministry of the Word
- A. The Pre-existence of the Word described, 1:1-5
    1. Co-existent, v. 1, 2
    2. Co-equal, v. 3-5
- B. The Word manifested to the Jews, and their rejection of Him, 1:6-11
    1. John the Baptist's witness for Him, v. 6-8
    2. His own witness rejected, v. 9-11
- C. The Word manifested to others, and their acceptance of Him, 1:12-18
    1. The spiritual reborn made children of God, v. 12-13
    2. These beheld the glory of God in Him, and recognized the grace of God in Him, v. 14-18.

THE PRE-EXISTENCE OF THE WORD DESCRIBED

Text 1:1-5

1 In the beginning was the Word, and the Word was with God, and the Word was God.
2 The same was in the beginning with God.
3 All things were made through him; and without him was not anything made that hath been made.
4 In him was life; and the life was the light of men.
5 And the light shineth in the darkness; and the darkness apprehended it not.

19

Queries

a. Who is the Word?
b. What relationship does the Word have to God?
c. Is the Word a created person, or is He Creator?
d. In verse 4 John uses the past tense, "was". Does this mean that "life" and "light" no longer exist in the Word?
e. What is the darkness?

Paraphrase

When the cosmos was created, the Word was already existent, and the Word was equal, intimate, and face to face with God. This same person was existing eternally in the bosom of the Father. All things came into existence through him, and separate from him not one thing was created that has been created. In the Word was the very essence of all life; and the life was the source of illumination for men. And this light is shining in the darkness and the darkness appropriated or perceived it not.

Summary

The Word (the expression of God), Jesus Christ, existed eternally with God. The Word was co-equal with God. The co-existent and co-equal Word was the agency with the Father in the creation of the universe. In the Word is the source of Life and Illumination. The Darkness does not wish to appropriate the True Light.

Comment

Our finite minds cannot comprehend eternity. John is condescending to our level of understanding. He gives us a point in time (the beginning) from which to reflect upon the eternal existence of the Word. All other things came into being, but the Godhead has enjoyed timeless existence. Jesus said the same thing in John 8:58 . . . "before Abraham came *(genesthai* — was begotten), I am *(eimi* — timeless existence)." Jesus also laid claim to pre-existence with the Father in His high priestly prayer, John 17:5.

The discerning reader will notice that John makes no argument for the existence of God. He boldly assumes that God does exist — just as the writer of Genesis (Gen. 1:1) begins by assuming the existence of God. Either God exists and is Creator of the cosmos — or the universe just happened!

What is the *Logos* (Word)? Probably the best way to define
the Word is to say that in the Word we see the expression of the
mind and the thought and the purpose of God. Just as our
thoughts and purposes are made known when we communicate
through words (Matt. 15:18), God's ageless purposes are made
known through His Word. cf. Heb. 1:1-2; Matt. 11:25-30;
John 5:19-20.

How is the Word "with God"? The Greek word translated
"with" is the word *pros*. As John used it here and other places
it represents equality and intimacy. The *Logos* was "face to face
with God"; He was "in the bosom of the Father" (v. 18), and
was "on an equality with God" (Phil. 2:6). There was perfect
fellowship (sharing) by the Father and the Word. The same
Greek word *pros* is used in I John 2:1 . . . "we have an Advocate
(face to face, intimately, etc.,) with the Father."

"And the Word was God" means that the *Logos* is of the
very essence and nature of God. As the writer of Hebrews expresses it . . . "the effulgence of his glory, and the very image
of his substance," (Heb. 1:3a). Paul wrote to the Colossians
that "in him dwelleth all the fulness of the Godhead bodily,"
(Col. 2:9).

When we understand that Jesus existed eternally in such a
state of oneness with the Father, we begin to understand that
God *was* and *is* always like Jesus Christ (minus His earthly body,
of course). Certain sects would teach today that Jesus Christ did
something to change God's attitude toward men. Jesus changed
a God of wrath in the Old Testament, they say, to a God of love
in the New Testament. Nothing could be more foreign to the
entire Bible. God has always been, and still is, a merciful, graceful and loving God (Heb. 13:8). Jesus Christ came to change
men's hearts and attitudes toward God!

In verse 3 of our text we have the astounding information
that the Word was the exclusive agent in the creation of our
universe. Whether John wrote this Prologue to combat Gnosticism
or not is a moot question. Be that as it may, this Prologue does
refute Gnosticism and many other "isms." The Gnostics were
an heretical sect arising at the very time some of the Apostles
were still alive. They believed and taught that matter is evil, and
only spirit is good. God is spirit, therefore God Himself could
not have created the world. Their philosophy was that God, at
some time or another, sent forth successive emanations from
Himself. Each successive emanantion was further away from,

more ignorant of, and more hostile toward the Eternal Being. At long last there came an emanantion (the "Demiurge") far enough removed from God that it could create evil matter, and God would be free of the taint of evil. Accept their absurdities and one must conclude that this world was created by a being who is ignorant of and hostile to, the One True God!

On the other hand, John's doctrine of the creation is the most reasonable. The *Logos* is the expression of the purposes and mind of God. The *Logos* enjoyed perfect fellowship with the Father. The *Logos* was the exclusive agency in the creation. Therefore, creation is an expression of the mind of the One True God. Jesus manifested the attitude of God . . . an attitude of infinite love. Matter is *not* evil! This universe is *not* antagonistic toward God! Of a truth, man's sin turns God's beauty into ugliness; man's foolishness turns God's gifts into instruments of his own destruction. This world was designed for man's good, but alas, man has abused it.

Other Scriptures testify that Jesus was Creator and is now Sustainer of our universe. Cf. Col. 1:15-17; Heb. 1:1-4; Gen. 1:26. JESUS IS THE GOD WHOM WE WORSHIP! Any church or organization that does not honor Jesus Christ as Deity does not honor the One God! "He that honoreth not the Son honoreth not the Father that sent him" (John 5:23b).

Verse 4 informs us that in the *Logos* was, and is, that unfathomable essence called LIFE. The Greek word *zoe* means "the very principle or essence of life." Jesus Christ not only created the universe, but He imparted to it life. This Life also includes "eternal life." Here is one place where science must humbly acknowledge its limitations. Science may be able to synthesize the elements until it comes near to composing a body — human or animal. But it cannot give that body life. It was the Godhead that created the body of man from the dust of the earth, and it was also the Godhead that "breathed into his nostrils the breath of life; and man became a living soul" (Gen. 2:7). Paul said, "in him we live and move and have our being" (Acts 17:28a). There is the answer to that impenetrable substance called LIFE. Science cannot furnish the answer. The famous Theory of Relativity and Einstein's formula revealed to us that our universe was created and does now subsist from the power or energy that is within the atom. But where does that power and energy come from? Hebrews 1:3b tells us that the Son is "upholding all things *by the word of his power.*" As the Psalmist also said, "By the

word of Jehovah were the heavens made, and all the host of them
by the breath of his mouth." Cf. Psa. 33:6-7; 148:5. Philosophy,
history and science cannot search it out. God's Word reveals it,
and this is all that anyone can know about Life!

Jesus gave many discourses on the Eternal Life that was His
to give to men and how He would give it. Cf. John 5:21, 26;
6:50-65; 10:1; 11:25-26, etc. The Lord also attested His authority to dispense this inscrutable substance when He reinvested
the decaying body of Lazarus with life. Cf. also His raising of
the widow's son at Nain (Lk. 7:11ff) and the raising of Jairus'
daughter (Mk. 5:2ff).

In the phrase "the life was the light of men," John uses the
Greek Imperfect tense for "was," which means continued action
in past time. The best commentary on this would be Peter's
indication that Christ by His Spirit illuminated the prophets of the
Old Testament period (and consequently all Israel), cf. I Pet.
1:10-11.

One author says that this phrase is interchangable. "The light
was the life of men" is also true. Life, when it is revealed,
becomes light. Power turned into electricity and made manifest
becomes light. Christ, the Power of God and the Word of God
manifested for us truth, love, knowledge, life and light. His
light is a revealing light. It reveals man as he really is. It also
reveals the love of God which is able to change man into what
he ought to be. His light is a guiding light that leads man through
the darkness of sin, ignorance error and death. Cf. Psa. 119:1,
2, 105; Prov. 6:23.

In the fifth verse, as may be noted from the paraphrase, the
word "shining" is in the present tense . . . continuing action. The
Light which illuminated men of old keeps on giving light. John
wrote in his first epistle, " . . . the darkness is passing away, and
the true light is already shining" (I Jn. 2:8b). The Life and
Light existed when the Spirit of Christ abode in the prophets of
old and shone forth. It existed in Jesus of Nazareth when God
became incarnate, and it shone forth. Life and Light is now
shining forth through the inspired Word of the apostles, and the
lives of men and women who have this Word "written and
engraven on their hearts."

There seem to be two schools of interpretation on the fifth
verse. Darkness, in John's writings, is synonymous with ignorance, hate, error, sin and death. So light is synonymous with
knowledge, love, truth, holiness and life. Here John records that

the Light is shining in the darkness and the darkness did not apprehend *(katelaben)* it. Some would translate the Greek word "overcome or overtake," while others say it means "apprehend or appropriate."

The first interpretation would have John mean that the darkness warred with the Light and made strong attempts to overcome the Light (John 12:35). Yet the Light kept on shining in spite of the darkness.

The second interpretation, which we have chosen in our paraphrase, seems to fit the context better. John seems to be speaking of the same Light and the same rejection and failure to appropriate in 1:9-11. Evil and darkness will, by its very nature, actively oppose truth and light and thus refuse to perceive it.

If darkness is opposed to all truth, opposed to all good, love and holiness, what then shall be the lot of those who are going to be sentenced to ETERNITY in "outer darkness"? For the redeemed, "the glory of God will lighten" the heavenly city . . . there will be no more sin, pain, tears, mourning or death. "And there shall be night no more; and they need no light of lamp, neither light of sun; for the Lord God shall give them light: and they shall reign for ever and ever" (Rev. 22:5). What do YOU want for yourself and others? Eternal LIGHT with God, or eternal DARKNESS with Satan and his angels?

Quiz

1. When was the Word in relationship to time?
2. What is a good definition of *Logos*?
3. How does v. 1-3 refute the Gnostic philosophy?
4. Where does life, in essence, originate?
5. Name two things light does as "the light of men."
6. How do you think the darkness "apprehended not" the light?

THE WORD MANIFESTED TO THE JEWS — THEIR REJECTION OF HIM

Text 1:6-11

6 There came a man, sent from God, whose name was John.

7 The same came for witness, that he might bear witness of the light, that all might believe through him.

8 He was not the light, but came that he might bear witness of the light.

24

9 There was the true light, even the light which lighteth every man, coming into the world.

10 He was in the world, and the world was made through him, and the world knew him not.

11 He came unto his own, and they that were his own received him not.

Queries

a. Which John is meant in verse 6?
b. How could "all . . . believe through him"?
c. Who is the "true light"?
d. Who are "his own"?

Paraphrase

There came a man with a commission and message from God; this man's name was John. John came for the purpose of giving testimony to what he had heard and seen concerning the Light. John's witness was given in order that all might come to believe on the Light through him. John was not the Light, but came for the express purpose of pointing out the genuine Light. The perfect Light, which reveals God to every man who will receive the revelation, was coming into the world. The Light was in the world prior to His incarnation, and the world which was made through Him testified to Him, but the world would not recognize Him. He came incarnate unto His own nation, and they that were His own peculiar people rejected Him.

Summary

John was not the Light, but was sent purposely to point out the Light. Even when the Light was manifested in the flesh, those who should have received Him rejected Him.

Comment

The Greek word for "sent" used here is *apostello,* from which we get our word "apostle." It usually means "one sent with a commission." *John* is a Hellenized form of *Jonathan,* which means gift of God. There is a great similarity between John and his Old Testament namesake. Both he and Jonathan gave up a great glory that could have been theirs in order that God's Anointed might have the pre-eminence. With Jonathan, it was David; with John the Baptist, it was Christ. Whenever the name John is used in the fourth Gospel it is always used to refer to

John the Baptist. The name of "John the son of Zebedee" is never mentioned.

Do you wonder why the Gospel writer would have to point out that John the Baptist was not the True Light? John had a tremendous following (Matt. 3:5). Many persons believed John to be the Christ (Lk. 3:15; Jn. 1:19). John even had disciples long after Christ had ascended, and in Ephesus, the very city where John was writing his Gospel account (Acts 19:1-3). In spite of the Baptist's continual affirmation that he was not the Christ, it was necessary to emphasize that Jesus Christ was the True Light. There were "preacher lovers" when John the Evangelist wrote his Gospel (I Cor. 1:12-13). John the Baptist's unfeigned humility in seeking to decrease and let Jesus increase prompted Jesus to remark, "Verily I say unto you, among them that are born of women, there hath not arisen a greater than John the Baptist" (Matt. 11:11). Every Christian ought to study intently the life of this "greatest of all born of women" and emulate his humility, self-denial and courage.

The grammar of the original Greek language in verse 7 indicates that John came for the very purpose of testifying. John was to point out the True Light and give what evidence he had that this was the Light. The object of belief was Jesus Christ — the agency or instrument through which the object is revealed was John. Faith still comes through the agency of the preached Word, (cf. Rom. 10:14-17; Jas. 1:21; I Pet. 1:22-25). The first disciples won by Jesus were of John's training (Jn. 1:35-42). Thus John was instrumental in bringing faith to all who subsequently believed on Jesus through the preaching of these apostles. John was *a* light (Jn. 5:35) but not THE Light.

In verse 8 we have repeated what was said in verses 6 and 7. What an opportunity John had to pass himself off as the Christ! John showed more unselfishness, perhaps, than any man that ever lived. More preachers today need to pattern their ministry after John the Baptist's. It is imperative that all Christians heed the injunction of these verses that no preacher or teacher, however great, is to be worshipped or followed . . . only Jesus Christ Our Lord.

Verse 9 is said to be the "Quaker Text" because they use it to substantiate their "Inner light" theory. Every verse of Scripture *must* be interpreted in the light of other Scriptures. The Bible nowhere teaches that every single person is enlightened whether he wants to be or not. Even here in this context (1:1-11), both before and after verse 9, the writer speaks of men rejecting this illuminating Light. Luther says of this passage, "There is only one light that lights all men, and no man comes into the world who can possibly be illumined by any other light." This interpretation takes account of the rest of the New Testament. Just as Jesus is the "Lamb of God that taketh away the sin of the world," He is also the "light of the world." But just as all the world will not avail themselves of His purifying blood, neither does every man receive His Light of Life. The word "true" in this verse could be better translated "genuine" or "perfect," as opposed to unreal and imperfect.

There is some disagreement among commentators as to *when* the Light was in the world (v. 10). In the Greek text, "was" is in the imperfect tense (continuous existence in past time). The world was made through Him, and He gave it Life and Order. This should have been enough evidence to direct men's minds toward One Eternal Being (Rom. 1:20-23). Yet the world (men) "refused to have God in their knowledge."

Verse 11 shows the extreme perversity of men in that even when The Light became Incarnate, His own (generally speaking) rejected Him. The pathos of the situation comes out in a literal translation of the text — "he came unto his own nation and they that were his own people did not receive him." He came to a nation that should have prepared itself for Him. He should have been welcomed like a king — but He was rejected. Israel, her people and all her institutions, existed only for His glory and His eternal purposes (cf. Zech. 2:12; Hosea 9:3; Jer. 2:7; 16:18; Lev. 25:23; Ex. 19:5; Psa. 135:4; Deut. 7:6; 14:2; 26:18 32:9).

They knew Him all right! The whole history of Israel was a training school (Gal. 3:24) to prepare the Jews to receive the world's Messiah. But they didn't want a meek, unmilitaristic and uncorruptible Messiah. The Jewish leaders wanted a Messiah that would help them in their graft — the Jewish people wanted a King that would put bread on their tables, and plenty of it. The parable of the wicked husbandmen (Matt. 21:33ff) represents the Jews as killing the Heir, not in ignorance, but because they *did* know who He was.

Here is the great tragedy: A people that had so long been nursed, disciplined and prepared to present the Messiah to the world for salvation, scorned and finally shamefully crucified the Incarnate Word. This is why Jesus' body was racked with great sobs over the city of Jerusalem (Lk. 19:41ff) . . . this is what caused Him to wish agonizingly that He could give them His protecting love, but "they would not" (Matt. 23:37ff). What pathos there is in this verse "he came unto his own home — and his own people gave him no welcome." It happened to Jesus long ago with Israel — and it is still happening today within New Israel, the Church!

Quiz

1. Why should it be emphasized that John the Baptist was not the Light?
2. Was John a light in any sense? Are we lights (Matt. 5:14)?
3. What is meant by "the light which lighteth every man"?
4. Can we see the evidence of a Creator in nature (cf. Rom. 1:20; Psa. 19:1; Job 12:7-10)?
5. Why is Israel's rejection of Christ so pathetic?
6. Do you think the Jews knew that Jesus was the Messiah (cf. Acts 3:17; I Cor. 2:8)?
7. Is Christ still rejected by "His own" today?

THE WORD MANIFESTED TO OTHERS AND THEIR ACCEPTANCE OF HIM

Text 1:12-18

12 But as many as received him, to them gave he the right to become children of God, even to them that believe on his name:
13 Who were born, not of blood, nor of the will of the flesh, nor of the will of man, but of God.
14 And the Word became flesh, and dwelt among us (and we beheld his glory, glory as of the only begotten from the Father), full of grace and truth.
15 John beareth witness of him, and crieth, saying, This was he of whom I said, He that cometh after me is become before me.
16 For of his fulness we all received, and grace for grace.
17 For the law was given through Moses; grace and truth came through Jesus Christ.
18 No man hath seen God at any time; the only begotten Son, who is in the bosom of the Father, he hath declared him.

Queries

a. What is meant by:
   (1) "born not of blood"?
   (2) "nor of the will of the flesh"?
   (3) "nor of the will of man"?

b. Why is there emphasis upon "grace and truth" in these verses?

c. Has any man ever seen God (cf. Ex. 33:17-23)?

Paraphrase

But as many as received the Light and trusted in His name and obeyed His commandments, He gave them the privilege and authority to become children of God; that is, those who have been born of God by spiritual rebirth and not physical birth. Physical lineage — blood descent, whether of the baser desire of the flesh or the nobler purposes of man — cannot inherit the Kingdom of God. And the Logos-Light took the form of a physical body and dwelt temporarily amongst us (and we saw with our own eyes His glory which is the same glory as of the Only-Unique Being from the presence of the Father) full of favor, mercy and truth. John bears witness of Him and has cried aloud, saying, This is He of whom I said, the One coming on the scene later than I, really comes before me, for He outranked me from eternity. For from His abundance all, including John the Baptist, received; and all give gratitude in exchange for that grace. For the Law, which was not merciful, came through Moses; but mercy and truth through Jesus Christ. No man has seen God at any time, the Only-Unique God, the One residing in perfect intimacy with the Father, That One has interpreted the mercy and love of the Father for us.

Summary

Those who received the Light were given the privilege and shown the way to become children of God. The Light became flesh, temporarily, to show them the way to the Father. The ultimate of grace and truth came only through Him. Neither the Law of Moses nor John the Baptist could reveal the way. The Only Son who enjoyed perfect union with the Father must alone show the way.

Comment

In verses 12 and 13 John puts "as many as received him" in opposition to them that were his own who did not receive Him. To those who received Him, He *gave* the right to become children of God. To "receive Him" is to "believe on His name." To "believe on His name" is to trust Him and obey Him. God offers us sonship of His own free love — we can never merit sonship by our works. What God offers, however, man must appropriate if he is to enjoy. As in the parable of the Prodigal Son (Lk. 15:11-32), the prodigal merited disinheritance by his self-willed rebellion — the father *gave* him back his sonship — the son had to "come to himself" and return to an obedient walk with his father to appropriate this sonship. Oh, what a joy it is to be sons of our Heavenly Father (I Jn. 3:1-3)!

Some would have verse 13 refer to the virgin birth of Christ, but the best contextual rendering would indicate that it refers to "as many as received him." Verse 13 is a climactic arrangement to show that it is utterly impossible for physical lineage to inherit the Kingdom of God. The Jews were sure that their descent from Abraham gave them sonship in the Messianic kingdom, but they were wrong (cf. Mt. 3:8-10; Jn. 8:31-44). For explanation of each phrase of verse 13 see the paraphrase of this section.

To become sons of God, we must be born of God. Without doubt, John is talking of the New Birth here. Jesus talks to Nicodemus of the same subject (Jn. 3:1-15). In essence, the New Birth is ours when we surrender our will to the will of Christ as revealed in the New Testament (read carefully I Pet. 1:17-25 in this connection). We cannot be born anew, or from above until the Spirit of God abides in us. The New Testament is explicit as to how this is intitially accomplished. Jesus said, "If a man love me, *he will keep my word:* and my Father will love him, and we will come unto him, and make our abode with him" (Jn. 14:23). The Word of Christ which offered the life-giving Spirit was preached by Peter and the other apostles on that great day of Pentecost (Acts 2). Some 3000 people were convicted of their sins and believed the testimony concerning a risen Lord. Having been convinced of their sin in rejecting God's Son, they cried out for forgiveness. Peter then told them, "Repent and be baptized every one of you in the name of Jesus Christ unto the remission of your sins; and ye shall receive the gift of the Holy Spirit" (Acts 2:38; cf. also Titus 3:4-7). We shall deal more

fully with the New Birth in the notes on John 3:1-5. Suffice it
to say here, the new-born babe in Christ is to be continually led
by the Spirit else he forfeits his sonship (cf. II Cor. 5:17; Rom.
8:1-17). The new creature must either grow, or wither and die
(cf. I Cor. 3:1-3; Heb. 5:11-14).

The next verse (14) might be considered the greatest single
verse in the whole New Testament. In the grammatical construction of the Greek language here John makes a point of saying
"the Word became flesh". Since he does not use an article with
sarx (flesh), this sentence cannot be translated "flesh became the
Word". Many modern cults would have us believe that our Lord
began from a human birth, like all mankind, and rather evolved
into someone divine. This verse also refutes the Docetists (ancient
and modern) who theorize that Jesus was only a phantom. His
human body was not a real body, they say He could not really
feel hunger, weariness, sorrow and pain. He was rather a
ghostly apparition, and not flesh. They are loathe to apply the
word *flesh,* with its connotations of weakness and frailty, to God.

It is even a weakness of many Christians today to emphasize
so strongly the deity of Jesus that they tend to forget that Jesus
Christ was fully a man as well. What a glorious meaning this
has for us — "the Word became flesh". Since we are flesh and
blood, and enslaved by the fear of death, Jesus shared with us
this nature in order that He might relieve us of this terrible fear
which chains all humanity. He conquered Satan and took away
his power of death! Furthermore, Jesus shared in our fleshly
nature, without sin, that He might become our Eternal High
Priest. We have a High Priest interceding before God on our
behalf Who has been "touched with the feeling of our infirmities
. . . tempted in all points like as we are . . ." (cf. Heb. 2:14-15;
4:14-16). Manifold are the blessings we partake of through the
incarnation. We see God's power *demonstrated* — to forgive sins
(Mk. 2:9-12), over death (Jn. 11:43-44), over disease (Lk. 17:11-
19), over the elements (Mt. 14:22-33).

This Word "became flesh and dwelt among us". The word
"dwelt" is translated from *skenao* which means literally "tabernacled or tented." John goes on to say parenthetically that "we
(the disciples) beheld his glory, glory as of the only begotten
from the Father . . ." This phrase would be full of meaning to
Israelites. When the "glory of God" dwelt with Israel, He dwelt
in their tabernacle and in their temple in the Holy of Holies (Ex.
40:34; I Kings 8:11). The "glory of God" means simply the

31

prescence of God. God's presence was among men in bodily form
— he ate, drank, conversed, slept, prayed with them. These twelve
men, in particular, saw and "handled" the "Word of life" for
approximately three years (cf. I Jn. 1:1-4). What the *Shechinah*
had been in the tabernacle (the dwelling of God in the midst of
God's people), the Word was then in human flesh — and the Holy
Spirit is now in the Word written on the hearts of men and
women (II Cor. 3:2-3; Heb. 8:10). Jesus says that His disciples
are given this glory — this presence of God (Jn. 17:22-23).

There seems to be a reference in "we beheld his glory," etc.,
to the transfiguration of Christ. John was one of the three privi-
leged to be an eyewitness to this glorious event (cf. I Jn. 1:1-4;
II Pet. 1:16-18). This glory which the disciples beheld (throughout the earthly ministry of Jesus — Jn. 2:11; 5:41; 11:4) was
so awesome and magnificent that it could be nothing less than
divine glory. Glory that an ONLY UNIQUE *(monogenes)* SON
has from His divine Father. (See *Special Study* on "He Gave
The Only Son He Had," pp.——.)

Endless application could be made concerning verse 14. But
we shall never drink of its sweet nectar to the full until we "know
as we are known." It can be accounted for on no less than divine
inspiration that John could express this great profoundity in such
terse and simple words — a mystery on which the greatest phil-
osophers have spent lifetimes — "the Word became flesh and
dwelt among us"!

Verse 15 is a quotation from John the Baptist. It has already
been pointed out in verse 8 that John the Baptist was not the
Light. It was necessary for the Gospel writer to make sure that
the *Voice* not be mistaken for the *Light*. Time and time again
John the Baptist cried aloud that he was not the Christ; he pointed
to the Nazarene, Who began His ministry after John. He emphatically stated that Jesus of Nazareth outranked him because
Jesus was the Lamb of God, the promised Messiah, the One Who
was eternal. John preached that he was merely a "way-preparer,"
and that his ministry would give way to that of the Christ.

The phrase in verse 16 seems to be partly explanatory on
behalf of the quotation from the Baptist. It is strange that John
the Evangelist would interject a quotation in the middle of such
a profound dissertation on the Incarnation. The author of this
Gospel, however, wants to show that *all*, including the "greatest
born of women (John the Baptist) received of the fulness of the
Son. Yea, even he who was "more than a prophet" needed grace

from the Lamb of God. The word for "fulness" is *pleroma* and
is the same word Paul uses in Colossians 2:9. There Paul says
that in Christ dwells all the fulness *(pleroma)* of the Godhead
(Deity) in a bodily form . . . and in Him are *all* made full. In
Christ dwells the ultimate of wisdom, power and love. His grace
is inexhaustible. We "have not because we ask not" (cf. Jn.
15:7; 16:23-24).

The next phrase, "and grace for grace," is one of varied interpretation. The most prevalent interpretation is "grace upon
grace," or "abundance of grace." One writer puts it, "like manna
fresh each morning — new grace for the new day and new
service." It can also mean "grace in exchange for grace." The
same Greek preposition *anti* (for) is used in Luke 11:11 "a serpent *for* a fish," and in Hebrews 12:2 where Jesus *in exchange for*
the joy set before Him endured the cross. Such an interpretation
would not be contrary to the tenor of New Testament teaching.
We give loving gratitude by our obedience in exchange for His
loving favors. The New Testament does teach that we only love
Him because He loved us first (cf. I Jn. 4:19).

We ask ourselves now, what is the connection between the
foregoing and verse 17? To some of his readers, John's statement that the fulness of God was in the incarnate Word would
disparage the Law of Moses. John explains — the Law was given
through Moses, and it was good and holy. Yet it was a law of
condemnation. Its purpose was to bring men to a trust in God
and not in themselves. The Law was given to demonstrate to men
that they did not have the ability to be righteous enough to earn
salvation (cf. Rom. 3:20; Gal. 3:10-11; 3:21). On the other hand,
through Jesus Christ came "grace and truth." Jesus brought the
favor of God which man *could* not nor *cannot* earn; The Law
said, "Do all this and live", Man could not do it (Jas. 2:10);
therefore, man merited the Law's penalty, death, eternal death.
Jesus says, "I *give* you life, eternal life; accept it by trusting and
obeying My words". (See Jn. 6:63). We have in Christ *grace,*
without which we stand condemned by the Law; we have in
Christ *truth,* which is the reality of all the shadows cast by the
Law of sacrifices and ceremonies.

The closing verse (18) to the Prologue is very well chosen.
It is a resume of the entire Prologue. John simply declares that
apart from Jesus, the incarnate Mind, no man has seen God (cf.
I Jn. 4:7-14). Not even the great lawgiver and prophet, Moses,
has had immediate knowledge of God. No man can ever see God

physically, for God is spirit. Moses merely saw the fading glory
of God as God passed by him. Paul was blinded by that glory
(Acts 9). But Christ has declared, revealed and interpreted God
to us. John uses an interesting word in the Greek for "declared".
He uses *exegesato,* from which we get our English words exegesis
and exegetical, meaning literally to lead out, or interpret. In other
words, Christ, through His incarnation, has interpreted God for
us. The Prologue is simply describing the interpretation which
the Word gave concerning the unseen Father (cf. Jn. 14:8-9).

This One, who has declared the Father for us is continually
in the bosom of the Father. To be "in the bosom" of someone
is an ancient way of saying "in perfect intimacy." It is used of
husband and wife, father and son or two friends who are in the
closest of communion with each other. There is perfect, continuing communion between the Father and the Son. He knows
whereof he declares. Proverbs 8:30 speaks of the close, intimate
relationship between God and Wisdom: "Then I was by him
(during the creation) as a master workman; And I was daily
his delight, rejoicing always before him." Compare also the intimate contact between Jesus and the Father in John 12:27-30.

Notice, in closing this great section, the awe-inspiring boldness
with which John writes concerning things that are beyond human
comprehension. Could we say that John claims inspiration for his
account of the Gospel? Indeed we could — indeed we *must!*

Quiz

1. What must we do to receive the sonship which God gives us?
2. What is a simple definition of the New Birth?
3. Which heretical sect in the early church denied that God came
   in the flesh?
4. Give at least two things which the Incarnation means for us.
5. How does the presence of God dwell in the church today?
6. What is the connection of verse 17 with the rest of the
   Prologue?
7. How may we say from the Prologue that John claims inspiration for his Gospel?

We come now to the second main division of the Gospel of
John. From 1:19 through the last verse of the twelfth chapter
(12:50), John the Evangelist shows how the Word was manifested in the flesh to His own and how they rejected Him. Jesus
is still in the "preparational phase" of His ministry (cf. Map No.

1, p. 17). We shall outline the remainder of Chapter One in
this manner:
   II The Word Manifested to the Jews and their rejection of
      Him. 1:19 — 12:50
      A. Preparation, 1:19-2:12
         1. Ministry of John the Baptist, 1:19-34
            a. The Jews investigate John's identity, 19-22
            b. John's answer, 23-28
            c. The Baptist's evidence for the Lamb of God,
               29-34
         2. Gathering of His first disciples, 1:35-51
            a. Andrew, Peter and an unnamed disciple, 35-42
            b. Philip and Nathanael, 43-51

THE JEWS INVESTIGATE JOHN'S IDENTITY
Text 1:19-22

**19 And this is the witness of John, when the Jews sent unto
him from Jerusalem priests and Levites to ask him, who art
thou?
20 And he confessed, and denied not; and he confessed, I am
not the Christ.
21 And they asked him, What then? Art thou Elijah? And he
saith, I am not. Art thou the prophet? And he answered, No.
22 They said therefore unto him, Who art thou? that we may
give answer to them that sent us. What sayest thou of thyself?**

Queries
   a. What are Levites?
   b. Why ask John the Baptist about Elijah and "the
      prophet"?
   c. Why would the "committee" need an answer?

Paraphrase
   Now this is what John testified, when the Jewish Sanhedrin
sent priests and Levites to John to obtain an answer from him
concerning his identity, and they asked him, Who are you? And
John vigorously and fully declared, I am not the Christ. Then
they asked him, What then is the case? Are you Elijah? And
he said, I am not Elijah as you look for him. Are you the prophet
like unto Moses? And he answered, No! Then they said to him,
Tell us then just who you are, for we must have an answer to

take back to them that sent us. Tell us, what do you say about yourself?

Summary

The Jewish leaders demand to know whether John the Baptist is the Messiah, Elijah or the prophet. John denies all three identities.

Comment

The Sanhedrin, largely controlled by the Pharisees, was the religious authority of that day. It was a council of 70 or 71 learned and influential religious leaders. The council was a mixture of Pharisees (strict law-keepers — traditionalists), Sadducees (skeptics, worldly, politicians), and Scribes (interpreters, lawyers). In the "committee" that was investigating John there were also Levites. The Levites were a sort of secondary priesthood. They performed the more menial tasks of the temple service, baking bread, leading temple music, etc. One of their main functions was to enforce the Law. They were the temple police force, and they carried out the sentences of the Sanhedrin when punishment was to be inflicted.

This great, magnetic, eccentric character was attracting multitudes. Crowds were trekking into the wilderness just to hear him preach. The whole nation was on tiptoe expectation because of his powerful message (Lk. 3:15). Thus the rulers of the Jews felt they must take this matter in hand before certain religious and political repercussions occurred. There had been certain religious fanatics before who claimed to be the Messiah (cf. Acts 5:36-37). These had mustered a small force of followers and revolted against their conquerors, only to suffer disasterous results to themselves and the nation at large. A revolt now, touched off by John the Baptist against Rome, would be disasterous. The Sanhedrin might be deposed! In fact, some of them might even loose their heads! This is what Caiaphas had reference to when he said of Christ, "it was expedient that one man should die for the people" (Jn. 18:14). Basically, this is why the rulers crucified Jesus. They feared that the popularity of Jesus might cause revolt and subsequent Roman intervention (Jn. 11:48). They would lose their hold on the nation's purse strings.

In addition to the fear of revolt, the rulers were interested in questioning John because of his frankness. He had said some very candid and revealing things about Pharisees and Sadducees (Mt. 3:7). Sending the Levites along indicates this committee would stand for no more attacks upon the character of the illustrious Doctors of Divinity of that day.

So they began their questioning by asking him if he was the Messiah. John emphatically stated that he was not the Messiah. The word used for "confess" in verse 20 is *homologeo* which literally means "to speak the same thing; to agree." Thus John's denial that he was the Christ was in perfect agreement with the truth. When we learn that we must "confess" Christ in order to be saved (Mt. 10:32-33), it means that our lives and our words must "speak the same things, or agree with," the commandments of the Lord (cf. Rom. 10:9-10). To confess Christ is not the mere mouthing of Scripture, formula or creed, but a profession by both word and action! (cf. Jas. 1:22; I Jn. 3:17-18).

What a man of God this John was! He willingly and joyfully kept himself in the background in order that all might see the only Son of God. The Baptist was what every true follower of Christ ought to be — a servant willing to lay all the acclaim and honor given him of men at the feet of Jesus.

"If you are not the Messiah, then you must be Elijah!" This was the next conclusion of the investigating committee. The Jews had a tradition that Elijah was to precede the Messiah and that he, Elijah returned in the flesh, was to set all matters aright. He was even to settle disputes between property owners and money lenders. They taught that anything disputed must wait "until Elijah comes". Of course, this is merely tradition, but is probably based on Malachi 4:5. They expected a literal, flesh-and blood Elijah to come and prepare the way for the Messiah. Therefore, John's denial here does not contradict Matthew 11:14 and 17:9-13, or Luke 1:17, where John the Baptist is said to have come "in the spirit and the power of Elijah."

1 :21 THE GOSPEL OF JOHN

COMPARISON OF JOHN THE BAPTIST AND ELIJAH

	Elijah	*John*
1. Place of abode	"Hide thyself by the brook" (I Ki. 17:3).	In deserts (Mt. 3:1).
2. Food	Ravens fed him (I Ki. 17:6).	Locusts and wild honey (Mt. 3:4).
3. Appearance	Hairy man (II Ki. 1:8).	Raiment of camel's hair (Mt. 3:4).
4. Message	Calamity to nation; call to Repentance (I Ki. 18:39).	Judgment to come; call to Repentance (Mt. 3:4).
5. Influence Over Multitudes	Personality tremendous and compelling (I Ki. 18).	Brought whole nation into wilderness (Mt. 3:5; Lk. 3:15).
6. Firey wrath on Enemies of True Religion	(I Kings 18:40).	(Matthew 3:7).
7. In the presence of Kings	Ahab and Jezebel (I Ki. 21:19).	Herod and Herodias (Mt. 14:4).
8. Rage of an Evil Woman	Jezebel (I Ki. 29:2).	Herodias (Mt. 14:5-8).
9. The Dark Hour	(I Ki. 29:4).	(Matt. 11:2).
10. Extraordinary End of Career	(II Ki. 2:11).	(Matt. 14:11).
11. Loyalty of Disciples	(II Ki. 16:17).	(Matt. 14:12).

The next question by these Jews was, "Are you *the* Prophet?" Moses had promised them *the* Prophet, like unto himself (cf. Deut. 18:15). This was a promise that the Jews taught their children as soon as they were old enough to understand. It was a promise no Jew ever forgot. Moses was their great deliverer, and ever since the captivities of the Jews they longed for *the* Prophet, Who they prayed would deliver them from their oppressions. Maybe the Jews thought the Prophet was another forerunner of the Messiah (Jn. 7:40) — maybe they thought he was to be the Messiah Himself. Whatever their ideas, John denied being *the* Prophet. It seems that even John himself was later puzzled as to whether Jesus was only a forerunner, and questioned whether he should look for another (Lk. 7:19).

This delegation from Jerusalem was getting nowhere fast! Their mission thus far was a failure. John's flat denial will not satisfy the "powers that be." They must bring an answer or suffer censure and embarrassment. The manner in which they ask, and the admitted purpose of their questioning shows they were not at all interested in the message of John and what it should mean to their spiritual condition. All they ask is, "What do you claim to be — the Sanhedrin wants to know?"

Quiz

1. Name three religious parties that make up the Sanhedrin?
2. Why would the Jewish rulers fear revolt against Rome?
3. What is the full import of the word "confess"?
4. In how many ways does John the Baptist compare with Elijah?
5. Give the Scripture references for Old Testament promises of "Elijah that was to come", and "the Prophet like unto Moses".

JOHN'S ANSWER

Text 1:23-28

23 He said, I am the voice of one crying in the wilderness, Make straight the way of the Lord, as said Isaiah the prophet.
24 And they had been sent from the Pharisees.
25 And they asked him, and said unto him, Why then baptizest thou, if thou are not the Christ, neither Elijah, neither the prophet?
26 John answered them, saying, I baptize in water: in the midst of you standeth one whom ye know not,

27 even he that cometh after me, the latchet of whose shoe I am not worthy to unloose.
28 These things were done in Bethany beyond the Jordan, where John was baptizing.

Queries

a. What would the prophecy which John applies to himself mean to his questioners?

b. Why do the Pharisees ask him about the fact that he is baptizing people?

c. Why does John emphasize that he baptizes in water — does he imply that the "one coming after him" will *not* baptize in water?

Paraphrase

John answered his questioners by saying, I am a voice of one crying loud and forcefully in the wilderness, Make straight the way of the Lord, just as the prophet Isaiah has prophesied. Those who had been sent to question John were from the Pharisees. And they asked him, Why then are you immersing if you are neither the Christ nor Elijah nor the Prophet? John answered them, saying, I am immersing in water: in your midst is standing One Whom you have not recognized, the One coming after me, Whose sandal thongs I am not worthy to untie. These things came to pass in Bethany which is on the eastern side of the Jordan river where John was immersing.

Summary

John's answer to the Jew's question is: "I am the prophecied 'way-preparer' for the Lord." Then John intimates that the Christ they seek stands unrecognized in their midst.

Comment

John takes Isaiah's prophecy (Isa. 40:3-5) and applies it to himself. The prophecy is given more fully in Luke 3:4-6; in Matt. 3:3, John the Baptist shows that the prophecy definitely foretold his ministry (cf. also Mk. 1:3). This committee undoubtedly interpreted Isa. 40:3-5 as Messianic, but they would hardly accept such a religious fanatic as John for the forerunner of their ideal Messiah. Their Messianic fancy was that of a king of military, political and economic grandeur. The custom of the country at that time sheds light upon the prophecy. When a conqueror was

40

about to travel through his province, the roads were leveled and made straight and put in order for his journey. A delegated subordinate always preceded the monarch to take care of this preliminary preparation. Thus, John the Baptist was the appointed "road preparer" for King Jesus. But the Jewish rulers hardly looked for either a spiritual king or a spiritual "way preparer."

It is interesting to note the word used by John for "one crying." It is the Greek word *boao,* an onomatopoeic word (a word formed by imitating the sound associated with the thing described, i.e., the name "Whippoorwill" to describe the bird), which came to describe the bellowing of oxen. In John's case it indicates that he was in the wilderness crying out with a strong, forceful and arresting voice, *"Repent,* for the kingdom of heaven is at hand."

John was literally in the wilderness of Judea doing his preaching. But there seems to be a spiritual application to the phrase "a voice of one crying *in the wilderness."* Especially is this true considering its prophetic background. This herald of God was also crying in a *wilderness* of wasted souls. "The wilderness" (a pathless, fruitless waste) fitly describes the spiritual condition of Jehovah's people. John sought to prepare the way by preaching, "Bring forth fruits worthy of repentance" (Mt. 3:8; Lk. 3:8).

It is still true today! All the preaching and teaching in the church must be done toward this end; that is, toward preparing the way for the Lord's entry into the heart of individuals. Genuine conviction of sin, a need for the Saviour, and a submissive will is preparing the way for the King of kings. That is what John the Baptist preached, and that is what the world needs preached today!

Verse 24 seems to be furnishing the reader the reason why the next question (v. 25) was asked of John. It would be within the realm of the Pharisses to ask such a question. Further, it is doubtful that the Sadducees would be the least bit interested in why John was baptizing.

Most critics hold that John merely adapted the Jewish "proselyte baptism" to his ministry. Ecclesiastical history, however, gives no clear-cut evidence that the Jews practiced proselyte baptism. To the contrary, ancient records seem to indicate that the Jews appropriated baptism to the ceremonies of making proselytes from the practice begun by John, and later from Christian baptism (cf. *Unger's Bible Dictionary,* pp. 985). It lends more force to the question of the Jews to John if we assume John is doing something foreign to religious custom and practice of that day.

Here was this desert hermit attracting the whole countryside to his preaching. And he brazenly set aside all the present customs and traditions of the ecclesiastical heads and commanded, "Repent and be baptized for the remission of your sins" (cf. Mk. 1:14; Lk. 3:3). Only as important a personage as the Messiah, Elijah or the Prophet would dare assume such authority as to introduce a new religious doctrine.

Furthermore, the Jews expected a general purification at the coming of the Messiah. At least they were inclined to interpret some of the Old Testament prophecies in this vein (cf. Zech 13:1; Ezek. 36:25). If John were not the Messiah, why then did he demand purity of life and practice baptism?

In studying verses 26 and 27, one must also consider parallel passages such as Mt. 3:10-12; Mk. 1:7-8; Lk. 3:15-17; and the next few verses of John (Jn. 1:29-34). John the Baptist emphasizes that he will baptize only in water because the One coming after him will have authority and power to baptize whom He will in the Holy Spirit and unquenchable fire. The Baptist does not imply that Christ will disregard water baptism. The New Testament plainly records that Jesus Himself was baptized in water, that He and his disciples taught water baptism, and that Christ commanded baptism for all subsequent believers (Mt. 3:13-17; Mk. 1:9-11; Lk. 3:21-22; Mt. 28:18-20; Jn. 4:1-2; Acts 2:38).

It would be well to pause here and define the word *baptize*. Every Greek Lexicon of any repute defines *baptizo* as having a primary meaning of "dip, plunge, immerse, submerge." In the Greek language (the original language of the New Testament) this word *baptizo* can never mean sprinkle or pour. It is to be feared that the translators of our English versions of the Bible have allowed religious prejudices to guide their translating. It is interesting to note how these translators contradict themselves. In II Kings 5:14 our English translators have rendered the verse thusly: "Then went he down and *dipped* himself seven times in the Jordan . . ." (speaking of Naaman and his cure of leprosy). The amazing fact is that they interpreted the word *baptizo,* here used in the Septuagint, to mean *dipped*. When these scholars came to the New Testament they merely transliterated (change of characters of one alphabet to corresponding characters of another alphabet) the word *baptizo*. "Consistency, thou art a gem!"

When John baptized, he immersed men and women in the

Jordan River. When men and women were told by the apostles that they must "repent and be baptized," the apostles meant that they must "repent and be immersed" in water. (Cf. Acts 2:38; 2:41; 8:34-38; 9:18; 10:47-48; 16:15; 15:33; 18:8; 22:16, etc.) No man or group of men has ever had nor will ever have authority to alter the scriptural plan of salvation (cf. Gal. 1:6-10). No "latter day prophet," no "earthly vicar," no, not even an "angel from heaven" is permitted to preach a revised gospel. Everyone who names the name of Christ as Lord is committed to "contend earnestly for the faith which was once for all time delivered unto the saints" (Jude 3).

John the Baptist said, "I immerse in water: but in your midst is standing One whom you do not recognize." In verse 28 John humbly explains that the multitudes are recognizing and acclaiming the wrong person. The One they are not recognizing is so far above John that John is not even fit to perform the lowliest servant's task for Him. The Eastern custom of taking the sandals from a guest's feet and bathing his feet was delegated to the lowest of the servants.

No man is a fit messenger of the Lord until he is able humbly to recognize his unworthiness. Let us remember the words of the Master, "Even so ye also, when ye shall have done all the things that are commanded you, say, We are unprofitable servants; we have done that which it was our duty to do" (Lk. 17:10).

The next matter for consideration is one of geography. Verse 28 speaks of "Bethany beyond the Jordan" as the location for these momentous events. Almost all the ancient manuscripts have "Bethany beyond the Jordan" here in place of the King James translation "Bethabara". One of the early Christian writers (Origen) could find no place in Palestine named Bethany when he visited there, but was directed to a village called Bethabara east of the Jordan. Origen is accused of taking the liberty of changing the original text. It is impossible, this far removed, to determine the definite geographical location. The attendant circumstances, however, point to a place on the east side of the Jordan, immediately north of the Dead Sea, in the vicinity of Jericho. There is a ford in the Jordan there, presumably the one used by Joshua and the children of Israel in their crossing (Josh. 3:16). For a more detailed presentation of this matter see Andrews, *The Life of Our Lord,* pages 146-151; McGarvey, *Lands of the Bible* pages 341-343.

Quiz

1. What does the prophecy in Isaiah 40:3-5 indicate of the nature of John the Baptist's ministry, i.e., how John could "prepare the way for the Lord"?
2. Why does John mention that it was the Pharisees that had been sent (verse 24)?
3. Was John's baptism an adaptation of Jewish proselyte baptism?
4. How must the Greek word *baptizo* be translated?
5. Must all who believe in Jesus be baptized? Give 3 Scripture references.
6. How do we know the Scriptures cannot be changed?
7. Where is the most probable location of "Bethany beyond the Jordan"?

THE BAPTIST'S EVIDENCE FOR THE LAMB OF GOD

Text 1:29-34

29 On the morrow he seeth Jesus coming unto him, and saith, Behold, the Lamb of God, that taketh away the sin of the world!
30 This is he of whom I said, After me cometh a man who is become before me: for he was before me.
31 And I knew him not; but that he should be made manifest to Israel, for this cause came I baptizing in water.
32 And John bare witness, saying, I have beheld the Spirit descending as a dove out of heaven; and it abode upon him.
33 And I knew him not: but he that sent me to baptize in water, he said unto me, Upon whomsoever thou shalt see the Spirit descending, and abiding upon him, the same is he that baptizeth in the Holy Spirit.
34 And I have seen, and have borne witness that this is the Son of God.

Queries

a. Why does John call Jesus the Lamb of God?
b. Did the descending Spirit really look like a dove?
c. Why does John emphasize "I knew him not"?

Paraphrase

The day following the questioning by the Jews, John sees Jesus coming toward him and says, Look! There is the Lamb of God, Who is taking away the sin of the world! This is the One

of Whom I said, a Man is coming on the scene after me Who
outranks me because He existed in eternity before me. I did
not know He was the Messiah at first; but in order that He might
be made manifest unto Israel, so Israel might know Him, I purposely came immersing in water. And John testified, saying, I
have seen the Spirit coming down as a dove out of heaven and
abiding upon Him. And I did not know Him, before this incident, as the Messiah; but the One who sent me to immerse in
water, that One said to me, the One upon Whom you shall see
the Spirit descending and abiding — this is the One Who im-
merses in the Holy Spirit. And I have seen and have testified
that this One is The Son of God!

Summary

John the Baptist points the multitudes to Jesus of Nazareth
as The Lamb of God. John then sets forth the God-given evidence
for his testimony.

Comment

It would be well to remark here that the author of the Fourth
Gospel bridges a gap of almost thirty years between verse 18 and
19. The boyhood, baptism and temptation of Jesus in the wilderness are all omitted between the account of the Incarnation and
that portion of John's ministry here recorded. Therefore, when
John the Baptist sees Jesus coming toward him, Jesus is returning to the scene of His baptism after having been in the wilderness of Judea for the temptation. It is only natural that Jesus
would come here to link up His ministry where that of John was
beginning to fade. Jesus took up "preaching the gospel of God,
and saying, The time is fulfilled, and the kingdom of God is at
hand: repent ye and believe in the gospel, (Mk. 1:14-15)" where
John left off.

There are a number of inferences connected with John's
utterance, "Look, the Lamb of God, that takes away the sin of
the world." (a) That John was thinking of the Passover lamb
(Ex. 12-13; I Cor. 5:7; I Pet. 1:19) since the Passover was near;
(b) that, being the son of a priest, he thought of the daily offer-
ing of a lamb (Ex. 29:38-42; Num. 28:4); or (c) that the Baptist was reminded of the lamb in Isaiah 53. We must agree with
Hendriksen when he says, ". . . why is it necessary to make a
choice?" Was not Christ the antitype of all three (I Pet. 1:19;
Acts 8:32-35)?

In the Old Testament, the priests were to place their hands on the head of each lamb offered, thus signifying that the lamb was suffering God's penalty upon sin which the Jew had merited by his disobedience. The lamb bore the sentence of death in place of the Israelite who deserved it. Amazing grace! This was the atonement of the Old Testament. It was typical of the atonement of the Lamb of God and the New Covenant. The atonement of the Hebrew was accomplished by the grace of God and the ransom of a lamb's blood. The Hebrew, however, had to appropriate that atonement to himself. He appropriated God's mercy through faith — a faith that caused him to obey God's plan of atonement. He might not understand fully the "how and the why" of placing his hand upon the head of the sacrificial lamb (Lev. 1:3-5), but trusting and believing in Jehovah to fulfil His promises, the Israelite obeyed.

When John the Baptist said that Jesus was the Lamb of God that makes atonement for the sin of the world, he did not mean irresistible or universal atonement. Such assumption contradicts plain scriptural teaching (cf. Mt. 7:14, 20-23, etc.). When, by faith, we are obedient to the plan of atonement or salvation ordained in God's New Testament, we are promised complete and eternal atonement. When we obey Christ's commands, we, like the Israelite of old, "lay our hands upon the Lamb of God" signifying that He pays the ransom for us — He suffers the penalty in our stead. We may not understand all the reasons for His commands, i.e., immersion in water (Acts 2:38), but if we TRUST Him, we will OBEY Him.

The atonement is a subject of "unsearchable riches." No commentator has yet fathomed its depths. As one reads the Scriptures concerning the subject, it becomes both awesome and beautiful. Christ took away our sin by bearing in His own sinless body the penalty of the Father upon sin (cf. Rom. 3:21-26; 5:1-11; 6:23 — Heb. 5:7-9; 10:1-39; Isa. 53). Christ bears away, potentially, every sin that shall ever be committed (cf. II Cor. 5:14-15).

In verse 31 John says that he did not "know" Jesus. Whether John knew Jesus as he would a kinsman, or whether he knew Him as a fellow Israelite, we do not know. The emphasis which the Baptist wishes to place is that he did not know Jesus as the Messiah — did not know Him thus until after the baptismal experience and the dove descending upon Him. At the baptism of Jesus the Spirit descended upon Him "in a bodily form as a dove and a voice spoke from heaven saying, Thou art my beloved

Son; in thee I am well pleased" (cf. Lk. 3:22). John really saw
a dove descend upon Jesus. These (the dove and the voice) are
the Divine manifestations which John saw and heard and which
he now bears witness to.

John also explains in verse 31 that one of the purposes of his
baptizing was that Jesus of Nazareth should be made manifest to
Israel as the Lamb of God — the promised Messiah. That Jesus
of Nazareth was the Saviour of the world was not the private
idea of John the Baptist, but He who sent John to baptize gave
him the signs of the dove and the voice from heaven. The testimony of John is that of an eyewitness, and rests upon miraculous
revelation. The fact that John was not aware of the diety of
Jesus beforehand precludes any possibility of collusion or agreement between Jesus and John to deceive the people.

Some comment is in order here regarding John's apparent
contrast between his water baptism and the baptizing which the
One following him shall perform. In the Synoptics, when John
is preaching to the public in general and the Pharisees in particular, he says, "I indeed baptize you in water . . . but he that cometh
after me . . . he shall baptize you in the Holy Spirit and in fire,
etc.," Mt. 3:11 (cf. also Mk. 1:8; Lk. 3:16-17). There are those
today who claim John meant that he baptized only in water, but
that Jesus would baptize (immerse) all believers in the Holy
Spirit and in fire. We believe that the Scriptures teach a baptism
of the Holy Spirit and of fire, but neither one are to be administered to all believers. By reading Luke 24:49, and by further
connecting it immediately with Acts 1:1-5 it becomes plain that
the baptism in the Holy Spirit is that which Jesus promised and
administered to the apostles on the day of Pentecost (Acts 2).
This was also administered to the household of Cornelius (Acts
10:44-48), signifying that the Gentiles were to be accepted into
the kingdom of God by the heretofore prejudiced Jews (cf. Acts
10:47; 11:16-18; 15:7-11). These are the *only* instances where
the Scriptures definitely speak of immersion in the Holy Spirit
after the ascension of Christ. Others received special gifts of
the Holy Spirit through the laying on of the hands of the apostles,
but there were no other baptisms in the Holy Spirit.

As for the baptism in fire, the context demands that we interpret John the Baptist's statement as referring to eternal punishment. In both Matthew 3:12 and Luke 3:17 John interprets his
foregoing statement concerning baptism in fire by saying, "the
chaff he will burn up with unquenchable fire." This is also true

of the verses preceding the mention of baptizing in fire. John first tells the Pharisees that "every tree therefore that bringeth not forth good fruit is hewn down, and cast into the fire"; then he goes on to tell Who is going to do the "casting into the fire" (cf. Mt. 3:10-11; Lk. 3:9-10). John is saying, "I am not the anointed One you are asking about — I merely baptize in water." The Baptist wants it emphatically understood that the One coming after him "is mightier than the forerunner," that it is He Who has authority to immerse in the Holy Spirit and in fire!

Quiz

1. What portion of Jesus' life is omitted between John 1:18 and 1:19?
2. How is the atonement provided for by Christ (the Lamb of God) appropriated to our souls?
3. Give two reasons why John "came baptizing."
4. What is the baptism in the Holy Spirit? in fire?
5. Only..has authority to administer these two baptisms.

ANDREW, PETER AND AN UNNAMED DISCIPLE

Text 1:35-42

35 Again on the morrow John was standing, and two of his disciples;

36 and he looked upon Jesus as he walked, and saith, Behold the Lamb of God!

37 And the two disciples heard him speak, and they followed Jesus.

38 And Jesus turned, and beheld them following, and saith unto them, What seek ye? And they said unto him, Rabbi (which is to say, being interpreted, Teacher), where abidest thou?

39 He saith unto them, Come, and ye shall see. They came therefore and saw where he abode; and they abode with him that day: it was about the tenth hour.

40 One of the two that heard John speak, and followed him, was Andrew, Simon Peter's brother.

41 He findeth first his own brother Simon, and saith unto him, We have found the Messiah (which is, being interpreted, Christ).

42 He brought him unto Jesus. Jesus looked upon him, and said, Thou art Simon the son of John: thou shalt be called Cephas (which is by interpretation, Peter).

Queries

a. Was the place where Jesus stayed near there?
b. Why did the two disciples say they were following Jesus? Was this really their purpose?
c. What did Jesus and these two talk about all that day?

Paraphrase

Again, on the next day, John and two of his disciples were standing near where John was immersing and John gazed intently at Jesus as He was walking near by. And John said, Look — the Lamb of God! And two of his disciples heard him speaking and they followed Jesus. Having turned suddenly, Jesus beheld them following Him and said to them, What purpose have you in following Me — what are you seeking? And they said to Him, Rabbi, (which is interpreted, Teacher) Where are You abiding? Jesus said to them, Come and see! And at about ten a.m. they went and saw where He was abiding, and they were with Him for the remainder of that day. Andrew, Simon Peter's brother, was one of the two disciples who heard John speak and followed Jesus. Andrew was the first of the two disciples to find his own brother, Simon, and say to him, We have found the Messiah (which is interpreted, anointed One). Then Andrew led his brother Simon to Jesus. Jesus gazed into his heart and said, You are Simon, the son of John. You shall be called Cephas (which is interpreted Peter — meaning Stone).

Summary

Two of the Baptist's disciples set about investigating the One whom he points out as "the Lamb of God." Having conversed with Him they are convinced that He is the anointed One of Israel. They allow no delay in leading their brothers to Him.

Comment

Again we marvel at the self-denial of John the Baptist. Did he not know that once he pointed out the Messiah he invited disaster to his own popularity? Did he not realize that once he proved Jesus of Nazareth to be the anointed One that his disciples would be likely to leave him and follow the King of Israel? Cer-

tainly he did; and yet he pointedly showed Jesus to his disciples!
There is nothing harder than to willingly take second place when
one has enjoyed first place.

Verse 38 shows an apparent hesitancy on the part of the two
disciples to join themselves rudely to Jesus uninvited. The tense
of the Greek word *strapheis* indicates to some commentators that
Jesus turned suddenly. When He turned, He asked them an important question, "What seek ye?" Notice that He said *"What,"*
not *"Whom* seek ye?" It has also been pointed out that Jesus
met these searchers halfway. It was God Who took the first step
in wooing man back to Himself. We still love God because He
first loved us (I Jn. 4:19). For those following Jesus today, the
Lord's question still rings true: "What seek ye?" — a good reputation? a set of religious rules? a Sunday club? or is it Jesus
Christ, the Son of God to be Lord of your entire being? (See
Gal. 2:20).

There are two interpretations of the disciple's reply, "Teacher,
where are you abiding?" One meaning behind the question might
be that they were caught unawares when Jesus turned suddenly,
and that was the only reply they could think of on the spur of
the moment. The other interpretation is that the disciples sincerely
sought His lodging place in order that they might go aside with
Him, away from the crowds into quiet and earnest conversation
concerning His messiahship.

The Lord was eager to satisfy their sincere and honest search
after the Christ of God. Lenski contrasts the ardent, "Come,
and ye shall see," of the King of Heaven and earth with the post-
ponements and procrastinations of earthly potentates. He did not
invite them merely to see His lodging place, but to "behold" the
One for Whom their hearts, as well as the hearts of their ancestors, had longed (I Pet. 1:10-12).

If the world could know where Jesus stayed, it would build
a shrine of stone and mortar. No one knows where it was. Perhaps it was the home of a friend, perhaps an inn — it may even
have been a booth (tabernacle) made of palm leaves. This day
and its revelations *were enshrined,* however, in the hearts of the
disciples who were there. For John (the other disciple), as he
writes this Gospel, remembers even the hour they arrived and
just how long they stayed with Him. John seems to use the
Roman mode of counting time, which would mean that 10 a.m.
was the hour of their arrival. Others contend that John uses
the Jewish notations of time, which would make the hour of

arrival 4 p.m. We refer you to the various works listed in the
Bibliography for a more extended study of the Evangelist's
method of counting time.

The Greek word *para* is the word used by the author to
describe the visit of these two disciples. This word means primarily "by the side of," and reveals the intense conversation that
must have been carried on.

In verse 40 the author finally mentions the name of one of
the two disciples. Andrew will always be known as Simon Peter's
brother (cf. Jn. 6:8). Almost immediately we ask, "Who was
the other disciple?" We are given no definite statement from
Scripture, but there is strong inference that it was John, brother
of James, son of Zebedee and author of the Fourth Gospel. It is
a trait of the author of this account never to mention his own
name or that of his relatives (cf. our Introduction, section on
"Authorship").

We are introduced to an outstanding characteristic of Andrew
in verse 41. Andrew was a personal evangelist. He was always
leading others to Jesus (cf. Jn. 6:8-9; 12:22). This is a characteristic that Jesus would have *all* His disciples cultivate (cf.
Mt. 28:19-20). What a man this was that Andrew led to the
Lord! We shall never fully know the fruit we bear indirectly
through those we lead to Christ until we "meet them in the air."
Andrew shares in all the subsequent fruits of Peter's labors!

In the phrase, "He findeth his own brother . . ." are also two
possible interpretations. The most prevalent one is derived from
the word *proton,* which means that Andrew sought his brother
first, before he did anything else. Some manuscripts, however,
have *protos* which means, perhaps, that Andrew was the "first"
disciple who went after his brother, and implies that John also
went after his brother James. We have chosen the latter interpretation in our paraphrase, for it fits the later call of the fishermen at Capernaum more readily (cf. Hendriksen on John, pp.
105-106, Vol. 1).

Andrew and John had made the greatest discovery of the ages
— they had found the Messiah of the Jews, the Son of David.
Andrew was excited, but the text seems to indicate that he could
not excite Peter with this news. The Greek word *egagen* implies
that Andrew had to coax Simon Peter — had to "lead" him to
where Jesus was. The zeal of Andrew is often found in new
converts. It is to the everlasting shame of the Church that this

zeal is often quenched by the pessimism and lack of faith of those older in the faith.

Jesus, with a searching gaze, looked on Peter's heart. The word John used to describe the Lord's manner of looking here is *emblepsas.* It is the same word used by Luke to describe Jesus' "look" at Peter in the courtyard after Peter had denied Him (Lk. 22:61). When Jesus looked upon Simon Peter, He saw not merely a fisherman from Bethsaida, but He saw the future sted-fast "Rock" (cf. Acts 4:19; 5:41). In the Greek language, *petra* was used for a "massive ledge of rock," while *petros* was a "detached fragment of the ledge, smaller." Simon is first nicknamed *Cephas,* which is Aramaic for Rock. Cephas is in turn interpreted in Greek as *Petros,* meaning small rock. The reader is referred to Matthew 16:17 where the distinction between the two Greek words is very clear. Simon is there (Mt. 16:17) called *petros,* but the truth contained in his confession is called *petra.*

Thus far we are told that Andrew, his brother Simon Peter, John, and probably his brother James, are the only disciples following Jesus. We shall see next how others join themselves to this little band. The conversation these first four had with Jesus becomes even more important, however, when one considers the Synoptic's account of their call (cf. Mt. 4:18-22; Mk. 1:16-20; Lk. 5:1-11). It is rather difficult to understand how four fishermen would leave their livelihood and immediately and unquestioningly follow an obscure Galilean as is pictured by the Synoptical accounts. This passage in John shows that there was a period of inquiry and association with Jesus before the Galilean call.

Quiz

1. Why did the two disciples following Jesus ask where He was abiding?
2. What was the time of day when they arrived at Jesus' lodging place?
3. Who was the "other disciple" with Andrew?
4. Give the basic characteristic of Andrew as shown in v. 41.
5. Give two possible interpretations of the phrase, "He findeth first his own brother" (v. 41).
6. How could Jesus know Simon's future character enough to call him "Rock"?
7. What bearing does this first call of the four fishermen have on the later Galilean call?

THE CALL OF PHILIP AND NATHANAEL

Text 1:43-51

43 On the morrow he was minded to go forth into Galilee, and he findeth Philip: and Jesus saith unto him, Follow me.

44 Now Philip was from Bethsaida, of the city of Andrew and Peter.

45 Philip findeth Nathanael, and saith unto him, We have found him, of whom Moses in the law, and the prophets, wrote, Jesus of Nazareth, the son of Joseph.

46 And Nathanael said unto him, Can any good thing come out of Nazareth? Philip saith unto him, Come and see.

47 Jesus saw Nathanael coming to him, and saith of him, Behold, an Israelite indeed, in whom is no guile!

48 Nathanael saith unto him, Whence knowest thou me? Jesus answered and said unto him, Before Philip called thee, when thou wast under the fig tree, I saw thee.

49 Nathanael answered him, Rabbi, thou art the Son of God; thou art King of Israel.

50 Jesus answered and said unto him, Because I said unto thee, I saw thee underneath the fig tree, believest thou? thou shalt see greater things than these.

51 And he saith unto him, Verily, verily, I say unto you, Ye shall see the heaven opened, and the angels of God ascending and descending upon the Son of man.

Queries

a. What did Moses write of Him "in the law and the prophets"?

b. What did Nathanael mean when he said, "Can any good thing come out of Nazareth? (v. 46)?"

c. What is the meaning of verse 51?

Paraphrase

The next day Jesus decided to go north to Galilee. Before leaving, however, He discovered Philip and said to him, Follow me. (Philip was from Bethsaida, the same city that Andrew and Peter were from). Philip, the same day, found Nathanael and said to him, We have found the One of Whom Moses wrote in the Pentateuch and of Whom the prophets also wrote. This One is none other than Jesus of Nazareth, the son of Joseph the carpenter. But Nathanael said, The Scriptures do not say, do they, that the Messiah shall come out of Nazareth? Philip answered, Come and see for yourself. As Nathanael was coming to Jesus, Jesus said, Look! A true son of Jacob in whom there is no deceit nor guile! Nathanael said to Jesus, How do you know what my character is? Jesus answered him, saying, Before Philip found you, when you thought yourself concealed under the fig tree, I could read your heart. Nathanael said to Jesus, Teacher, you are indeed the Son of God — the King of Israel. Jesus said to Nathanael, You believed when I told you I saw you under the fig tree. You shall see greater things than these. I tell you truly, You shall see the way into Heaven and a measure of its glories revealed through the Son of man.

Summary

Jesus gathers two more disciples. Philip, neighbor of Andrew and Peter, and Nathanael, a true Israelite. Nathanael's quick faith is to be rewarded by visions of Glory.

Comment

This is the fourth day from the time the Jews questioned John the Baptist. Jesus has spent almost a week in the vicinity of John's place of baptizing. Time is drawing near for Him to commence His public ministry. The Lord has decided to go north into the province of Galilee. It may be that while He is preparing to go Philip comes to Him. It may be that Philip had called Andrew and Peter aside and was talking to them when Jesus approached him with the challenge, "Follow me." The two from Bethsaida (Andrew and Peter) had probably told Philip, their fellow townsman, the Messianic news. Philip seems to be the type of man who always wants to "get to the bottom of things" (cf. Jn. 6:5-7; 12:21; 14:8-9), and was probably seeking Jesus when Jesus found him.

Philip, too, is a personal evangelist. We cannot help noticing a strong emphasis on personal evangelism in this first chapter of John. Each one wins one. *Now* it takes more than one hundred to win one.

Who is Nathanael? The best answer is that he is the Bartholomew of the Synoptical Gospels. The name Nathanael means gift of God. His home town was Cana of Galilee (Jn. 21:2). We assume Nathanael and Bartholomew to be the same man since Bartholomew is never mentioned in John's Gospel, and Nathanael is never named in the Synoptics. It is amazing that Nathanael

lived his youth at the same time Jesus lived His, in Cana of Galilee — only about 3 miles from Nazareth the boyhood home of
Jesus — yet he had never heard of Jesus. This fact shows how
perverse the wild fantasies of the Apocryphal Gospels are.

These two men, Philip and Nathanael, were undoubtedly students of the Old Testament Law and Prophets. Nearly every
male Israelite studied them from childhood through old age.
When Philip told Nathanael of finding the One of Whom Moses
and the prophets wrote, Nathanael's heart must have pounded as
he recalled the words of Deuteronomy 18:15, Isaiah 53, Daniel
9:24-27, Jeremiah, the Psalms and a host of other references.
There is an invaluable lesson here for students of God's Word
today. The Old Testament cannot be properly understood without seeing Christ as the very core and substance of the Law and
prophets (cf. Lk. 24:27, 32, 44; Jn. 5:39, 46; Acts 3:18; I Pet.
1:10).

Verse 46 has always been one of varied interpretation. Three
interpretations are usually offered: (a) that Nathanael was expressing civic pride and rivalry since he was from the neighboring
village of Cana, (b) that Nazareth was notoriously evil and
Nathanael was uttering a proverbial denunciation, or (c) that
Nathanael is questioning, what seems to him, a wrong interpretation by Philip of the Messianic prophecies. The third interpretation seems to have the weight of the context in its favor (cf.
Jn. 7:52). Philip does not try to argue Nathanael into his position but bids him, "Come and see!"

Nathanael, being a man with an "honest and good heart" (Lk.
8:15), comes to see. Jesus, seeing him coming, tells His other
disciples, "Look! a true son of Jacob." The word Jesus used for
"guile" here is *dolos* which means "bait, snare, deceit, or guile."
It is evident that throughout the entire conversation with Nathanael Jesus keeps referring to the history of Jacob, father of all
Israelites. He contrasts the guileless character of Nathanael with
the deceitful practices of Jacob. Such trickery was also found in
most of the descendants of Jacob (cf. Gen. 34; Mt. 23:16-22).
Many of the Jews of Jesus' day had no scruples against cheating
and deceiving in their business transactions. Few of the rulers had
guileless characters. Nathanael's moral excellence caused Jesus
to exclaim, "Look! a true Israelite, in whom is no deceit" (cf.
Rom. 2:28-29, 9:26).

Nathanael is surprised that Jesus knows how he thinks and
how he lives. Those who seek to follow Jesus now would do well

to remember that He still sees the most hidden recesses of their hearts (cf. Jn. 2:24-25; Psa. 139). The guileless Israelite frankly asks Jesus where He received His information. Perhaps Nathanael silently wonders if Jesus had learned of him through Philip. The Master quickly shows that this would be impossible for He saw Nathanael's heart before Philip found him.

Jesus even names the place where Nathanael thought he was hidden from the eyes of strangers. It seems to have been the custom of the Jews to seek the shade of the fig tree as the most peaceful and obscure place to sit and meditate and pray (cf. I Ki. 4:25; Micah 4:4). Was Nathanael praying and meditating under the fig tree? Did he often pray that the Holy One of God should soon come? From the Lord's estimate of his character these things could not be far wrong. Now Nathanael is face to face with One Who knows his secret longings — Who has heard his prayers — Who reads his heart. This must be the Son of God — the King of Israel.

Most of our English versions have translated verse 50 as a question. This interrogative form tends to disparage the value of Nathanael's unhesitating faith. We might get the idea from a question that Jesus doubts that Nathanael could believe so soon — or that Jesus doubts the surety of his faith. To the contrary, Jesus praises the man's faith by promising to reward it with even greater manifestations of His glory.

Verse 51 is hard of interpretation. The best exegesis is that Jesus means He is the antitype of Jacob's ladder. In other words, He will be revealed to Nathanael as the Way to Heaven (Jn. 14:1-6). He will be shown to His disciples, and eventually the world, as the Mediator between God and man. The Lord could hardly have reference to a literal ascent and descent of angels upon His Person. There were times when the angels did literally minister unto Him (cf. Mk. 1:13; Ik. 22:43; Mt. 28:2-4; Jn. 20:12, 13), but Nathanael was not sufficiently close to Jesus at any of these incidents to see the angels.

"This record of the actual opening of Jesus' ministry is full of victory. He does not declare Himself in spectacular fashion to the multitude, but a little group of select and eager men begin to have an insight into His glorious personality. They recognize Him as the Lamb of God, the Messiah, The Son of God and the King of Israel. He declares Himself the Son of man, and opens up an absorbing vista of His coming ministry." (R. C. Foster in *Studies in the Life of Christ*, Vol. 1).

THE GOSPEL OF JOHN

Quiz

1. What type of man was Philip?
2. Who was Nathanael? Where did he live?
3. What is the necessary relationship of Christ to the Old Testament?
4. Who does Jesus think of as He talks to Nathanael?
5. What is the teaching of Psalm 139?
6. What do we assume Nathanael was doing under the fig tree?

EXAMINATION

(Introduction and Chapter One)

1. Who wrote the Fourth Gospel?
2. Give 4 evidences to substantiate your answer to question one.
3. Name the two papyri which are so important to the Fourth Gospel.
4. How near to the original manuscript of the Fourth Gospel do these papyri take us?
5. Give two reasons for saying that the Fourth Gospel is not "silent" about the virgin birth of Christ?
6. How is the Prologue (1:1-18) an abridgment of the entire Fourth Gospel?
7. What does the author mean by saying that the "world was made through" Christ (cf. Jn. 1:10)?
8. Name two heretical sects whose doctrines are refuted by the Prologue.
9. Give the scriptural limitations for the second main division of the Fourth Gospel.
10. What was the essence of the preaching of both John the Baptist and Jesus (cf. Mt. 3:1-2; Mk. 1:14-15)?

Fill in the blanks:

1. John the apostle has been called "the apostle of......................"
2. John's purpose in writing his Gospel is to show that Jesus is
....
3. "In the........................was the Word, and the Word was ....God, and the Word was........................"
4. God........................and........................always like Jesus Christ (Heb. 13:8).
5. "He came unto his................, and they that were his................ received him not."

6. Every verse of Scripture must be interpreted in the light of the entire.. .
7. "And the Word became............................, and............................ among us."
8. "For the........................was given through Moses;........................ and........................came through Jesus Christ."
9. To become sons of God we must be............................anew of God.
10. "Behold, ..., that taketh away the sin of the world!"

True or False?

1. ....Our finite minds cannot comprehend eternity.
2. ....John the Baptist was very unpopular.
3. ....The baptism of fire is promised to believers.
4. ....Nathanael was Andrew's brother.
5. ....James was Simon's brother.
6. ....Philip was Andrew's brother.
7. ....The four fishermen received only one call from Jesus.
8. ....The Old Testament may be very clearly understood without a knowledge of Christ.
9. ....Nathanael was the brother of Bartholomew.
10. ....Jesus declared Himself in a spectacular manner to all of Judea immediately after His baptism.

EXPOSITORY SERMON NO. 1

THE BIRTH OF CHRIST INTERPRETED

John 1:1-18

Introduction

I. TELL BIRTH STORY BRIEFLY (Luke 2).
   A. John's Prologue gives the definition of Christmas.
   B. Especially consider verse 14.
II. WHO IS THIS CHILD BORN 2000 YEARS AGO IN A STABLE IN BETHLEHEM?
   A. Who is He, that men have celebrated His birth for 2000 years?
   B. Who is He of Whom thousands of books have been written?
   C. Who is He in Whom all of history centers, past and present?

III. JOHN STATES THREE THINGS ABOUT THIS CHILD IN HIS PROLOGUE

A. He is the eternal Word of God.

B. He was made flesh to bring life to men.

C. He is the complete and final opportunity for man's salvation.

LITTLE DID THE SHEPHERDS OR THE WISE MEN KNOW THE SIGNIFICANCE OF THIS CHILD . . . EVEN WE DO NOT REALIZE THE FULL SIGNIFICANCE OF HIS BIRTH BECAUSE MANY DO NOT RECOGNIZE THE FINALITY OF HIS REVELATION!

Discussion

I. HE IS THE ETERNAL WORD OF GOD

A. *Logos* is defined as "the thought, purpose and expression of the mind of God."
Just as our thoughts and purposes are made known when we communicate by words,
SO GOD'S AGELESS PURPOSES ARE MADE KNOWN THROUGH CHRIST (Eph. 3:9).

B. "The Word was with God" — the Word was of the very essence and nature of God.

1. Heb. 1:3.
2. Col. 2:9.
3. GOD WAS, AND EVER SHALL BE, ALWAYS LIKE JESUS REVEALED HIM — merciful, graceful, loving, yet wrathful against sin and hypocrisy.

C. The Word was an equal agent in creation (v. 3).

1. Heb. 1:2-3.
2. JESUS IS THE GOD WHOM WE WORSHIP! HE WAS THE CREATOR COME IN THE FLESH!
   a. Let that knowledge burst afresh on our minds.
   b. We cannot deny the divinity of Jesus and still honor God (cf. Jn. 5:23).
   c. WHERE DOES THAT LEAVE ALL RELIGIONS THAT BELIEVE JESUS TO BE A PROPHET . . . A GOOD MAN, BUT NOT DIVINE?

II. HE BECAME FLESH AND DWELT AMONG US TO BRING LIFE AND LIGHT
- A. Blessed word! . . . "He *tabernacled* among us."
  1. Our God is not aloof . . . not unsympathetic.
     a. Every heathen concept of gods is of unsympathetic gods always seeking to do harm and hurt to man.
  2. God could have sent Logos into world and then quickly withdrawn Him.
     a. BUT HE CAME . . . HE KNEW WEARINESS, THIRST, SADNESS, TEARS, TEMPTATION, PERSECUTION, YEA — DEATH.
     b. He is not a high priest that cannot be touched with our infirmities.
        WE ARE DRAWN CLOSER TO HIM BECAUSE HE DID COME AND TARRY IN THE FLESH.
- B. In Him was life.
  1. It was necessary for Him to come in the flesh . . . in order to condemn sin in the flesh.
     a. MAN COULD NOT FULFIL THE LAW OF GOD . . . THUS THE LAW BECAME A CONDEMNATION TO MAN.
     b. THEREFORE, GOD SENT HIS SON . . . IN FLESH . . . TO CONQUER SIN AND SUFFER THE PENALTY OF SIN.
- C. Many rejected Him . . . and still do . . . BUT TO ALL WHO RECEIVE:
  1. HE GIVES THE RIGHT TO BECOME CHILDREN OF GOD.
     Notice that He gives — we do not earn.
  2. YET WE MUST ACCEPT HIS GIFT.
     a. This we do by being born of God (new birth).
     b. Compare Jn. 3:3-5; Titus 3:5; I Pet. 1:22-23, etc.
  3. Jesus gives both authority and power to live this new life . . . faith, hope, prayer and obedience.

III. HE CAME AS A COMPLETE AND FINAL REVELATION OF GOD
- A. In times past God spoke partial revelations (Heb. 1:1).
  1. But at the end of the ages, in the fulness of time He spoke to man in His Son (Heb. 1:2).

a. The Law was given through Moses, but grace and truth came through Jesus Christ.

B. The Law was only a shadow of the reality of God's truth.

    1. It was all realized in Christ.

C. He is the only opportunity for men forevermore.

    1. "Except ye believe that I am He, ye shall die in your sins."

THIS MEANS THAT MEN WILL BE SEPARATED FROM GOD, AND THE WHOLE WEIGHT OF THE PENALTY FOR THEIR SIN WILL FALL UPON THEIR OWN SHOULDERS . . . THEY WILL PAY THIS PENALTY FOR ETERNITY.

    2. All men will eventually live eternally — either in heaven or hell.

        a. But Jesus gives Life with a capital L. He brings life and immortality to light through His resurrection.

HIS BIRTH WOULD MEAN LITTLE WITHOUT HIS DEATH AND RESURRECTION!

OUR HOPE AND FAITH AND POWER TO LIVE A CHRISTIAN LIFE IS ALL BASED UPON HIS VICTORY OVER DEATH!

JESUS HAS COME . . . AND GOD IS LIKE JESUS . . . WE OUGHT TO SHOUT WITH THE MULTITUDE OF THE HEAVENLY HOST: "GLORY TO GOD IN THE HIGHEST!"

Conclusion

I THUS WE SEE THAT THE BABE BORN 2000 YEARS AGO WAS:

A. He who put the stars in the heavens;

He who created our delicate bodies from dust and breathed life into them;

He who upholds all creation by the word of His power.

B. It means that:

We no longer need to fumble and miss the way; HE IS THE WAY.

We no longer need to grope for the truth; HE IS THE TRUTH.

We no longer need wonder how life ought to be lived;
HE IS THE LIFE.

II BUT WE ONLY BELIEVE THIS ON THE BASIS OF
HIS RESURRECTION.

   A. IF THERE WERE NO KNOWLEDGE OF RESUR-
       RECTION TO INCORRUPTION, there would be
       very little sense to life on this earth. It would then be
       sensible to adopt Solomon's philosophy.

   B. Jesus has proved that there is an eternal life beyond the
       grave. Thus we see that all his statements about heaven
       and hell are true!

SOME MAY LAUGH AND SCOFF NOW, BUT WHEN
DEATH COMES, WHO IS GOING TO TAKE THEIR
HANDS AND LEAD THEM ACROSS THE DARK, BLACK
CHASM WHERE NONE BUT HE HAS RETURNED TO
TELL ABOUT?
SURRENDER AND TRUST HIM ... JESUS WILL LEAD
YOU ACROSS! THAT IS THE REASON WHY THE
CHILD WAS BORN IN BETHLEHEM 2000 YEARS AGO.

CHAPTER TWO

Some commentators make the first miracle of Jesus recorded in this chapter the beginning of His public ministry. We prefer, however, to consider the miracle at the marriage feast as the final preparation for His public ministry. Verse eleven of this chapter indicates that He performed this miracle especially to prepare His disciples for the public ministry to follow. Furthermore, this miracle goes unnoticed as far as the multitudes are concerned, and was not intended to be an open manifestation. Therefore, we continue in our outline with the Preparation Period:

A. Preparation (cont.) 1:19-2:12.
   3. First miracle 2:1-11.
      a. Mary's expectations rebuked by Jesus vv. 1-5.
      b. Miracle performed vv. 6-11.
   4. Residence moved to Capernaum 2:12.

MARY'S EXPECTATIONS REBUKED BY JESUS

Text 2:1-5

1 And the third day there was a marriage in Cana of Galilee; and the mother of Jesus was there:

2 and Jesus also was bidden, and his disciples to the marriage.

3 And when the wine failed, the mother of Jesus saith unto him, They have no wine.

4 And Jesus saith unto her, Woman, what have I to do with thee? Mine hour is not yet come.

5 His mother saith unto the servants, Whatsoever he saith unto you, do it.

Queries

a. Why would Jesus go to a wedding?
b. What was Mary expecting from Jesus?
c. Did Jesus rebuke His mother?

Paraphrase

The third day after finding Philip and Nathanael, Jesus arrived in Cana of Galilee. There was a wedding feast in Cana, and Mary, the mother of Jesus, was attending the feast. Jesus and His disciples, having also been invited, were in attendance.

And when the wine was all gone, the mother of Jesus said to Him, The hosts have no more wine. Jesus replied, Woman, what have you to say about My work? This is not the proper hour for My public manifestation. His mother then said to the servants, Whatever He may say to you, do it!

Summary

Jesus, His disciples and His mother all attend a wedding feast in Cana of Galilee. Mary is anxious for Jesus to declare Himself. Jesus warns His mother that she is not to lead Him but to follow Him.

Comment

Cana was a small village about three or four miles northeast of Nazareth. The place is now called Kefr Kenna. J. W. Mc-Garvey, author of *Lands of the Bible,* visited there in 1879 and inspected an ancient building which had been converted into a chapel. This building was alleged to have been the very place where Jesus made the water into wine. They even pointed out to Brother McGarvey two stone mortars containing water which were used to immerse infants. They were supposed to be the very jars used by the Lord in His miracle. The caretakers of this chapel seemed to be unaware that these two jars could hold only about six gallons apiece, whereas the scriptural water jars held approximately 20 gallons each.

By "the third day" John probably means it was the third day after Jesus "decided to go into Galilee" (1:43) that He finally arrived in Galilee. He went directly to Cana of Galilee where he had been invited to a wedding. Cana would be about 60 or 70 miles north of Bethany beyond Jordan (as located on Map 1, pp. 17). Contrary to the contention of some commentators, it would be possible for Jesus and His disciples to walk 70 miles in two full days and a part of a third. Besides, He could have been advancing north toward Galilee day by day as He gathered His first disciples.

Mary was probably there as one invited to assist, much as certain ones are invited today to attend to the festivities of the wedding reception of a relative or a friend. It is not certain why Jesus was invited. Perhaps the newlyweds were personal friends or relatives of His mother; maybe the invitation came through Nathanael whose home was here in Cana.

The point is that Jesus took His disciples to Cana that they might see His glory. There is also the possibility that He took this opportunity to show these former disciples of John the Baptist the contrast between His type of ministry and that of their former teacher. The Baptist's disciples came later and asked Jesus why His disciples did not fast (Mt. 9:14ff), i.e., why His ministry differed from that of John the Baptist. Jesus was not eccentric and ascetic like John the Baptist, but neither was He a "glutton and a wine-bibber" (Mt. 11:19). As Trench points out, Jesus had a "harder and a higher task" than the Baptist. Jesus mingled with men in their daily living and sought to sanctify and purify their everyday activities (cf. Lk. 14:7-14), while John withdrew from the common activities of men. Jesus gives divine sanction to the joyous activities of human existence — profitable activities such as marriage, family life and etc. Our Lord never countenanced revelry or sensual gratification. His paramount emphasis was that of the Spirit (Mt. 6:33; Jn. 6:63). Jesus gives sanction to the wholesome activities of this world only insofar as they constantly lead us to a higher and holier walk with God.

If Mary was there as one assisting in the affairs of the festivities, her concern was only natural when the wine began to "fail". This would be very embarrassing according to the Eastern customs of hospitality. Just what Mary expected Jesus to do we are not expressly told. It may be safely inferred, however, from Jesus' answer (v. 4) that she desired something extraordinary from Him. For years Mary had observed such things as the astounding miracles surrounding her Son's birth — the prophecies of Simeon and Anna, Jesus confounding the teachers in Jerusalem — and she "kept all these sayings in her heart" (cf. Lk. 2:51). She had probably been informed of the miracles surrounding His baptism. Now Jesus appears with six disciples, and it seems to her that He is ready to announce Himself to the world and make some drastic changes in the present social order. Mary has decided that this is His opportunity to do so, and she hints that He should avail Himself of this moment. Mary felt that the Lord needed some "motherly advice" on how to carry out His work.

In verse 4 we see that Jesus understood Mary to be dictating the course of His ministry. A literal translation of His answer would read "Woman, what to me and thee?" As Lenski puts it, Jesus was saying, "Woman, what is there in common for us in this matter?" or, "This is my affair, not thine." In the word "Woman" there is no rebuke or insult for He used the same word tenderly remanding her to the care of the beloved John (cf. Jn. 19:26). But in the phrase "what have I to do with thee" there *is* a rebuke. He cannot allow even His mother to dictate His affairs. It was necessary for the Lord later to remind His family that they must not interfere with His ministry. When His friends thought Him "beside Himself" they seem to have reported to Mary and her sons (Mk. 3:21). His family came seeking Him apparently to take Him home for a forced rest. But Jesus would not even walk through the crowds to talk to them. They came, it appears, to interrupt His work, and He was very explicit in showing that He was subject to the influence of no human, not even His mother (cf. Mk. 3:31-35). Jesus is Lord of *all!* Everyone must depend upon Him as the *only* mediator (I Tim. 2:5). Much earlier than the Cana incident, we remember, Jesus as a lad of twelve indicated to His mother and Joseph that he was not to be restricted by parental interference because "he must be about his Father's business" (Lk. 2:48-50).

He informs His mother that His "hour is not yet come." He has an hour set in the Father's economy for each task which has been given Him. When that hour comes, He acts, and not until then. Jesus never allows anyone to rush or hurry Him (cf. Jn. 7:6, 8, 30; 8:20; 12:23; 13:1; 17:1).

It is inspiring to witness such immediate submission as was evinced in Mary's directions to the servants. Her decision to simply trust Jesus has now prepared her for a manifestation of His glory. It is not inconsistent, therefore, for Jesus to perform the miracle when He had previously rebuked Mary's impertinence. Mary's lesson can be applied to our lives today. James writes, "Ye ask, and receive not, because ye ask amiss, that ye may spend it in your pleasures" (Jas. 4:3). When we seek the Lord's blessings for carnal pleasure or vanity we "receive not." But when we resign ourselves to His will (I Jn. 5:14-15) we receive "exceeding abundantly above all that we ask or think."

Quiz

1. Where is Cana?
2. Explain how Jesus could have made the journey to Cana in three days.
3. How did Jesus' ministry differ from that of John the Baptist?
4. Why do we think that Mary expected a miracle from Jesus?
5. Name two incidents where Jesus rejected the intervention of His family into His affairs.
6. What is the lesson for us in this section?

THE MIRACLE PERFORMED

Text 2:6-11

6 Now there were six waterpots of stone set there after the Jews' manner of purifying, containing two or three firkins apiece.
7 Jesus saith unto them, Fill the waterpots with water. And they filled them up to the brim.
8 And he saith unto them, Draw out now, and bear unto the ruler of the feast. And they bare it.
9 And when the ruler of the feast tasted the water now become wine, and knew not whence it was (but the servants that had drawn the water knew), the ruler of the feast calleth the bridegroom,
10 and saith unto him, Every man setteth on first the good wine; and when men have drunk freely, then that which is worse: thou hast kept the good wine until now.
11 This beginning of his signs did Jesus in Cana of Galilee, and manifested his glory; and his disciples believed on him.

Queries

a. What is "the Jews' manner of purifying"?
b. Was this a drunken feast?
c. Is this Jesus' *first* miracle?

Paraphrase

Now there were six stone water-jars which had been set there for purifying purposes (Jewish ceremonial purification) and they were capable of containing about 20 gallons apiece. Jesus commanded the servants, saying, Fill the water-jugs with water. The servants then filled the jars full to the brim. Jesus

next commanded the servants, saying, Draw out a portion and
carry it to the ruler of the feast. The servants carried a portion
to the ruler and when he tasted the water which had been made
wine, and did not know where it came from (but the servants
that had drawn the water knew), the ruler of the feast called the
bridegroom and said, You know the proverb that says, "A man
sets his good wine out first then when the taste is blunted, he sets
out the poor wine," but you have kept the good wine until last.
This is the first sign that Jesus did and He did it in Cana of
Galilee, and He manifested His glory and His disciples believed
on Him.

Summary

Jesus miraculously changes water into wine, primarily to manifest His divine glory. His disciples believed on Him as a result.

Comment

Six 20-gallon water-jugs, set aside for purification rites, indicates a large crowd. John, writing for Gentile readers, feels it
necessary to note that the jars were there "according to the Jews'
manner of purifying." The Jews washed their hands and their
pots and pans before and after eating to cleanse themselves
ceremonially, (Mt. 15:1-11). This was one of their traditions
added to the law of Moses (cf. Mk. 7:1-9; Lk. 11:37-41). The
Jews were very careful to wash before meals in case they had
touched a Gentile, or rubbed against a publican or a harlot in the
marketplace.

What would be the thoughts of the servants and Mary when
Jesus commanded that the jars be filled with water? It would be
fruitless to speculate. Just as it is pointless to speculate about
the extent of the miracle, i.e., whether the water became wine
only when they drew it out of the jars, or, whether all the water
in each jar became wine and remained so. The point is, Jesus
performed a miracle! The radical critics claim this miracle runs
counter to the laws of nature; therefore, they attack the credibility of the account.

Trench, in his *Notes on the Miracles of Our Lord,* page 116,
explains it this way: "He who each year prepares the wine in the
grape, causing it to absorb, and swell with, the moisture of earth
and heaven, to transmute this into nobler juices of its own, did
now concentrate all those slower processes into a single moment,
and accomplish in an instant what usually He takes many months

to accomplish . . . He was working in the line of His more
ordinary operations, the unnoticed miracles of everyday nature."

We cannot doubt the miracle of the grape as it grows through
the "slower processes" before our very eyes though we cannot
explain it. We ought not to doubt the same result attained in an
instant by your Lord when the record rests upon irrefutable testimony of eyewitnesses.

The skeptics and the sensualists consider this miracle to be
ammunition for their attacks upon the Bible along another line.
They charge Jesus with immoral action, and claim that He made
intoxicating wine. The burden of proving that Jesus did make
intoxicating wine is with those who make the accusations. They
are the ones who say the wine was intoxicating. John does not
say so! It is a prejudiced and unscholarly determination that
says the Greek word *oinos* (the word used here) must always
mean intoxicating wine wherever the word is used. In fact, New
Testament and classical usage show that the word may mean a
number of things. Thayer shows that *oinos* is even used of the
vine itself (cf. Rev. 6:6) rather than the juice. In classical Greek,
usage may be cited to show *oinos* designating the grape itself,
the juice still within the grape, the fresh pressed juice, and unin-
toxicating drinks. A corresponding word in the Hebrew language
is *yayin*. When Hebrew scholars translated the Hebrew Old
Testament into the Greek language (known as the *Septuagint*),
they used the Greek word *oinos* to express the meaning of their
word *yayin*. The word *oinos* is used in the Septuagint as a generic
term for wine — fresh, cooked, fermented juices alike. (Cf. Num.
6:4; Judges 13:4 where "wine" is used for the grape itself).

Aristotle, Pliny and Nicander speak of *oinos* that does not
intoxicate. Classical writings could be cited to show that the
ancients knew of five ways of keeping grape juice from fermenta-
tion, and they called such preserved juice *oinos*. No one should
use this instance to justify drinking today unless he can prove
absolutely that the wine Jesus made is *just like* the wine they
propose to drink!

Of course, the question is always posed as to what the ruler
of the feast meant by his speech in verse 10. The ruler seems
to be chiding his host in verse 10 by reminding the bridegroom of
a well known custom. It was, and is, a common practice to pass
off an inferior wine when men's taste becomes blunted by even
a small amount of drinking. It is obvious that the ruler was not
drunk. He recognized the difference in the juice instantly. It is

only the perverse mind that could imagine Jesus condoning drunken revellry, let alone using His power to furnish men something destructive to their physical and spiritual well-being.

Modern man cannot possibly use the Cana miracle to justify indulgence in any of the detestable liquor of today (cf. ICor. 8:13; 10:31-33; Rom. 14:15-17, 21). Those who buy from liquor manufacturers today are supporting an industry which has contributed to the loss of thousands of lives physically, and the eternal damnation of thousands of souls spiritually.

In verse 11 we learn that this is the first miracle Jesus performed. His second was the cure of the nobleman's son (cf. Jn. 4:54). One commentator defines "sign" as "a miracle viewed as proof of divine authority and majesty." A "sign" points to the divine Doer instead of the deed. This seems to be the very purpose of the miracle — to point His disciples to the divine Son. Note how John, one of the eyewitnesses of this miracle, puts everything else secondary to the manifestation of Jesus' deity.

It would be well to here define the word disciple. Disciple comes from the word *manthano*, which means "I learn." A disciple then is one who learns, a pupil, a follower. It is best defined as a learner, one who accepts the instruction of his teacher and makes it his way of life. The miracle at Cana shows us that Jesus did not require His disciples to have perfect knowledge or perfect faith in order to begin following Him. What the Lord wants is a disciple with a willing mind and an honest heart — willing to learn and honest enough to apply the lesson to his own life!

Quiz

1. Why did the Jews purify themselves before meals? Was this a law of Moses?
2. Why should we believe miracles recorded in the Bible when we cannot understand them or explain them?
3. Name three things that the Greek word *oinos* (wine) may mean other than intoxicating wine.
4. Give two reasons why men today may not use this miracle to justify drinking intoxicating beverages.
5. Is this Jesus' first miracle? Explain.
6. Give a good definition of the word disciple.
7. What was the primary purpose of this miracle?

JESUS MOVES HIS HEADQUARTERS TO CAPERNAUM

Text 2:12

12 After this he went down to Capernaum, he, and his mother, and his brethren, and his disciples; and they abode there not many days.

Queries

a. Where is Capernaum?
b. Why did He go there and what did He do?
c. Who are "his brethren"?

Paraphrase

After the wedding feast at Cana was over, Jesus went down from the hills of Galilee unto the city of Capernaum on the shore of the Sea of Galilee. And He remained there a few days, He, and His mother, and His brothers and His disciples.

Summary

Jesus moves to Capernaum, abiding there a few days with His entourage as He awaits the time of the Passover.

Comment

We have entitled this part of the outline, "Jesus Moves His Headquarters to Capernaum" because He ever after makes this city a pivotal point for the larger portion of His ministry. One must, of course, study the Synoptics to realize this, since nearly all of His Galilean ministry is recorded in those accounts. One thing seems evident — He never returns to Nazareth to live, only to preach and be rejected. After John the Baptist was delivered up to prison, Jesus "withdrew into Galilee; and leaving Nazareth, he came and dwelt in Capernaum, which is by the sea . . ." (Mt. 4:12-13). The Gospel of Luke tells us that Jesus did not own a residence (Lk. 9:58). He probably made Peter's home His headquarters here in Capernaum (cf. Mk. 1:31). Whatever the case, Capernaum seems to be the headquarters for all His activities until He finally ends His public ministry in Galilee and comes to the Feast of Tabernacles (Jn. 7:2, 3, 10). Once He arrives in Judea at this feast, He never again returns to Galilee except for a few days preaching "in the borders of Galilee" (cf. Lk. 17:11 and Map 6, p. ...., Vol. 2).

There is a great deal of controversy among commentators as to the most probable location of Capernaum. The two most likely places are the ruins of modern Tell Hum or Khan Minyeh. Most scholars prefer Tell Hum. For extended discussion on this subject consult any good Bible dictionary (cf. also Andrews, *Life of Our Lord,* pp. 224-230). Capernaum was located on the north side of the Sea of Galilee, west of the Jordan River entrance into the sea. The ruins of Tell Hum are very interesting. Most of its buildings were built of black basalt with the exception of a white synagogue. This synagogue probably dates back to about 200 A.D. but it was built on still more ancient ruins which date back to the very time of Christ. These ancient ruins may be those of the same synagogue that the centurion erected for the Jews (cf. Lk. 7:5) and the one in which Jesus healed the withered hand (Mk. 3:1-6). Capernaum was the home of the four fishermen; it was a customs station (Mt. 9:9), and a residence of a high officer of the king (Jn. 4:46). A Roman garrison was probably stationed there under the command of the centurion mentioned above. So completely has this city perished, as was prophesied by the Lord (Mt. 11:23), that the very site is a matter of much dispute today.

This verse (12) affords an opportunity to discuss the question of the Lord's brethren. The question would probably never have been raised had not the Roman church made the perpetual virginity of Mary a dogma. First consideration must be given to what the New Testament reveals on the subject of the Lord's brothers and sisters. They are mentioned in Mt. 12:46-50; 13:55-56; Mk. 3:31; 6:3; Lk. 8:19; Jn. 2:12; 7:3; Acts 1:14; I Cor. 9:5; Gal. 1:9. There were four brothers, James, Joseph, Simon and Judas. None of the accounts tell us how many sisters He had or what their names were. The Greek is very precise concerning this matter. His brothers and sisters are always called *adelphoi* (brothers and sisters) — not *anepsioi* (cousins) or *sungeneis* (kinsmen). Notice also they are always called His brothers and sisters, not sons and daughters of Mary. Further, they are always connected with Mary in the particular relationship of being her very own children; members of her household and under her direction — not merely her nieces and nephews.

Amazingly enough, the theory of the perpetual virginity is even held by many Protestant writers. There is strong inference against this theory in the Scriptures. First is the inference that there were later sons born to Mary because Jesus is called the "firstborn son" in Luke 2:7. Secondly, there is the inference that Joseph later "knew" Mary in the husband-wife sexual relationship after the virgin birth of Jesus — "he knew her not until she brought forth a son" (Mt. 1:25).

The number of days Jesus stayed in Capernaum is not certain. We are told that it was "not many days." The couple in Cana had a spring wedding, probably sometime in April. Jesus attended this wedding, spent a few days in Capernaum then joined the thousands of pilgrims going to Jerusalem for the Passover, which was also in April.

And so we come to the end of the period of preparation. When Jesus arrives at the Passover He will declare Himself to the rulers in no uncertain terms. There He will begin His public ministry — His open manifestation to the multitudes and the Jewish rulers.

Quiz

1. Describe Capernaum.
2. Why does John mention that Jesus went to Capernaum?
3. Tell all that the Scriptures say about Jesus' brethren.
4. What does the New Testament say about the "perpetual virginity" of Mary?

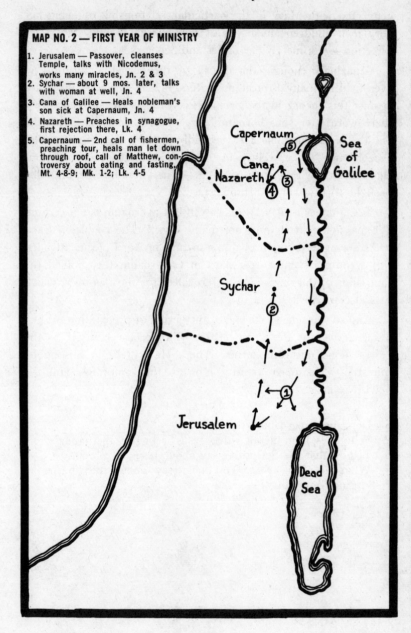

MAP NO. 2 — FIRST YEAR OF MINISTRY

1. Jerusalem — Passover, cleanses Temple, talks with Nicodemus, works many miracles, Jn. 2 & 3
2. Sychar — about 9 mos. later, talks with woman at well, Jn. 4
3. Cana of Galilee — Heals nobleman's son sick at Capernaum, Jn. 4
4. Nazareth — Preaches in synagogue, first rejection there, Lk. 4
5. Capernaum — 2nd call of fishermen, preaching tour, heals man let down through roof, call of Matthew, controversy about eating and fasting, Mt. 4-8-9; Mk. 1-2; Lk. 4-5

In our outline we are still under the second main division of the Fourth Gospel. We come now to the next point under that main division, namely, The Public Ministry — First Year. A primary purpose of John in writing his account was to supplement the other three gospel accounts. Therefore, many of the incidents of His public ministry will have to be obtained from the Synoptics. We shall endeavor to mention these omitted incidents from time to time as we connect the events of the Fourth Gospel. It is suggested that the reader frequently consult the maps in this commentary to get a comprehensive view of Jesus' public ministry as the text is being studied.

II The Word Manifested to the Jews and their Rejection of of Him. 1:19-12:50 (cont.)

    B. The Public Ministry — First Year 2:13 - 4:54

        1. Early Judean Ministry 2:13-35

            a. Cleansing of the Temple 2:13-17

            b. Results of the Cleansing 2:18-22

            c. General Judean Ministry 2:23-25

CLEANSING OF THE TEMPLE

Text 2:13-17

13 And the passover of the Jews was at hand, and Jesus went up to Jerusalem.

14 And he found in the temple those that sold oxen and sheep and doves, and the changers of money sitting:

15 and he made a scourge of cords, and cast all out of the temple, both the sheep and the oxen; and he poured out the changer's money, and overthrew their tables;

16 and to them that sold the doves he said, Take these things hence; make not my Father's house a house of merchandise.

17 His disciples remembered that it was written, Zeal for thy house shall eat me up.

Queries

    a. What is the "passover of the Jews"?

    b. Why were oxen, sheep and doves being sold in the Temple? Why were money changers there?

    c. How was Jesus able to cleanse the Temple unresisted?

Paraphrase

Now the time for the passover of the Jews was near and Jesus left Capernaum and went up to Jerusalem. There, in the temple courts, He found some who were selling, for sacrificial purposes, oxen, sheep and doves. He also found some who had set up their change-making enterprise in the temple and were sitting, conducting their business there. Jesus made a whip of ropes and drove the sheep and the oxen out of the temple courts. Then he scattered the money of the money-changers, turned over their tables, and said to the ones who were selling the doves, Carry these things out of here! Stop making my Father's house a market place! His disciples then remembered what had been written in the Scriptures, "Zeal for thy house will consume me."

Summary

Jesus goes up to the Passover to worship. He finds the Temple being desecrated, and he manifests His wrath at such hypocrisy. His disciples interpret it as a fulfillment of messianic prophecy.

Comment

The majority of commentators agree that this cleansing of the Temple is the first of two such incidents in the ministry of Jesus. The very nature of John's gospel would indicate this. (a) John writes to fill in what the other Gospel writers have omitted. He omits some events of greater significance than the cleansing of the Temple, i.e., the transfiguration, the birth of Jesus, etc. Would it fit John's pattern then to repeat what all three of the other writers record (cf. Mt. 21:12-13; Mk. 11:15-18; Lk. 19:45-46)? (b) John is the most chronological of the four. Why would he violate all of his chronology and insert here at the beginning of Jesus' ministry an event which the other three definitely place at the last Passover of His ministry? (c) John gives the most detailed account of the last Passover of the four writers. If John is merely repeating the Synoptical cleansing, why did he not put it in his detailed account of the last Passover? (d) Again, in all three accounts of the second cleansing the Jewish rulers are represented as seeking to destroy Jesus. There is no mention of such an intensified animosity here in John's account of the first cleansing of the Temple.

Jesus left Capernaum, some 680 feet below normal sea level, and traveled "up" to Jerusalem, some 2500 feet above sea level. When people are said to be going "up" and "down" by the Gospel writers, it is meant that the people are going "up" and "down" in altitude — not in a north-south map-wise manner. The Lord's reason for going to Jerusalem was that the time for the Passover was near. We shall deal with the details of this feast in later chapters. Here it will be sufficient to notice only a few significant things connected with the Passover: (a) it was one of three feasts which every male Jew above the age of twelve must attend — the other two being the Feast of Tabernacles and the Feast of Pentecost; (b) Passover was the most important of all the feasts; (c) it commemorated the Israelite deliverance from Egyptian bondage, and more specifically the passing over of the death angel (cf. Ex. 12 and 13); (d) the feast was to be held on the fourteenth day of the month Nisan (corresponding to our April); and, (e) many sacrifices were required for those who worshipped at the feast (Num. 28:16-25).

Great multitudes of Jews attended the Passover. Jews from all over the civilized world made pilgrimages to Jerusalem for this feast. Josephus, in his account of the destruction of Jerusalem in 70 A.D., tells us that there were approximately 3 million Jews in the city when Titus the Roman general beseiged it at Passover time. This Jewish historian adds that some 260,000 lambs were slain that year during the one week of the Passover celebration. Remember, also, that a great number of oxen would be sacrificed that week.

We begin now to get a picture of the magnitude of the scene which greeted Jesus as He entered the city of David. Some three million people there for the "Independence Day" celebration of the Jews — all crowded into Jerusalem until her very walls were groaning. People slept on the housetops and in the courtyards — anywhere they could find a place that was reasonably safe from robbers. The Law of Moses provided for the people to bring their own animals (if they had any) to the Passover. They were to present them to the priests for approval and subsequent sacrifice on the worshipper's behalf. Most of the worshippers preferred to purchase a suitable animal (one without spot or blemish) at the feast. This was much more convenient than bringing their own animal. Money-hungry priests had taken advantage of this attitude and they abused their authority to approve or disapprove the sacrificial animal until they had cornered the market! It is probable that had the worshippers gone to the trouble to present a lamb of his own flock the priests would have rejected it as unfit for sacrifice. The people's only recourse then was to purchase an animal from the vending stalls of these racketeers. Of course, with such a complete control of the market, the racketeers would be able to coerce exorbitant prices from the starving populace. One commentator says the Sadducees made a profit of about $300,000 each year from this market. It is also said that, at one time, the price of a pair of doves was about four dollars when they were really worth only about a nickle a pair. The people were being fleeced in the name of religion.

The changers of money also had a racket. Every male Jew above 20 was required to pay a Temple tax (cf. Ex. 30:11-16; Mt. 17:24-27) of a half-shekel. Only Jewish coinage was acceptable for the tax — Gentile money was polluted. Everyone who did not have Jewish money was obliged to get it changed. This afforded another means of extortion for the Jewish rulers.

There are two Greek words used in the New Testament which are translated "temple." One word *(hieron)* signifies "the entire building with its precincts, or some part thereof"; the other word *(naos)* usually means the inner sanctuary of the Temple. John uses the former word *(hieron)* here. Most scholars think that the animal markets were in the court of the Gentiles. This was the outermost precinct of the Temple. The rulers would most likely set up their markets here, not wishing to desecrate the courts where only Jews were allowed. Jewish pride shows its haughty contempt for the Gentiles by bringing the stench and filth of the animals into the court of the Gentiles. One writer describes the scene thusly: "And this was the entrance court of the Most High! The court which was a witness that that house should be a House of Prayer for all nations had been degraded into a place which for foulness was more like shambles and for bustling commerce more like a densly crowded bazaar; while the lowing of oxen, the bleating of sheep, the babel of many languages, the hucksterling and wrangling, the clinking of money and of balances (perhaps not always just) might be heard in the adjoining courts, disturbing the chant of the Levites and the prayers of the priests!" (Farrar, *The Life of Christ,* pp. 445ff). It was not merely the presence of the animals that was offensive

78

THE GOSPEL OF JOHN

to the Lord. His righteous ire was aroused because of the dishonest merchandizing and the desecration of the only place the Gentiles might seek the presence of God. Men seeking God (cf. Jn. 12:20) were denied His presence! We would do well to search our own practices as the people of God today. Is there anything in our lives — pride, carelessness, irreverence — that keeps the seeking stranger from the presence of God? Remember the wrath of the Lord as he displays it here against such action. Compare also Matthew 23:13.

Zealous for His Father's house and His Father's children, Jesus deliberately fashioned a whip from some rope-like pieces of twisted reeds. Then He quickly and decisively drove the animals out as the traders were fleeing from His countenance. In almost the same motion He turned and began upsetting the tables of the money-changers. It was a scene of bedlam: the animal traders trying to control and protect their property — sheep and oxen running helter-skelter — men shouting and swearing — bankers on their hands and knees greedily scurrying after the tinkling coins as Jesus went from table to table overturning them. The Lord then issued two thundering commands: "Take these things out of here!... Stop making my Father's house a market place!' The word translated "house of merchandise" is the Greek word *emporiou*, from which we have the English word emporium. The Jews were literally making God's holy Temple an animal emporium. It was a scene so suddenly violent that the disciples were fearing for the Lord's safety, and they remembered an appropriate prophecy of Scripture, "Zeal for thy house will eat me up." Another interpretation is that the disciples saw further manifestation of the Deity of Jesus in this incident and remembered the Messianic prophecy of Psalms 69:9. Why not apply both interpretations to the utterance of the disciples? They recognized His fulfillment of the Messianic prophecy, but on the other hand they feared that His fanatic zeal would eventually bring about His death. The Greek word for zeal is *zelos* from which we also get the word jealous. Christ was very jealous for His Father's house — that it not be made a shelter for unrighteousness.

There are those who would have us believe that Jesus struck the men with His "scourge of cords." It is true that the Lord revealed holy anger at the conduct of these men, but striking them with a whip would not be in keeping with the character of His teaching. His answer to Pilate would seem to preclude such physical combat on His part . . . "if my kingdom were of this world, then would my servants fight . . . but now is my kingdom not from hence." (Jn. 18:36). Compare also His instruction to Peter concerning "taking up the sword" (Mt. 26:51-56). His only use for the whip was to drive out the dumb beasts, for they could not respond as He would have them to His spoken commands. In the second cleansing of the Temple the hucksters fled before His righteous countenance — He brandished no scourge there. The awesome manifestation of His glory drove the men out — just as it was manifested to the officers who could not arrest Him because "never man so spake" (cf. Jn. 7:45-46).

The public ministry of our Lord begins with explosive suddenness. No doubt the multitudes, along with the disciples, were electrified. Some of the multitude might even have recalled the prophecy, "Behold I send my messenger, and he shall prepare the way before me: *and the Lord, whom ye seek, will suddenly come to his temple* . . . But who can abide the day of his coming? and who shall stand when he appeareth? . . . and he will purify the sons of Levi . . ." (Malachi 3:1-3). The rulers were probably so surprised and so shamed that they were not able to grasp immediately the significance of this manifestation. Nevertheless, they counterattacked at once, touching off a controversy that grew and increased in fierceness until they were satisfied with nothing less than His death. This was the beginning of a struggle that continued for three years. The rulers would hardly let it rest for a moment. They followed Jesus wherever they could, seeking ever to ensnare Him . . . to destroy Him. The world hated Him because He "testified of it, that its works were evil" (Jn. 7:7).

Quiz

1. Give three reasons for believing that this is the first of two recorded instances where Jesus cleansed the Temple.
2. What was the Passover feast to commemorate?
3. About how many people attended the feast in Christ's day?
4. How were the animal traders taking advantage of the worshippers?
5. Why were the money-changers there?
6. Where was this merchandizing probably taking place?
7. Do you think Jesus struck the men with His scourge? Explain.
8. Give two Old Testament prophecies connected with this incident.

RESULTS OF THE CLEANSING

Text 2:18-22

18 The Jews therefore answered and said unto him, What sign showest thou unto us, seeing that thou doest these things?

19 Jesus answered and said unto them, Destroy this temple, and in three days I will raise it up.

20 The Jews therefore said, Forty and six years was this temple in building, and wilt thou raise it up in three days?

21 But he spake of the temple of his body.

22 When therefore he was raised from the dead, his disciples remembered that he spake this; and they believed the scripture, and the word which Jesus had said.

Queries

   a. Why did the Jews ask the question (v. 20)?

   b. What is the meaning of Jesus' answer in verse 19?

Paraphrase

The Jews said therefore to Jesus, What Messianic sign do you show us? do you have any credentials for these presumptuous actions in our temple? Jesus answered them, saying, Destroy this Sanctuary of God, the place where God's Presence dwells, and I will raise it up in three days. The Jews therefore said, It has taken forty-six years to erect this Sanctuary, and do you claim to be able to re-erect it in three days? But Jesus was speaking of the Sanctuary of His body, and when He was raised from the dead His disciples remembered these words of Jesus and applied them to His resurrection. When the disciples had witnessed the Resurrection and had seen this prophecy fulfilled, they believed more firmly that the Old Testament Scriptures were fulfilled in Jesus, and that His Word was the Word of God.

Summary

Jesus' authority to reform their Temple is challenged. The rulers demand from Him a wonderful sign of Messianic proportions. Jesus predicts a future sign. They are now destroying God's typical Sanctuary by evil practices and will eventually seek to destroy the Incarnate Sanctuary of God by crucifying Him. But in three days He will raise the new Sanctuary up!

Comment

At every manifestation of Jesus' glory the "wheat" is separated from the "chaff." The cleansing of the Temple is no exception. Those of honest heart find spiritual nourishment for their faith ((vv. 17, 22). Those concerned with satisfying the vanities of life become more hardened in their carnality (v. 20). Here Jesus gave an answer at which the Jews scoffed and used to reject His authority. The disciples, however, laid His answer up in their hearts and later their faith was strengthened! Jesus often clothed His greatest spiritual lessons in enigma for the very purpose of separating the spiritual followers from the carnal followers (cf. Mt. 13:10-16; Jn. 6:60-65).

When they regained their composure, the Temple traders turned on this presumptuous Galilean (v. 18) and demanded that He show proper credentials for His reformatory actions. Undoubtedly some of the rulers of the Temple were among those asking for His authority. There seems to have been a general expectation that a prophet (Elijah or Jeremiah) would come to prepare for the Messiah by confirming present religious practices or changing them. Perhaps they even recognized that this Galilean might possibly be the Messiah Himself!! If so, they must have some amazing and extraordinary signs to confirm their suspicions. According to Jewish tradition, the arrival of the Messiah was to be heralded by great wonders and upheavals. These rulers are like the great multitudes of followers in Galilee (Jn. 6). Jesus told them that they were only following Him because He had filled their hungry stomachs. When He told the multitudes that He came to feed them on His Word (Jn. 6:63), they turned away from Him. These rulers in Jerusalem refused all the signs of His deity because He would not conform to their carnal ideas concerning the Messiah of the Jews. Christianity is not primarily concerned with relieving hunger or suffering. The New Testament church is not primarily concerned with national or international politics. Christianity IS concerned primarily with saving men's souls by bringing them to trustful obedience to the doctrines of Christ (Jn. 14:15, 21, 23; 15:1-6, 14; Heb. 5:9, etc.).

There is a tendency on the part of some interpreters to apply the answer of Jesus (v. 19) exclusively to His physical body. However, the context demands that a certain amount of literal application to the Jewish temple be included in His answer. As Wescott sees it, "there are two distinct ideas which have to be brought into harmony here." Jesus is referring to both the actual Temple and the Sanctuary of His body. The Jews were at that very moment destroying God's Temple, the place where the presence of God dwelt, by their unholy desecration of it. But this Sanctuary of stone was only a figure of the Person of Jesus Christ — the Incarnate Presence of God dwelling among men (Jn. 1:14). They are now desecrating the typical Sanctuary and will eventually destroy the fulfillment, even Jesus.

When they shall have rejected and put to death the Christ — the fulfillment of the type — what further use will there be for the type (the Sanctuary of stone)? The crucifixion of Jesus, in Whom dwelt the fulness of God, brought with it necessarily the destruction of the Temple. Why should God allow a rebellious Israel to keep the type when they spurn the Antitype? Thus the Jews brought about the destruction of their Temple and the judgment of God upon themselves (cf. Mt. 27:25). When the Lord expired upon the cross, the veil of the Temple was torn in two, signifying that it was all over with Israel and their typical Sanctuary (Mt. 27:51). Henceforth God may be worshipped anywhere if the worship is "in Spirit and in truth" (cf. Jn. 4:23).

Jesus warned that the unfaithfulness of the Jews and their rejection of Him would end in terrible judgment upon the nation and complete destruction of their Temple (Mt. 23:37; 24:1-28). He intimated that these very rulers of the Jews would see such judgment come upon their nation (Mt. 26:64). As Lenski so aptly puts it, "Thus the sign the Jews demanded will be theirs indeed . . . a sign of final judgment."

The Messiah perishes — the Temple and the Jewish economy falls — the Presence of God is withdrawn from His people. The Messiah lives again — the true Sanctuary of God rises — the Presence of God is restored among His new people. God's presence among men was restored by the glorification of Christ and the giving of the Holy Spirit to believers (Jn. 7:37-39; Acts 2). God does not dwell in temples made with hands (Acts. 7:48; 17:24), but the church (the universal body of Christ) is the temple of God. Every Spirit-filled believer is a living stone in God's spiritual house (I Pet. 2:5; cf. also I Cor. 3:16; II Cor. 6:16; Eph. 2:21-22). Every Christian's body is individually a "temple of the Holy Spirit" (I Cor. 6:19-20).

The Jews scoffingly interpreted His words literally. It had taken them forty-six years to partially reconstruct the temple.

Would this Galilean rebuild it in three days? Preposterous! The reconstruction of the Temple was begun by Herod the Great in about 20 B.C. This is forty-six years later, and it is still unfinished. It was not completed until 64 A.D., thirty years after the crucifixion of the Lord Jesus. And then, only six years after its completion (70 A.D.) it is so levelled by the Roman destruction that, according to the Jewish historian Josephus, "one stone was not found upon another."

The Jews, their carnal minds closed to any spiritual comprehension of Christ's words, scoff at Him for predicting that He will do in three days what they have not even finished in half a lifetime. When Jesus was on trial for His life, bribed witnesses brought lying testimony against Him by perverting these words of prophecy (cf. Mk. 14:57-58; 15:29-30).

Even the disciples did not then realize the significance of His words. John, writing years after His death and resurrection, records that the disciples remembered this prophecy after they had witnessed the resurrection. Their retrospective look at a fulfilled prophecy was spiritual food — nourishment for their faith.

Quiz

1. Why did Jesus clothe His answer in enigma?
2. What kind of sign did the Jews demand of Jesus?
3. Is there any reference to the literal Temple of the Jews in Jesus' answer? Explain!
4. Give three Scripture references which show that the Jews brought about judgment upon themselves.
5. Where is the Sanctuary of God today? Cite Scripture references to prove your answer.
6. How long did it take to complete the Jewish temple? When was it destroyed?
7. Was this prediction of Jesus ever repeated? Where?

GENERAL JUDEAN MINISTRY

Text 2:23-25

23 Now when he was in Jerusalem at the passover, during the feast, many believed on his name, beholding his signs which he did.

24 But Jesus did not trust himself unto them, for that he knew all men,

25 and because he needed not that any one should bear witness concerning man; for he himself knew what was in man.

Queries

a. Why did Jesus "not trust himself unto them"?

Paraphrase

Now when Jesus was in Jerusalem, He did many signs during the seven days of the feast. Many of the people at the feast marvelled at these signs which they beheld Him doing and believed Him to be a prophet sent from God. But Jesus did not entrust them with the essence of His message and cause, for He knew the heart of every one of them. Jesus did not need that anyone should tell Him of the nature of man, for He was able to search their hearts and know what was in their very thoughts.

Summary

Jesus knows who His true believers are by looking on their hearts.

Comment

In John 2:23 through 3:36 we have recorded a rather general Judean ministry. There is one exception — the specific conversation with Nicodemus (3:1-21). The Judean ministry begins, of course, in Jerusalem, in the Temple, and continues for at least the duration of the Passover in the city. This ministry branches out into the land of Judea (3:22) and it lasts for about eight or nine months. We are able to calculate the length of time from the fact that Jesus began the Judean ministry at Passover time, and He is next found in Samaria about four months before the harvest (Jn. 4:35). Harvest time and Passover time are identical and the Jews count their religious year from Passover to Passover. Thus Jesus was in Samaria about four months before the end of the year, or about eight months after the beginning of the year.

During the Passover feast (also called the Feast of Unleavened Bread, and which lasts seven days) Jesus performed many marvelous signs. What they were, we are not told. One of the Jewish rulers was convinced by these signs that Jesus was "a teacher sent from God" (3:1-2). The multitudes also beheld these signs and many are said to have "believed on his name." Just how sincere their faith was seems to be debatable,

considering the attitude the Lord had toward them (v. 24).
Jesus had very little success in Judea throughout His entire
ministry. It appears that those who believed on him here were
interpreting His signs as harbingers of an impending militant
Messiah who would spark a revolution and throw off all their
oppressions. The serious student of the life of Jesus must famili-
arize himself with the situations and the expectations of the
times in which Jesus lived, or he cannot appreciate the attitude
of the multitudes toward Christ's marvelous signs.

The average Jew was poverty-stricken. He suffered at the
hands of the Roman overlords, at the hands of the tax-collectors
(publicans), and under the heavy yoke of the religious bigots in
Jerusalem (cf. Lk. 11:46). The Jewish nation had a proud
heritage. It had enjoyed pre-eminence under David and Solomon,
but during the hundreds of years since Solomon, this nation had
suffered oppression and slavery at the hands of her conquerors.
Israel had become the byword (Deut. 28:37; I Ki. 9:6-7) and the
laughing stock of the heathen and the barbarian. It had been some
four hundred years since God's last direct communication with
His chosen nation. The people had doubtless heard and repeated
rumors of the miraculous signs attending the birth of the son of
a priest down in Jerusalem (John the Baptist). The multitudes
would tell over and over again the story which had been started
by some shepherds, of a babe born some thirty years ago in the
city of David, and of the signs surrounding His birth. Suddenly,
the one who came "in the spirit and power of Elijah" burst on the
scene with his soul-searching preaching. Josephus says of him that
"he had great influence over the people who seemed ready to do
anything that he should advise." One day when the crowds had
come out to hear him, he pointed to a Galilean and cried, "Behold,
the Lamb of God." A few days later this same Galilean appeared
suddenly in the Temple at Passover time and challenged the very
throne of religious authority. And so this multitude of Judeans
who were beholding His signs were anticipating these signs as
omens that He was about to declare Himself the long awaited
King, the One who would forever relieve their poverty, their
political oppression and their religious burdens.

This is what Jesus saw when He looked on their hearts, and
this is why He would not entrust them with His cause. He
could not trust such carnally minded people with the full revelation of His teachings. Many would follow Him only as long as
He would produce miracles and signs, but when He began to talk

about their making His Word their spiritual food — about self-denial and surrender — they would "go back and walk with him no more" (Jn. 6:66). Men were never able to deceive Jesus by outward appearance — He knew just what was in the heart of anyone with whom He came in contact (cf. Jn. 1:42, 47-48). He later read the thoughts of His disciples, of Nicodemus, and of the woman of Samaria (cf. Mk. 9:33-35; 14:30; Jn. 3; Jn. 4). Enthroned in heaven, He still sees the motives and schemes of men's hearts (cf. Acts 5 and 9; Rev. 1-3).

There is a second possible interpretation of Jesus' refusal to trust Himself to them. Some commentators believed that Jesus avoided a situation where He must trust His physical person to them because of the enmity He had aroused in attacking the merchandizers of the Temple courts.

These three verses offer an excellent study of the meaning of the word believer. The English words believe and faith are derived from the Greek word *pisteuo*. It generally means "believe, trust, be persuaded, adhere to and have faith." The Greek noun *pistis* (faith, belief) is used in the New Testament in a number of ways. It may be used to mean obedience (cf. Rom. 4:12), or it may be used to mean the enlightened conscience of the individual Christian (cf. Rom. 14:22-23). But in the context before us we have two other clear definitions of the word. In verse 23 many believed on his name without really surrendering their wills to Him. Although they beheld the miraculous signs which He did, their belief was probably a carnal hope in a worldly Messiah. It *is* possible to accept the miracles of Jesus as actual facts and still not trust Jesus with one's soul to the point of surrender and obedience. The brethren of Jesus accepted the fact that He was doing miraculous works (Jn. 7:3-4), but since He did not fit their ideal as the materialistic type of Messiah, they would not believe on Him. In verse 24, the same word, *pisteuo*, is used, and the translators translated it trust. Trust is the best definition of *pisteuo*. There can be no faith and belief without trust. When we trust someone, we have confidence in his person and in his word — confidence that his word is true. When the Lord invites us to believe in Him, He invites us to have confidence in His Word. When He promises us eternal life, it is always conditioned upon our confidence and trust in His Word as the Truth. How can one completely confide in and trust His Word without obeying its commands? It is impossible — faith without obedience is dead!

Jesus had no confidence in these Judeans, and would not trust them because their belief was only superficial and carnally motivated. Their faith was one of accepting the factual evidence but refusing to surrender their hearts in trusting obedience to His Word. How do *you* believe in Jesus? Do you trust Him with a confidence that loves to obey?

Quiz

1. How long was Jesus' first Judean ministry? How do we know this?
2. Considering the expectations of the people in Jesus' time, what would they believe, having beheld His signs?
3. What is meant by "he knew all men"?
4. What does the word believe *(pisteuo)* means?

EXPOSITORY SERMON NO. 2
John 1, 2
JESUS MANIFESTS HIS GLORY

Introduction
I. PROLOGUE
  A. A condensed version of the entire Gospel of John.
    1. Pre-existence of the Word
    2. The Word manifested to Jews; their rejection
    3. The Word manifested to others; their acceptance
  B. The Prologue summarized in 1:14
II. JOHN THE BAPTIST'S WITNESS TO THE LAMB OF GOD
  A. Jesus' glory evidenced to John
    1. The Spirit's descent seen by John
    2. God's voice heard by John
  B. John taking second place to Jesus
    1. John pointing out Jesus to his own followers
  C. John's disciples following Jesus
    1. Talking with Him for whole day
    2. Beginning to get a glimpse of His glory

Discussion
I. HIS GLORY SHOWN IN SEARCHING HEARTS OF DISCIPLES
  A. Peter nicknamed "Rock": Peter's future known (Lk. 22:31-32; Acts 4:19; 5:29)

B. Nathanael — prime example
   1. Seen by Jesus as an Israelite without guile (Something to strive for today)
   2. Thinking himself hidden under fig tree
   3. Nathanael convinced of Jesus' glory (v. 1:49)
C. The Holy Spirit still manifesting God's glory through the Word
   1. The living and active Word of God . . . (Heb. 4:12)
   2. The converting power of the Word of God
      TO THE GLORY OF GOD . . . NOT OF THE PREACHER

"JESUS NEEDED NOT THAT ANYONE SHOULD BEAR WITNESS CONCERNING MAN: FOR HE HIMSELF KNEW WHAT WAS IN MAN" (Jn. 2:25).

II. HIS GLORY SHOWN AT CANA WEDDING FEAST
A. Majesty shown in rebuking His mother Jn. 2:4
   1. Mary seeking to dictate His affairs
   2. At age 12 His warning to Joseph and Mary that He has a task to perform
   3. Later warning to Mother and brethren He is not to be influenced by men (Mt. 12:46-50)
   4. Obedience to Jesus enjoined upon ALL . . . EVEN HIS MOTHER (cf. Lk. 11:27-28.)
B. Mary's resignation to His will 2:5
   1. Jesus then not inconsistent in performing miracle
   2. NECESSITY OF DOING THINGS HIS WAY . . . ACCORDING TO HIS WILL
      a. Not asking to spend in own pleasure
      b. Mary's desire . . . her own pleasure
C. The Miracle 2:7ff
   1. Disciples belief on Him as a result 2:11
   2. Skeptics rejection of the miracle
   3. Same One able to step up wine process by miracle still glorified in nature every day
   4. FAITH PRODUCED BY ALL OF HIS MIRACLES
      a. To show His control over nature, etc.
      b. HIS SUPREME MIRACLE, THE RESURRECTION
         1) RESURRECTION THE BASIS OF OUR FAITH

2) BY IT WE TRUST HIM TO RAISE US, IF WE OBEY!

III. HIS GLORY SHOWN AT CLEANSING OF TEMPLE
  A. No miracle here!
    1. Miracles not always needed to show His glory
    2. Here His Majesty shown in righteousness
    3. HIS SINLESS LIFE MANIFESTS HIS GLORY
       When on trial . . . "If have done any evil, bear witness . . . etc."
  B. His glory manifested in His wrath at ungodliness

Conclusion

I. ALL THESE MANIFESTATIONS TO INSTILL TRUST . . . FAITH
  A. Faith *is* trust . . . . hope that is seen is not hope
     Faith that understands all is not faith
     The testimony of honest men found here

II. THESE MANIFESTATIONS ARE WARNINGS
  A. Our very thoughts seen by Jesus . . . deeds without love unavailing
     The hypocrisy of Church-going without faith and love
  B. The need of obeying, not dictating to Him
  C. His wrath against sin (Jn. 3:36)

III. MEN NOT REQUIRED TO HAVE *ALL* KNOWLEDGE OR *ALL* FAITH TO BECOME HIS DISCIPLE!
  A. A willing mind and honest heart and lead by Him to growth.
  B. Disciples defined as learners, trusters,
  C. HIS PROMISE CAN BE YOURS . . . ONLY TRUST HIM
    1. "Verily, verily, I say unto you, He that heareth my word, and believeth him that sent me, hath eternal life, and cometh not into judgment, but hath passed out of death into life."
  C. WHEN DEATH COMES TO A DISCIPLE OF CHRIST WHO HAS TRUSTED AND OBEYED . . . . DEATH BECOMES BUT THE DOOR TO PARADISE, A SHARING IN THE GLORY OF THE SON!

CHAPTER THREE

The third chapter of John's Gospel is very precious to the believer. It contains the teaching of the Lord on the new birth; it contains the "golden text" of the Bible (3:16); it contains the final testimony of John the Baptist to Christ. In this third chapter may be found the grand scheme of redemption. God's part (v. 16-17) and man's part (v. 3-5) in this redemptive plan is made plain. Chapter three falls naturally into two sections as outlined below:

II The Word manifested to the Jews and their rejection of Him. 1:19-12:50 (cont.)
  B. The public ministry — first year 2:13 - 4:54 (cont.)
    2. Conversation with Nicodemus 3:1-21
      a. Teaching on the Kingdom and new birth 3:1-8
      b. Earthly mysteries compared with heavenly mysteries 3:9-15
      c. More heavenly mysteries 3:16-21
    3. Further Judean ministry and John the Baptist's final testimony 3:22-36
      a. John's witness concerning himself 3:22-30
      b. John's witness concerning Christ 3:31-36

TEACHING ON THE KINGDOM AND NEW BIRTH

Text 3:1-8

1 Now there was a man of the Pharisees, named Nicodemus, a ruler of the Jews:

2 the same came unto him by night, and said to him, Rabbi, we know that thou art a teacher come from God; for no one can do these signs that thou doest, except God be with him.

3 Jesus answered and said unto him, Verily, verily, I say unto thee, Except one be born anew, he cannot see the kingdom of God.

91

4 Nicodemus saith unto him, How can a man be born when he is old? can he enter a second time into his mother's womb, and be born?

5 Jesus answered, Verily, verily, I say unto thee, Except one be born of water and the Spirit, he cannot enter into the kingdom of God.

6 That which is born of the flesh is flesh; and that which is born of the Spirit is spirit.

7 Marvel not that I said unto thee, Ye must be born anew.

8 The wind bloweth where it will, and thou hearest the voice thereof, but knowest not whence it cometh, and whither it goeth: so is every one that is born of the Spirit.

Queries

   a. Why did Nicodemus come to Jesus by night?
   b. What does "water and Spirit" have to do with being born anew?
   c. How does the wind illustrate the birth of the Spirit?

Paraphrase

Now there was a man in Jerusalem by the name of Nicodemus. He belonged to the sect of the Pharisees and was a member of the Sanhedrin, the ruling body of the Jews. This man came to Jesus during the night, and said to Him, Teacher, we know that you are a teacher come with God's approval; for no teacher is able to substantiate his teaching with the miraculous signs which you are doing unless God is with him. Jesus said to Nicodemus, I tell you positively, Unless a person be born anew, he cannot participate in the kingdom of God. Nicodemus asked Jesus, How is it possible for a man to be born anew when he has already been born once? can he enter a second time into his mother's womb, and be born again? Jesus replied, I tell you positively, Unless a person be born of water and of Spirit, he cannot become a citizen of the kingdom of God. Physical birth, although renewal were possible, could not avail for an inheritance in the kingdom of God. Spiritual rebirth, however, brings forth a child of the Spirit and a child of Promise. Do not let the mysteriousness of a spiritual rebirth astonish you, Nicodemus. You are aware of the reality of the wind, for you see it act upon objects and you hear its sound, but cannot fathom its origin or destination. Just so may you be aware of the reality of the working of the Holy Spirit, by the action He causes in the spiritually reborn.

Summary

Nicodemus comes to Jesus, convinced that He is a teacher come from God, to see what He has to say about the glorious future of Israel. Jesus tells this Pharisee that the Kingdom of God belongs to those born of "water and of Spirit" — not the fleshly sons of Abraham. Jesus illustrates the mystery of the working of the Holy Spirit by the mystery of the wind.

Comment

What of this "ruler" who came and talked with Jesus "by night?" All we know of Nicodemus is that: (a) he was a Pharisee; (b) he was a ruler of the Jews (probably a member of the Sanhedrin — the Senate of the Jews); (c) he came to Jesus by night; (d) he was an esteemed teacher in Israel; (e) he later spoke on behalf of fairness in judging Jesus (7:50); (f) he boldly assisted Joseph of Arimathaea in removing the body of Jesus from the cross and in burying it (19:39); (g) he was willing to admit the verity of Jesus' miracles and that Jesus was a "teacher come from God."

Some students of the Scriptures are inclined to question Nicodemus' courage from the single phrase, "the same came unto him by night." Of course, there is the reference in John 19:39 to this same incident, but as a matter of fact, we do not know why this ruler of the Jews came to Jesus by night! It may be that he came in the night simply to have privacy and leisure. The Sanhedrin had religious jurisdiction over every Jew in the world (Mt. 23:1-3) and they were to investigate everyone suspected of being a false prophet — was this his reason? Contrariwise, Nicodemus leaves us with the impression that he did not believe Jesus to be a false prophet but a true prophet! It is remarkable that Nicodemus came at all! It may be that Nicodemus was too busy during the day to come; it may be that Jesus was too busy during the day for Nicodemus to get sufficient answers for his questions. Even though we must guess as to the reason why Nicodemus chose the night for his visit instead of the day, one fact stands out plainly — Jesus did *not* reprove him for his night visit. He who came to "seek and to save that which was lost" never smothered the faintest spark of belief but ever strove to fan it into a burning fire of faith and devotion.

We pause here, in the continuity of the context, to give the reader a brief history of Pharisaism. It was a sect which seems (according to Josephus) to have originated some years before the Maccabean wars. This party began with a group of men whose righteous indignation had been aroused against the worldliness and paganism creeping into Israel through Hellenism (Greek cultural influence). About 200 B.C. this group of men reacted against the infiltration of idolatry and immorality and were called *hasidim* or Pietists. It seems they acquired the name Pharisee or Separatist about 135 B.C. In order to join this party, a young man had to take a pledge of entry "that he would devote all his life to studying and observing every detail of the traditions of the elders and the law of Moses." The Pharisees produced men of high morality, in most instances, and they were essentially a believing sect. They believed in God, man as a free moral agent, a general resurrection, angels, rewards and etc. They produced men like Saul of Tarsus who "lived in all good conscience" as to the letter of the Law. Their main fault was in swinging the religious pendulum, through reaction to evil, to the opposite extreme. They rebelled from the extreme liberalism of the Hellenists — but they fell into the extreme of self-righteousness and meritorious conservatism. They made religion a matter of outward conformity to traditions, rites and ceremonies. As Jesus said, "outwardly they appeared beautiful, but inwardly they were full of hypocrisy and iniquity." They changed the great principles of God's law into legalistic by-laws and a meritorious keeping of regulations. They "strained the gnat and swallowed the camel"; they tithed to the last tiny dill seed but neglected the weightier matters of the law — justice, and mercy, and faith, (cf. Mt. 23: Lk. 11). One good example of their emphasis on externals is their absurd regulations concerning the Sabbath. The Law merely says, "remember the Sabbath day to keep it holy," and that no servile work shall be done on that day. The Pharisee decided to define work. One form of work, he decided, was tying knots. Then he had to define which knots were work and which were not. "The following," says the Mishnah, "are the knots the making of which renders a man guilty; the knot of camel drivers and that of sailors; and as one is guilty by reason of tying them, so also of untying them." Knots which could be tied or untied with one hand were legal. "A woman may tie up a slit in her shift and the strings of her cap and those of her girdle, the straps of shoes or sandals, or wine skins." Notice now the absurdity of their regulations carried to a logical end: If a man wanted to tie up a goat or donkey, he could not use a rope. He might tie up his animal with a woman's girdle or her shoe strings, for these were legal knots. A woman could not look in a mirror, for she might remove a fallen hair from her shoulder, which would be classified as "bearing a burden on the Sabbath." No one could gargle on the Sabbath, for that would be practicing medicine. Such rules and regulations were matters of life and death; by conforming to such absurdities they were sure they were pleasing God! To such a religious sect belonged Nicodemus.

For an honest-minded man, with a sensitive conscience, such a religion soon becomes unsatisfying and often disgusting. It is a religion of sham. Nicodemus appears to be an honest and sensitive man. Could it be that this "teacher of all Israel" had been dissatisfied with his externalized religion for the last few years? Could it be that he had secretly, but eagerly, listened to the preaching of John the Baptist? Perhaps he had also heard the teaching, as well as having seen the signs, of Jesus and wanted to earnestly discuss them with Him.

There also seems to be leaping within his heart of the hope that these signs of Jesus somehow proclaim the impending arrival of the kingdom promised to the Branch out of Jesse and the Son of David. He, as one of the chief Pharisees, wants to make preliminary arrangements, perhaps, for his place of honor in that kingdom.

Whatever the cause of Nicodemus' coming, Jesus brushes aside his inadequate estimate of Him, and answers the thoughts of this man's heart. Jesus knew his problem, even if we do not!

There are two problems in verse three: (a) does the Greek word *anothen* mean "from above" or "anew"? (b) what does Jesus mean by "cannot see"? As to the first problem, Nicodemus' reply (v. 4) seems to indicate that he took Jesus to mean "anew" or "again." But we cannot definitely prove that this is what Jesus meant merely by Nicodemus' reply. The Greek word may mean both "from above" or "anew." Actually, Jesus seems to indicate both meanings — a heavenly or spiritual birth which is a new birth. By the word *see* Jesus probably means participate or have part in. The same Greek word is used to express participation in death (cf. Lk. 2:26; 9:27; Acts 2:27; Heb. 11:5). Thus, any man who is not born again has no part in God's promised kingdom. Physical lineage will not do. Just because

Nicodemus was a Jew, a descendent of Abraham, did not mean he would be a member of Jehovah's new dispensation (cf. Gal. 3rd and 4th chapters). His circumcision as an Israelite was useless in the new kingdom (Gal. 5:15) — he must become a new creature.

Jesus' answer undoubtedly startled Nicodemus. That any descendent of Abraham, Isaac and Jacob should be excluded from the kingdom of promise was absolutely foreign to the Jewish thinking. Nicodemus could not comprehend what Jesus meant. It was not the Lord's fault. Nicodemus was simply carnally minded — he could not think spiritually. "Now the natural man receiveth not the things of the Spirit of God; for they are foolishness unto him; and he cannot know them, because they are spiritually judged (discerned)" (I Cor. 2:14). Thus in verse four Nicodemus exclaims incredulously, "How"?

Just what does Jesus mean by born anew? There are veiled references to the new birth in the Old Testament. Ezekiel, chapters eleven and thirty-six, speaks of a new heart and a new spirit which God will give His people. He will "put His Spirit within them and cause them to walk in His statutes." In Ezekiel 18:31, Israel is commanded, "Cast away from you all your transgressions, wherein ye have transgressed; and make you a new heart and a new spirit: for why will ye die, O house of Israel?"

The phrases, new birth, regeneration, new creature, born again, run through the New Testament as its absolute requirement for entering the kingdom of God!

1. "Begotten again unto a living hope by the resurrection of Jesus Christ from the dead" (I Pet. 1:3).
2. We purify our souls by obedience to the truth, and we are begotten again, of incorruptible seed through the Word of God (I Pet. 1:22-23).
3. We are brought forth of God by the Word of truth (Jas. 1:18).
4. God saved us through the washing of regeneration and renewing of the Holy Spirit (Titus 3:5).

5. We have "put off the old man . . . and have put on the new man, that is being renewed unto knowledge after the image of him that created him" (Col. 3:10).

6. We are to "put away . . . the old man . . . and be renewed in the spirit of our mind . . . put on the new man that after God hath been created in righteousness and holiness of truth (Eph. 4:22-24).

7. Circumcision or uncircumcision avails nothing . . . "but a new creature" (Gal. 6:15).

8. If any man is in Christ, "he is a new creature: the old things are passed away; behold they are become new" (II Cor. 5:17).

9. When we have buried the old man through repentance and baptism, we "rise to walk in newness of life" (Rom. 6:1-6).

10. "Except ye turn, and become as little children, ye shall in no wise enter into the kingdom of heaven" (Matt. 18:3).

In verse five, then, Jesus answers Nicodemus' "How"?
The new birth is one of "water and Spirit." There cannot be a separation of the terms "water and Spirit." There is no article (the) in the original language with either word. Regeneration is one single action. That is, the initial act of the new birth is completed at the time a person submits in faithful obedience to baptism in water for the remission of sins (Acts 2:38). Of course, after having become babes in Christ, we must continue to feed on His Word and grow spiritually (I Cor. 3:1-2; Heb. 5:11-14; I Pet. 2:2) — baptism does not make a person "eternally secure."

As will be seen from the ten Scripture references to the new birth, regeneration comes when the Holy Spirit confronts a man through the preaching or reading of God's Word and when that man crucifies (puts to death) self (cf. Gal. 2:20; 5;24; 6:14) and comes forth from the world into the kingdom of God. When the seed, which is the Word of God, falls upon good and honest hearts, men will change their minds and their lives (by faith and repentance) and will change their state (by baptism). Such men have been spiritually transformed (cf. Rom. 12:2).

We do not propose to limit the working of the Holy Spirit to the agency of the written or spoken Word alone! He may work in and through men and women apart from the Word as He pleases. Of one thing we are certain — the Holy Spirit is the One who convicts men of "sin, of righteousness, and of judgment" (cf. Jn. 16:8). This He does through the agency of the written Word of the apostles, for He is the Holy Spirit of promise which should "guide the apostles into all the truth." He is the same Holy Spirit which spoke through Peter and the eleven on the day of Pentecost and three thousand souls were "pricked in their hearts" from conviction of their sin (Acts 2:36-38) and were subsequently "born anew of water and Spirit." The Holy Spirit did not act there apart from the spoken Word, nor does He now, in both convicting sinners and showing them the way of salvation.

It is unquestionable that Jesus means baptism in water when he says "born of water . . ." This is the same Jesus who later *commands,* "Go ye therefore, and make disciples of all the nations, baptizing them into the name of the Father and of the Son and of the Holy Spirit: teaching them to observe all things whatsoever I commanded you . . ." (Mt. 28:19-20). The New Testament is plain that the apostles understood Jesus to mean baptism in water (cf. Acts 8:36-39; 10:47; I Pet. 3:20-21, etc.). To refuse to repent (change the mind, the will and the actions) and still claim to have been born anew would be mocking God. And, in like manner, to refuse the positive command of Christ to be baptized (immersed) in water and still claim to have been born anew is sheer mockery!

In verse six Jesus shows Nicodemus the impossibility of his suggestion of physical rebirth (v. 4). Even if it were possible to have a physical rebirth, it would produce only flesh, "and they that are in the flesh cannot please God" (cf. Rom. 7:18 — 8:17). This leaves Nicodemus and all the Jews, with their physical birthright from father Abraham, outside the kingdom. Paul says that only those born after the Spirit are children of promise (cf. Gal. 3:7, 14; 4:6, 7, 28).

Jesus must have seen astonishment in the face of this learned teacher. Nicodemus cannot grasp the *how*. He is stumbling over the *how* as so many after him have. "Do not be astonished," says Jesus in verse seven, "at the mysterious working of the Spirit, for He is invisible." The Master Teacher then illustrates the Spirit's unseen nature by the wind. No man knows where the wind originates, nor its ultimate destination. Yet we know the reality of the wind from the effect it has upon certain objects. We see it blow the leaves from the trees in the fall and we hear it whistle and moan through the branches and we know the wind is there. Just so, we may know the reality of the working of the Holy Spirit when we observe the conviction and the change wrought in the lives of men through Him and hear His voice speaking forth from those who speak the Word of Christ in the spirit of Christ. Those who have experienced the birth of the Spirit will let flow from within their inner life, rivers of living water unto thirsty men (Jn. 7:38-39), and such a life will bear the fruit of the Spirit (Gal. 5:22-24).

Here is an analogy of the new birth as compared with the physical birth. This analogy is given merely in the interest of stimulating thought and meditation. It is axiomatic that an analogy cannot prove any argument — it merely illustrates. Further, we do not presume to say that Jesus had such an analogy in mind when He said, "Ye must be born anew." Remember, however, that John says of this same Jesus, "all things were made through him (physical life) . . . in him was life; and the life was the light of men (spiritual life)." He is the Giver of life in both realms, and it may be that such a comparison was in His mind as He spoke to Nicodemus.

AN ANALOGY OF THE "NEW BIRTH"

BIRTH CYCLE	NATURAL BIRTH	SPIRITUAL BIRTH
Seed	Living sperm	Living Word of God Lk. 8:11
Place of planting	Womb	Heart (the will) Lk. 8:15
Signs of life	Action	Repentance and Confession Lk. 3:8-15 Lk. 19:8-9
Change of state	Delivered forth in water — translated into the world	Baptized in water — translated into the kingdom of God Rom. 6:1-6
Life comes by Circumcision	Breath of life Of the flesh	Holy Spirit Rom. 8:11 Of the Heart Rom. 2:28-29
Nourishment	Milk — then solid foods	Sincere milk of the gospel I Pet. 2:2, then solid food — Heb. 5:13-14; I Cor. 3:1-2
Relationship	Son, child of the father, heir	Son by adoption, child of God the Eternal Father, joint heir with Christ Gal. 4:5-7

It is interesting to note that the phrase "kingdom of God" is found only twice in the entire Fourth Gospel (verses 3 and 5 of the third chapter). In John 18:36 Jesus tells Pilate that His kingdom is not of this world, but one must go to the Synoptics to find "kingdom of God" repeated again and again.

In view of the supreme importance of this subject, we introduce here, before continuing our commentary, a "SPECIAL STUDY" entitled "The Kingdom of God" by Seth Wilson. Bro. Wilson is Dean of Ozark Bible College, Joplin, Missouri, and it is through his Christian courtesy that we reproduce his essay here.

100

SPECIAL STUDY NO. 1

The Kingdom of God
— by Seth Wilson

The New Testament says much about the kingdom, mentioning it 140 times by the term "kingdom," besides the other terms and phrases used. The whole message of the great prophet, John the Baptist, was the importance of the coming kingdom and of personal preparation for it. Jesus taught more about the kingdom than He did about any other subject. He taught men to pray for the kingdom to come (Mt. 6:10). He said it was the greatest treasure in the world, one for which any one should joyfully sell all other possessions that he might gain the kingdom (Mt. 13:44-46). He told us all to "Seek first the kingdom of God and his righteousness; and all these things shall be added unto you" (Mt. 6:33). He made it more important than the food and clothing which are necessary to physical life. Surely it matters much whether we believe in the kingdom and know it, not only in theory, but in vital experience.

What is the Kingdom of God?

It is not easy to give a definite and brief answer which would be satisfactory to all students or true to all the Scriptural uses of the phrase. *Its essential idea is the reign or government of God over the lives of men.* Sometimes it comprehends the characteristics and advantages of the complete submission of an individual life to the rule of God. Sometimes it refers to the whole community of men who obey God on earth. Sometimes it has reference to heaven itself as a place where God reigns in perfect peace, wisdom, and glory. But regardless of all other circumstances, it is always essentially the rule of God in the hearts of men.

Other terms and phrases are used for the same idea, and are freely interchanged with "the kingdom of God." Matthew uses the words "kingdom of heaven" about 29 times, although it is not used in any other New Testament book (cf. Mt. 13:11 with Mk. 4:11; and Mt. 13:31 with Mk. 4:30-31, etc.). It is also called "his kingdom (the son of Man's)" (Mt. 13:41; 15:28); "my kingdom" (Christ's) (Jn. 18:36; Lk. 22:29-30); "the everlasting kingdom of our Lord and Saviour Jesus Christ" (II Pet.

1:11) ; "the kingdom of God's dear Son" (Col. 1:13) ; "the kingdom of Christ and of God" (Eph. 5:5) ; "my (Christ's) church"
(Mt. 16:18) ; the "church of God" (I Tim. 3:5, 15) ; "the church"
(Eph. 1:22 ; 3:10, 21 ; 5:23-32) ; "the church of the first born
(ones)" (Heb. 12:23) ; or as congregations viewed distributively
"churches of God" (I Cor. 11:16) ; (I Thess. 2:14), and
"churches of the saints" (I Cor. 14:33), and "churches of
Christ" (Rom. 16:16).

These various expressions are not identical in their limits
and points of emphasis, but they do overlap in that all of them
have reference to the realm of God's rule through Jesus Christ.
That reign will some day be complete and unchallenged, and will
continue so eternally ; but it also exists now and has for many
centuries in the midst of those who resist it or deny its present
reality.

The kingdom is not represented as coming all at once fully
formed and in its ultimate glory, but this term is used for the rule
of God in different stages, and for the growing control of Christ
over men through the gospel — "first the blade, then the ear, and
then the full grain in the ear" (Mk. 4:26-29). Study the other
parables of the seed and of the leaven. Chiefly, of course, it looks
forward to the glorious consummation, the complete subjection of
all things to God, the eternal state of righteousness, peace, and
blessedness that will result when God is given full control. Jesus
came to establish the kingdom by revealing the righteousness,
mercy, and goodness of God's will, and by winning the hearts
of men to surrender themselves to Him — by redemption of sinners and reconciliation of their hearts to God, by putting the law
of God into their minds and hearts through faith and love and
regeneration of the Holy Spirit — (Heb. 8:10-11 ; Jn. 3:5). The
government of God is truly desirable. Pray that it may prevail
upon earth as it does in heaven (cf. Psalm 19:7-14).

John the Baptist, Jesus, and the apostles (before the cross)
preached that the kingdom was just at hand, to be expected
and prepared for immediately. It was certain to come before that
generation died (Mt. 16:28 ; Mk. 9:1). In a sense it was already
come (Mt. 12:28) in the person of the King, and it was suffering
violence from the days of John the Baptist (Mt. 11:12 ; Lk.
16:16). The rule of God and the principles of His realm were
being presented in the preaching of Jesus, and Jesus could say,
"Lo, the kingdom of God is in the midst of you" (Lk. 17:21).

This was said to the unbelieving Pharisees who did not have the kingdom in their hearts, but it was in the midst of them, in that its King was there proclaiming its laws and swaying His authority over them or at least some who were standing among them. Moreover, whenever it came to men, it was to come not with great demonstrations of force, "not with observation, but as in inward growth (Mk. 4:26-28). It was to spring from seed, which is the Word of God (Lk. 8:11), and to be brought about by preaching of the Word (Mt. 13:18-23). It was to begin small and grow to be very great (Mt. 13-31-33). During the growing stage it takes some "bad" as well as "good," who have to be separated by the angels at the end of the world (Mt. 13:47-50). The sons of the kingdom are the righteous (Mt. 5:20), who grow in the world side by side with the wicked (Mt. 13:38-41). Yet it is not a kingdom of this world (Jn. 18:36). It must be entered by a new birth of the Spirit (through faith in and submission to the word of the Spirit) and of water (baptism into Christ) (Jn. 3:5; Eph. 5:26; Titus 3:5; I Pet. 1:23). And the least in the kingdom is greater than the greatest born of women (Mt. 11:11). Having part in it is equivalent to having "eternal life" and being "saved" (Lk. -8:18, 25, 26).

One thing is evident — that Jesus did not mean to set up a worldly, materialistic, or military kingdom. The devil offered Him the kingdoms of the whole world, but He refused them (Mt. 4:8-10). The Jews and even the apostles wanted that kind of kingdom, but Jesus disappointed them. After the feeding of the five thousand, they sought to take Him by force and make Him king, but Jesus refused. The very next day He preached a sermon on the spiritual and eternal purpose of His ministry which was so unacceptable to them that multitudes went away and followed Him no more (John 6). This same idea presents itself at the time of the Triumphal Entry, when the people in all the clamor and excitement of a mob, gathered together as a whole nation at Jerusalem for the Passover, and welcomed Jesus into the city as "the King that cometh in the name of the Lord" (Lk. 19:38), and as bringing in the kingdom of His father, David (Mk. 11:10). If he had wanted a kingdom of force, or of material wealth, or of political organizations, He could have had it (cf. Mt. 26:53; Jn. 18:36-37). Because of materialistic ambitions of the people regarding the Messiah, Jesus avoided telling plainly that He was the Christ, and He had to teach of His life's purpose and His kingdom by parables in order to hold their attention and try to make plain the unwelcome message of a spiritual kingdom, instead of temporal.

One group of passages represents the kingdom under the figure of a place. This is the case in all expressions involving the act of entering into the kingdom (Mt. 5:20; 7:21; 18:3). It is better to enter into the kingdom of heaven with one eye than, having two, to be cast out (Mk. 9:27). Men are said to be near or far from it (Mk. 13:34). Those who enter are those who are reborn and who do the will of God, who have by relationship with the Saviour and by their characters a certain fitness for it (Lk. 9:62; Mt. 7:21; Jn. 3:5). But after entrance has been secured, it is a place of enjoyment, as in Mt. 25:34, and a place where even Jesus Himself eats and drinks, as in Mt. 26:29.

In a second class of passages the kingdom is represented as a possession. It is said to belong to the poor in spirit and to those persecuted for righteousness (Mt. 5:3, 10; Lk. 18:16). It will be taken from the Jews and given to a nation bringing forth the fruits thereof (Mt. 21:43). It is the gift of God (Lk. 12:32). It is the most valuable of possessions, and it is the height of wisdom to seek and the summit of prosperity to secure it (Mt. 6:33; Lk. 12:31).

A third class of passages represents the kingdom as an organization, or body, composed of a certain class of men.

A fourth class designates it as an order of things, or a dispensation. The special new feature of the dispensation thus announced was its spirituality. Its members are in it by choice and by their perfect willingness to do God's will. Thus its law is written on their hearts and in their minds (Heb. 8:10-12; Rom. 12:1-2).

The kingdom did come in the generation of the apostles as Jesus said it would (Mk. 9:1). It did come with power on the day of Pentecost after His resurrection. Peter was given the keys (Mt. 16:19). Paul went everywhere preaching the kingdom of God (Acts 20:25), although he determined to know nothing save Jesus Christ and Him crucified (I Cor. 2:2). Philip preached the kingdom of God, and the faith of the Samaritans caused them to be baptized into Christ and become members of the church (Acts 8:12). Paul says God "translated us into the kingdom of his dear Son" (Col. 1:13), and John says "he made us to be a kingdom" (Rev. 1:6). The church is a kingdom. Today, in our dispensation, it is THE kingdom. It is certainly not a democracy as to its nature. Christ is the obsolute monarch over all things pertaining to the church and to the kingdom (Eph. 1:22).

Quiz

1. Tell five things you know of Nicodemus.
2. Why do you think Nicodemus came to Jesus by night?
3. What was the main fault of the Pharisees?
4. Did Jesus say, "Ye must be born *anew*," or did He say, *"from above"?*
5. Give at least five Scripture references in the New Testament concerning new birth, or regeneration.
6. How is one born "anew" (cf. verse 5)?
7. In what way did Jesus illustrate the working of the Holy Spirit in the new birth process?
8. Essentially, what is the kingdom of God?
9. When did the kingdom of God come?

EARTHLY MYSTERIES COMPARED WITH HEAVENLY MYSTERIES

Text 3:9-15

9 Nicodemus answered and said unto him, How can these things be?
10 Jesus answered and said unto him, Art thou the teacher of Israel, and understandest not these things?
11 Verily, verily, I say unto thee, We speak that which we know, and bear witness of that which we have seen; and ye receive not our witness.
12 If I told you earthly things and ye believe not, how shall ye believe if I tell you heavenly things?
13 And no one hath ascended into heaven, but he that descended out of heaven, even the Son of man, who is in heaven.
14 And as Moses lifted up the serpent in the wilderness, even so must the Son of man be lifted up;
15 that whosoever believeth may in him have eternal life.

Queries

a. Who is the "we" of verse 11?
b. What are "earthly things" and "heavenly things"?
c. Why is the comparison made with the "serpent in the wilderness"?

105

Paraphrase

Nicodemus said to Jesus, How is it possible for all these things to come to pass? Jesus replied to Nicodemus, Are you *the* teacher of Israel and do not understand these things? I tell you positively, that John the Baptist and I are speaking that which we fully know, and we are testifying to that which we have actually seen with our own eyes, and yet none of you are receiving our testimony. If I have told you the earthly things of the kingdom which happen within the realm of human experience and you continue to disbelieve, how shall you believe if I tell you of the heavenly counsels of an Omniscient God? No mortal has ever ascended into heaven to obtain first hand knowledge of God's eternal will except He that has come down from heaven, even the Son of Man. And in like manner as Moses lifted up the brazen serpent in the wilderness, even so it is necessary that the Son of Man be lifted up in order that everyone who looks unto Him in believing obedience may be cured of sin's deadly bite and may have eternal life.

Summary

Nichodemus is curious as to the exact manner of working of the Holy Spirit in the new birth. Jesus tells him that inability to comprehend the secret actions of the eternal God is no excuse for unbelief. What is necessary for man to know, God has revealed through His Son.

Comment

Nicodemus' continual "how"? (v. 4, 9) is like that of so many men and women today. He cannot understand the secret doings of an Infinite God and therefore he refuses to obey the mysteries of this God which have been revealed and which may be empirically known. There are those today who will admit the historical verity of the death, burial and resurrection of Jesus of Nazareth but they will not give their souls over to God in trustful obedience to His Word because they cannot probe into and prove to their senses every unveiled mystery of an omnipotent God.

In verse 10 Nicodemus is informed that he should have had some knowledge concerning the subject under discussion, i.e., regeneration. The use of the article the in the Greek language emphasizes indentification. Since the article is used with both "teacher" and "Israel" in verse 10, the emphasis is that Nicodemus was one of *the* esteemed teachers in all Israel. He may even have been *the* leading teacher of the day, as Gamaliel was a few years later. The Pharisees were supposed to be the spiritual leaders of the nation — they were supposed to be the experts in the Scriptures. Nicodemus' ignorance of the subject of regeneration was inexcusable and should have been embarrassing. The "law and the prophets" spoke again and again of Jehovah's demand for a renewal of heart and mind (cf. Deut. 30:6; Psa. 51:10-12, 17; Isa. 1:16-20; 57-15; Jer. 24:7).

There are various interpretations of the plural *we* in verse 11: (a) Jesus speaks of Himself and the twelve disciples; (b) Jesus refers to Himself and the Old Testament prophets and writers; (c) Jesus means Himself and His forerunner, John the Baptist. We prefer the latter of the three as the most likely meaning. Both Jesus and John the Baptist knew the Spirit for they were filled with the Holy Spirit; both had seen the Holy Spirit in a visible manifestation (Mt. 3:16; Mk. 1:11; Lk. 3:22; Jn. 1:33-34); both were sent to testify as to the work of the Holy Spirit and to preach repentance and regeneration. Both were eyewitnesses of the working of the Holy Spirit — Jesus' testimony being greater than John's, of course, for He had descended from Heaven and from intimate communion with the Father. Jesus and the Baptist went about testifying as eyewitnesses to the reality of the Holy Spirit, but the Pharisees rejected their testimony and their message of repentance and were, in essence, calling both Jesus and John liars! The cause for rejection by the Pharisees is made plain in Luke 7:29-30. When the outcasts of society heard John's message of repentance they "justified God" (put God in His rightful place of Divine authority) and were baptized of John. But when the Pharisees heard, they "rejected the counsels of God" (dethroned God) and refused John's baptism. The Pharisees rebelled because they did not want to "bring forth fruits worthy of repentance" (cf. Lk. 3:7-14).

The omniscient Teacher now shows the mortal teacher it is unless to discuss Heavenly mysteries. Nicodemus cannot even understand earthly things. There are two general interpretations of what is meant by "earthly things" in verse 12: (a) that Jesus means the wind, or (b) that He means the earthly things within the kingdom of God, e.g., things that may be experienced such as faith, repentance, baptism, and renewal of mind and heart. We prefer the second interpretation, for it fits the context better. If

Nicodemus could not understand that a "new heart and a new spirit" was necessary to be pleasing unto God (something he should have known from the Old Testament), how much more incredible would be God's eternal purposes to such a carnal mind! It was evident even then to Jesus that the cross would be a "stumbling block to the Jews and foolishness to the Gentiles." How could Nicodemus understand it was necessary that the Son of Man be lifted up, like Moses lifted up the serpent in the wilderness — he could not even understand the Prophets whom he had pledged to study all his life!

Even when mortal man asks, "How can these things be?" God's wisdom is so infinite and unsearchable that none can know except they ascend into heaven and sit in personal conference with him. None except the Son of man and the Holy Spirit have ever enjoyed this intimate bosom-acquaintance with the Father. Paul informed the Corinthians the wisdom he spoke was God's wisdom, infinitely greater than men's eloquence. Such wisdom God had "hidden since the foundations of the worlds," but it had been given unto the apostles by a special revelation of the Spirit "which searcheth the deep things of God," (cf. I Cor. 2:6-11). The last phrase of verse 13, "who is in heaven," is omitted in many ancient manuscripts. It is omitted in the most recent Codex — the Bodmer Papyrus (see Introduction). Most authorities believe it to be a scribal gloss and we have, upon textual evidence above, omitted it from our paraphrase.

The incident referred to by Jesus in verse 14 is found in Numbers 21:4-9. The Israelites were in the wilderness country south of Mt. Hor, near to the Red Sea and the land of Edom when they began to rebel against Moses and God. The Lord sent fiery serpents among the people, and many were bitten and died. The people repented of their murmuring and came begging Moses to intercede on their behalf for mercy. Jehovah God then revealed His plan of salvation to Moses who was to tell it to the people. Moses would fashion a serpent from bronze and raise it up on a pole or a standard. Every Israelite who obeyed God's plan and looked upon the brazen serpent would be cured and restored to life. Commentators have wrested Jesus' use of this incident as an illustration in order to carry out their own analogies. There seems to be at least two main points of analogy or illustration which are revelant to the context: (a) just as the brazen serpent was the *only* cure for the deadly bite of the fiery serpents, so the "lifting up" of the Son of Man is necessary — a must — as the *only* remedy for the deadly bite of sin (cf. Jn. 8:28; 12:-32) ; (b) God provides the remedy for sin through His Son and only that man who looks upon Him in trusting obedience will be saved. Although God provided the children of Israel with a cure for snake bite, not one would have lived had they stubbornly refused to look upon the brazen serpent. "Obvious!" a reader says. Yet how many today who have been bitten by "that old serpent, the devil" are refusing to do the obvious thing and obey the gospel? Did the Israelites hold back, like Nicodemus, harping on the "how can this be?" Did they demand an explanation of the scientific and medical relationship between a bronze serpent and cure of snake bite? Indeed they did not! These people were saved, not because they understood God's requirement, but because they trusted God and obeyed His demand to look upon this brazen serpent. Whom among mortals can explain fully the relationship between Christ's death on the cross and His commandment to "believe and be baptized" with salvation? How is this possible? — it is not possible for us to fully comprehend — but it is possible for us to trust and obey! This was the lesson Nicodemus needed to learn, this was the lesson the disciples had to learn and the lesson we must all learn. "Trust and obey, for there's no other way . . ."

Quiz

1. Why should Nicodemus have known of the subject of regeneration?
2. Give three Old Testament Scripture references that speak of regeneration.
3. What is the best interpretation of *we* in verse 11? Why?
4. What are the "earthly things" that Nicodemus could not believe?
5. Give the two main points of comparison between the brazen serpent and the "lifting up of the Son of Man."

MORE HEAVENLY MYSTERIES

Text 3:16-21

16 For God so loved the world, that he gave his only begotten Son, that whosoever believeth on him should not perish, but have eternal life.

109

17 For God sent not the Son into the world to judge the world; but that the world should be saved through him.

18 He that believeth on him is not judged: he that believeth not hath been judged already, because he hath not believed on the name of the only begotten Son of God.

19 And this is the judgment, that the light is come into the world, and men loved the darkness rather than the light; for their works were evil.

20 For every one that doeth evil hateth the light, and cometh not to the light, lest his works should be reproved.

21 But he that doeth the truth cometh to the light, that his works may be made manifest, that they have been wrought in God.

Queries

a. Why did God "so love the world?"
b. How is the unbeliever judged already?
c. What is the significance of the contrast between "doing evil" and "doing the truth?"

Paraphrase

For God so dearly loved mankind, that He gave His Son, His Only-unique son, in order that everyone continuing to trust in Him may not be eternally separated from the presence of God, but may have eternal life. For God's primary purpose in sending His Son into the world was not to sentence and condemn the world but in order that the world might be saved through the agency of His Son. The man who continues to trust in Him is not condemned. The man who continues to disbelieve is condemned already because he has not trusted himself to the Only Son of God in whose name only is salvation possible. But this is the inevitable condemnation of the unbeliever, that the Light has come unto the world and men deliberately chose to love the darkness rather than the Light; for their works were evil. For everyone who practices worthless things hates and resists the Light and comes not unto the Light in order that his works may not be shown for what they really are. But the one who continually does the truth comes to the Light in order that his works may be made manifest because they have been wrought in God.

Summary

God, motivated by infinite love, sent His only Son unto fallen mankind, not to condemn but to save everyone who believes in His Son. The unbeliever brings condemnation upon himself by purposely rejecting the *only* life-giving light. The believer purposely manifests his works to glorify God.

Comment

Verse 16 has been called the Golden Text of the Bible, Everyman's Text, and other equally descriptive names. It is probably the most famous verse of the New Testament, and the most often quoted. In fact, verses 16-21 do contain the heart of God's new will. We see in this Golden Text that "God is love." Until we have experienced, in a measure, the same unselfish love, we cannot know God as we ought (cf. I Jn. 4:7-12). We see (v. 16) God's love wooing mankind back unto His glorious fellowship, for He made the initial advances — we love Him only because "He first loved us" (cf. I Jn. 4:19). This text shows God loving us, not for His sake alone, but for our sakes. True love "seeketh not its own" (cf. I Cor. 13:1-7). God's love is that of a Father who is happy only when His prodigal child has returned to His fellowship (cf. Lk. 15:11-24). Augustine said, "God loves each one of us as if there was only one of us to love . . . Love is the highest characteristic of God, the one attribute in which all others harmoniously blend. Although our finite minds cannot grasp the limitlessness of His love, we are informed of it in His revealed Word. God's love for men is declared in both the Old Testament and the New Testament (cf. Deut. 7:13; Isa. 63:9; Hos. 14:4; Rom. 5:8; I Jn. 4:10). Here are outlines of this famous verse by two famous men:

Wm. Hendriksen, author of *New Testament Commentary* "God's Love": 1. Its character (so loved, 2. Its Author (God), 3. Its object (the world), 4. Its Gift (his Son, the only-begotten), and 5. Its purpose (that whoever believes in Him should not perish but have everlasting life).
R. C. Foster, author of *A Syllabus of the Life of Christ* "Doctrinal Elements of John 3:16": (1) Love of God (2) Jesus, the Son of God, deity of Jesus (3) Atonement (gave His Son) (4) Man lost in sin (5) Plan of salvation suggested (6) Eternal reward and punishment.

A few commentators have contended that Jesus' words cease at verse 15, and that from verse 16 through 21 we have the reflective words of the author, John. There are two reasons for believing to the contrary, that these words are further words of teaching by Jesus to Nicodemus: (a) the conjunction "for" establishes a causal relation between this and the preceeding discourse (vs. 1-15); (b) the close connection of thought, i.e., "heavenly things" concerning the "scheme of redemption"; and, further, there is not the slightest notice indicating that the record has passed from direct conversation in v. 15, over to the writer's reflection in v. 16. Before passing on to the next verse, it will be well to note that "perish" does not mean "annihilate." That the wicked who die merely cease to exist, or are annihilated, is absolutely denied by the Scriptures. The New Testament is plain and positive in its teaching that those who refuse to believe and obey and who depart this world in such a state look forward to a "certain fearful expectation of judgment, and a fierceness of fire . . ." (Heb. 10:27). The unsaved dead will be condemned to eternal punishment (cf. Mt. 18:8; 25:41, 46; Jn. 5:29; II Thess. 1:7-9; Jude 6-7). We must also note that the promise of eternal life is to whosoever *continues* to believe in the Son. The word "believe" is in the Greek present tense, and indicates continued action.

From the sublime contemplations of the love of God, we are abruptly faced with judgment — condemnation. Verse 17, according to one commentator, "is an attempt by Jesus to correct a Jewish misinterpretation of the prophecies concerning the coming of the Messiah." A long standing Jewish interpretation of Messianic prophecies held that the purpose for the coming of the Messiah was to "condemn the world," i.e., to judge the Gentile nations which had oppressed Israel. Amos, the herdsman-prophet from Tekoa, seems to be crying out against such a gross misinterpretation (Amos 5:18-20). The verse before us (v. 17) clearly teaches Christ's primary purpose in the first coming into the world was to provide a way of salvation for mankind. Skeptics are quick to sieze upon this verse and compare it with John 5:22, 27; 9:39; 12:47, 48 and declare the Bible contradicts itself. A moment of unbiased contemplation of all the passages dealing with the purpose of Christ's coming will show there is no contradiction. Jesus came to save, not to judge the world. He came to judge the world (at the Incarnation) only insofar as it would not allow itself to be saved. He still judges (condemns or sentences) the world when His good news of salvation is rejected by men. This same principle is applied in our everyday living. It is possible for us to offer to share something with a fellow-man, and, when he deliberately rejects our offer, his rejection turns out as a judgment upon him. A favorite illustration of this same principle goes: "A visitor was being shown around a famous art gallery by one of the attendants. In the gallery were masterpieces beyond all price, works of genius and fame. At the end of the tour the visitor said: 'Well, I don't think much of your pictures.' The attendant answered, 'Sir, I would remind you that these pictures are no longer on trial, for they are masterpieces, but those who look at them are '." When the Jews rejected Paul's message they "judged themselves unworthy of eternal life" (cf. Acts 13:46). The gospel is *never* on trial, but those to whom the gospel is preached are *always* on trial. Jesus Christ was not on trial as He faced Annas, Caiaphas, Herod and Pilate in succession — but these judges were being judged!

In verse 18 comes the wonderful news of pardon for the believer, and the awful sentence of doom for the unbeliever. This verse shows why God did not need to send His son to condemn the world. Since the Son was sent with the message of salvation, the man who disbelieves and disobeys brings about his own condemnation. On the other hand, the man who accepts the testimony of Christ and obeys His Word "has passed out of death into life." The word *kekritai* is the Greek word for judged — condemned and the word from whence comes the English critic, crisis, critique, etc. That this word means condemned here is evident from verse 17 where it is placed in apposition to saved. The tense of the Greek in verse 18b shows that the unbeliever is condemned just as long as he continues to disbelieve and disobey. The men or women who even now refuse to surrender in loving obedience to the demands of the gospel walk the face of this earth with the sentence of eternal condemnation ever present upon them! God does not need a special day to determine a man's destiny — that is determined by the man's own will and sealed at death. Notice that Jesus places all of mankind in only two categories: the believer and the unbeliever — the saved and the condemned. We cannot here enter into a lengthy discussion of the possibility of the unevangelized heathen being saved through ignorance of the gospel. Suffice it to say the New Testament indicates even the heathen has had sufficient law of conscience given to him so that "he may be without excuse" (cf. Rom. 1:18-32; Ept. 2:11-12). The point Jesus seems to emphasize for Nicodemus is that salvation is possible *only* through trust in God's Son. Unless Nicodemus accepts the *only* way, he stands condemned, regardless of his Jewish blood and ancestry from Abraham. This point needs emphasis in every generation. Family ties, traditions and family religion will not avail unless they be conformable to revealed truth!

The next verse (v. 19) is very revealing! Jesus shows that the condemnation which abides upon the unbeliever is just — it is what the unbeliever deserves — and He further reveals the inner moral wrong which makes this condemnation deserved. The Greek word for loved in verse 19 is *agapae* which means a love of intelligence and purpose . . . a deliberate love. Thus a man who deliberately loves the darkness is morally rebellious and makes his own choice! When the light comes and convicts this man of his sins he will purposely reject the light and deliberately love the darkness. Such a man inevitably condemns himself and receives a just punishment (cf. II Thess. 2:9-12). Unbelief stems from a moral wickedness and not from ignorance! Paul recognizes as the basic cause of rejecting of the truth "having pleasure in unrighteousness."

The Lord further shows that the one who has deliberately chosen the darkness cannot remain at peace with the light. This principle is expressed by Jesus — "He that is not with me is against me; and he that gathereth not with me scattereth" (Mt. 12:30). The lover of darkness *must* hate the light. There are two different Greek words used for evil works in verses 19 and 20. In v. 19 the word *ponera* which denotes an active wickedness, and in v. 20 the word is *phaula*, which denotes worthlessness — the one positive the other negative. Even the one who is useless and inactive in the cause of righteousness is evil in the Lord's sight! The remaining words of Jesus in this 20th verse focus like a gigantic searchlight upon the very deepest recesses of the heart of the one who loves darkness. Such a man hates and wars against the light because the light reveals his works for what they really are — evil, dishonest and worthless. The verb convicted *(elencho)* means more than reproved. It means expose, show up, bring to light, show what is actually the case (cf. Eph. 5:13). As Lenski says, "We see here the inner, self-contradiction and self-

THE GOSPEL OF JOHN 3:20-21

condemnation of all such doers of evil who in unbelief act contrary to Christ and the gospel. They choose the worthless but
they do not want its worthlessness revealed. They want to be
undisturbed in thinking the worthless valuable." The evil-doer
does not want others to see him, nor does he want to face himself.
Jesus recognized this in the Pharisees who deliberately rejected
His word when He said, *"Because* I say the truth, ye believe me
not" (Jn. 8:45).

Now what of the man who does the truth? He gladly comes
to the light. The man who abides in the truth purposely comes
to the light that he may manifest his works to show that they
have been wrought in God. He is not afraid to have the pene-
trating searchlight of truth play upon his works for they have
God as their source and they are good works. The disciple of
Jesus is to purposely show his good works before men that they
may glorify the Father who is in heaven (cf. Mt. 5:16).

Thus ends Jesus' conversation, as far as we know, with this
teacher of Israel. We would like to know more of Nicodemus
than what is briefly told in two later passages (Jn. 7:50-51;
19:39). The important Personage for us to know, however, is not
Nicodemus but the One who is now teaching Nicodemus, even
Jesus.

Quiz

1. What is the nature of God's love (cf. I Cor. 13:5)?
2. Give three Old Testament references to the love of God.
3. What reasons may be given for contending that verses 15-21
   are a continuation of Jesus' teaching?
4. What is meant by the word perish?
5. What was the primary purpose for Jesus' coming into the
   world?
6. How does the unbeliever bring about his own condemnation?
7. Into what two categories does Jesus place all mankind?
8. What kind of choice is made by the man who loves darkness?
9. Name two types of evil as mentioned in these verses.
10. How does the unbeliever contradict himself?
11. Why does the doer of the truth come to the light?

JOHN'S WITNESS CONCERNING HIMSELF

Text 3:22-30

22 After these things came Jesus and his disciples into the land of Judea; and there he tarried with them, and baptized.
23 And John also was baptizing in Enon near to Salim, because there was much water there: and they came, and were baptized.
24 For John was not yet cast into prison.
25 There arose therefore a questioning on the part of John's disciples with a Jew about purifying.
26 And they came unto John, and said to him, Rabbi, he that was with thee beyond the Jordan, to whom thou hast borne witness, behold the same baptizeth, and all men come to him.
27 John answered and said, A man can receive nothing, except it have been given him from heaven.
28 Ye yourselves bear me witness, that I said, I am not the Christ, but, that I am sent before him.
29 He that hath the bride is the bridegroom: but the friend of the bridegroom, that standeth and heareth him, rejoiceth greatly because of the bridegroom's voice: this my joy therefore is made full.
30 He must increase, but I must decrease.

Queries

a. Why is Jesus' growing popularity mentioned?
b. Why does he ask the question about purifying?
c. How does John's analogy of the bridegroom and the friend of the bridegroom apply?

Paraphrase

After His ministry in the vicinity of Jerusalem, Jesus and His disciples went out into the countryside of Judea and He spent some time there with His disciples and immersed. But John the Baptist was also immersing in Aenon near Salim, because there was an abundance of water there; and people were continuing to come and be immersed — for John had not yet been cast into prison. John's disciples, therefore, began a disputation with a Jew concerning the subject of ceremonial cleansing. They came to John and said to him, Teacher He that was with you beyond the Jordan, the One to whom you have borne witness, look, He is immersing and everyone is flocking to Him! John

116

answered and said to them, A man is not able to claim any
authority if it has not been given unto him from heaven. You
yourselves are my witnesses that I said positively, I am not the
Christ but I was sent in advance of the Anointed One. The One
having the bride, He is the Bridegroom. But the friend of the
Bridegroom, the one who stands and listens for the Bridegroom's
coming, rejoices greatly on account of the approaching voice of
the Bridegroom. This, therefore, is the fulfillment of my work
and thus my joy is fulfilled when all the people flock to Him.
He must continue to grow in esteem and following while I continue to decrease in following.

Summary

Jesus' ministry and popularity grows. John the Baptist's
disciples exhibit jealousy. The Baptist exhibits humility and
devotion to Jesus, refusing to be jealous of Him.

Comment

After attending the Passover week and performing many
signs and after a considerable ministry in the vicinity of Jerusalem
(including the conversation with Nicodemus), Jesus goes out into
the countryside. The most likely place to go with his disciples
in order to baptize would be near Jericho where the Jordan was
forded. It is evident from John 4:2 that Jesus baptized no one
personally, but He is said to have baptized when actually His
disciples performed the rite. There was Divine wisdom in this.
The apostle Paul was forced to contend with division in the
Corinthian church a few years later which had resulted from
certain Christians taking pride in having been baptized by certain
preachers and apostles (cf. I Cor. 1:14ff). It is asked, "What
baptism would Christ and His disciples administer?" The only
reasonable answer is that they were administering John's baptism
of repentance and preparation. The baptism into His death (Rom.
6:3) .could not have been instituted until after His death. The
baptism instituted and commanded by Jesus at His ascension (Mt.
28:19-20; Mk. 16:15-16) was not a carry-over of John's baptism.
John's baptism was not valid after Pentecost (Acts 2) and this
is evident from Paul's instruction to some untaught disciples of
the Baptist (Acts 19:1-7) and from the instruction given to
Apollos (Acts 18:24-26). The list of parallels below which show
the differences in the two baptisms is taken from *Studies in the
Life of Christ*, Vol. 1, by R. C. Foster:

CHRISTIAN BAPTISM	JOHN'S BAPTISM
1. Demands explicit faith in Jesus as Son of God, as well as repentance	Was preceeded by repentance
2. In the name of Father, Son, and Holy Spirit	On the general authority of God, no known formula
3. Permanent, remaining in force to the end of time	Temporary, preparing for the appearance of Christ
4. Universal — "all nations," "every creature"	For the Jews only
5. Inducts one into the kingdom and into Christ	Only in preparation for the coming kingdom
6. "For the remission of your sins."	Unto repentance and remission of sins (in promise?)
7. Followed by the "gift of the Holy Spirit"	Not connected with the gift of the Holy Spirit

In verse 23 we are informed that John changed his place of baptizing. Before this time he was "beyond the Jordan" (v. 26) which means the eastern side of the Jordan. There is much discussion as to where Aenon is located. No definite location can be established. The most acceptable location is about eight miles south of Scythopolis on the western banks of the Jordan. The primary discussion of this verse centers around the phrase, "because there was much water there." The pedo-baptists claim the phrase means "many waters, or an abundance of springs." They do this, of course, to discredit the "much water" as an inference for immersion. They say John chose a location with an abundance of water that the multitudes might have sufficient drinking water. But the whole emphasis of this context is upon baptizing. The demand of the New Testament for immersion as the only Scriptural mode of baptism cannot be denied by such egregious reasoning as the pedo-baptists have used with this verse (cf. also comment on 1:23-28).

As John writes his gospel, he is aware of Matthew's sequence of events in the ministry of Jesus and John the Baptist. John would know that Matthew has John the Baptist cast into prison just after the temptation of Jesus (Mt. 4:11-12). Here, in

John's gospel, Jesus and the Baptist are represented as preaching and baptizing simultaneously at least six months after the Lord's temptation. John, the author, is aware that those who later compare his gospel and Matthew's account may stumble and so he interjects the phrase anachronistically, "for John was not yet cast into prison." The interjection of verse 24 shows there was a considerable lapse of time between Matthew 4:11 and 12, and during this time Jesus and John were both preaching and baptizing.

As in the case when most great spiritual leaders gain a following, there arises, unsanctioned by the leaders, jealousy between the followers. Verse 25 informs us of John the Baptist's disciples beginning a disputation or argument with a Jew (probably one who favored Jesus and His ministry) over the question of cleansing. From verse 26 it seems the whole disputation was over the authority and cleansing efficacy of the two baptisms. The disciples of John began the controversy and probably challenged the Jew because he had been baptized by Jesus' disciples. That Jesus could baptize without consulting John they could not understand, and undoubtedly argued that the Jew had not been purified or cleansed because he had not been baptized by John. John's disciples probably brought the Jew with them when they came to their Teacher, expecting John to set this man right about the correct administrator of the rite of baptism.

The real trouble of these particular disciples of John was jealousy, not theological problems. Jesus was gaining popularity, and He and His disciples were preaching and baptizing and were not companying with John and his disciples. Jesus' disciples had the same trouble with the "unknown miracle-worker" (Mk. 9:38-39.). They could not understand how one could do good and practice religion and not company with them. Anyone who is doing the revealed will of God, whether he belongs to our immediate circle of fellowship or not, is for us and for Christ, and he is a child of God!

The Baptist's answer, verse 27, was probably unexpected by the disputing disciples. They were saying John should have the pre-eminence and that Jesus was a usurper. But John replies that authority and pre-eminence is divinely bestowed. In God's eternal scheme of things everyone has a place. John knew he had a definite place — his place was to be a preparer, a forerunner. Even John's own disciples testified publicly of John's previous denial that he was the Christ.

119

John now uses a familiar Old Testament figure to illustrate his secondary position to Christ. The bride is expressive in the Old Testament of the people of Israel in their close relation to God (cf. Isa. 54:5; Hos. 2:18; Psa. 45). The bride belongs to the bridegroom. Christ is the Bridegroom, and His people are the Bride (cf. Eph. 5:32; II Cor. 11:2; Rev. 21:2, 9; 22:17). In the Jewish marriage ceremonies, the friend of the bridegroom often had certain tasks to perform in advance of the final union. The friend would then stand and wait for the approach of the groom. Upon hearing the groom's voice the best man could rejoice in a task completed and rejoice again when the groom voices his joy upon receiving the bride. John then tells his disciples, "Since you have come to me and told me that all people are flocking to Him, the Bridegroom, my joy is made full." The Bridegroom is receiving His Bride with joy and the friend of the Bridegroom also rejoices!

Verse 30 will stand forever as a monument to this great man, John the Baptist. It exemplifies his whole life of service in behalf of the Christ. As Barclay says, "we would do well to remember that it is not to ourselves that we must try to attach people; it is to Jesus Christ. It is not for ourselves we seek the loyalty of men; it is for Him." (Wm. Barclay in *The Daily Study Bible,* "The Gospel of John," Vol. 1). Note the word must in this verse. The word is a translation of the Greek word *dei* which, in turn, is from the Greek verb *deo* meaning "I am bound." John says, then. "I am bound, I must decrease while He is bound to increase." John is merely submitting to the eternal plan of God by giving Jesus the pre-eminence.

Quiz

1. Where did Jesus go with his disciples to baptize?
2. Did Jesus baptize anyone? Explain.
3. Name at least 4 differences between John's baptism and Christian baptism.
4. Where is Aenon?
5. How are Matthew 4:11-12 and John 3:24 reconciled?
6. What probably caused the disputation concerning purifying?
7. How is v. 27 to be interpreted?
8. What was the joy of John the Baptist v. 29?

JOHN'S WITNESS CONCERNING CHRIST

Text 3:31-36

31 He that cometh from above is above all: he that is of the earth is of the earth, and of the earth he speaketh: he that cometh from heaven is above all.

32 What he hath seen and heard, of that he beareth witness; and no man receiveth his witness.

33 He that hath received his witness hath set his seal to this, that God is true.

34 For he whom God hath sent speaketh the words of God: for he giveth not the Spirit by measure.

35 The Father loveth the Son, and hath given all things into his hand.

36 He that believeth on the Son hath eternal life; but he that obeyeth not the Son shall not see life, but the wrath of God abideth on him.

Queries

a. Who is "he that cometh from above" and "he that is of the earth"?

b. What is the meaning of "He giveth not the Spirit by measure"?

c. What is the significance of the word obey?

Paraphrase

The One coming from above is far above all men: but he that comes from the earth remains on an earthly level and is above no one and he speaks from an earthly standpoint. The One coming from heaven is above all men: He is bearing witness to that which He has seen and heard in the very presence of God and no one is receiving His witness! The person who has received the Son's witness has acknowledged that God is true. For the One Whom God sent is speaking the words of God, for the Father does not give the Spirit to the Son in part. The Father loves the Son and the Father has given all things into His hand. The person continuing to believe in the Son with a trustful obedience is continually possessing eternal life, but, conversely, the one continuing to disobey the Son shall not see life, but the wrath of God remains upon him in his disobedient state.

Summary

The Baptist points out that Jesus comes with the full revelation of God's will. The person who accepts Jesus' words acknowledges that Jesus is God's true Representative.

Comment

Although it is not certain whether verses 31-36 are the words of John the Baptist or John the Apostle, contextually they seem to be the words of the Baptist. John the Baptist is certainly capable of uttering such high and lofty phrases when speaking of the Son of God (cf. Mt. 3:11-12; Mk. 3:7-8; Lk. 3:16-17; Jn. 1:26, 27, 29-36; 3:27-30).

Assuming these to be the words of John the Baptist, they are his final testimony to the Sonship of Jesus. These words of witness to Jesus' deity are but a continuation of the witness John is giving his disputing disciples. These disciples must recognize, as did Andrew, Peter, Philip and the other early disciples of John, that the Lamb of God has come and He is the pre-eminent One. Thus, the Baptist points out, since Jesus came from the "bosom of the Father" He is superior to every mortal. He is above even a great mortal like John the Baptist, for this prophet was earthly in origin like all other mortals (cf. Mt. 11:11). These loyal (but jealous) disciples of John must see that the "one to whom all men are flocking" is the One Who has come down out of heaven with the complete and final counsel of God (cf. Jn. 1:9-15; 3:11-13). The Baptist states an axiom which not only applies to ordinary fallible men, but also in some instances to Spirit-inspired mortals when he says, "he that is of the earth . . . and of the earth he speaketh." John the Baptist and some of the apostles, when left to their own falible reasoning, reverted occasionally to carnal thinking and speaking (cf. Mt. 11:2-3; Gal. 2:11-14).

The Baptist continues, in verse 32, to explain to his disciples that Jesus has come from the very presence of the supreme God and Father with the message of absolute truth. The message of Jesus does not vary; it contains no conjectures and is not frustrating. His message is the exact will of God for men which the Son heard directly from the Father (cf. Jn. 5:19; 7:16, 29; 8:26, 38, 40; 15:15). What a blessed knowledge! He Who speaks to us through the gospels speaks the words which He heard in the council-halls of heaven. He has interpreted for us (Jn. 1:18) the divine plan of redemption, and He became God's oath, sworn in blood, to show that the promises of God are immutable (Heb. 6:17). Then the Baptist, in the last phrase of this verse, shows the superlative guilt of one who rejects Christ's testimony. John does not mean every man, without exception, when he says "no man receiveth his witness." This is plain from the following verse (v. 33). It is so monstrous to the Baptist that even one man should reject the message of Christ that he is moved to say, "no man receiveth his witness."

John says there were some who did receive the witness of Jesus, and thereby acknowledged that "God is faithful and will fulfill all that he has promised." Those few of Israel who did accept Jesus as the Son of God realized God was fulfilling His promises through Jesus and they "set their seal" that God was true to His word. Up to this time, John the Baptist, Peter, Andrew, Philip, Nathanael, and undoubtedly John and James had all received the witness concerning Jesus as the promised Messiah. Another principle is implied in this verse (v. 33). The person who will not receive the witness of Jesus is actually calling God a liar. Jesus told the Pharisees that although they claimed God as their Father, in reality Satan was their father because they rejected the Son's witness (cf. Jn. 8:38-47). To reject the witness of Jesus is to call God a liar (I Jn. 5:10). To dishonor the Son is to dishonor the Father (Jn. 5:23b).

Verses 34-35 are John's climactic conclusions to convince his untaught disciples that Jesus is the One to be followed and adhered to. John is convinced that Jesus is the One whom God sent. Except for one or two instances, the phrase *hon apesteilen ho theos* ("The one whom God sent") is always applied to Jesus (cf. Jn. 3:17; 5:36; 6:29; 7:29; 8:42; 9:7; 10:36; 11:42, etc.) Upon others who spoke on behalf of God the Spirit came only in measure. God spoke by others "in divers portions and in divers manners," but the Son was the "effulgence of his glory and the very image of his substance," and the Spirit was given to the Son without measure. The Baptist was an eyewitness to this and he "saw the Spirit descending and remaining upon Him" (Jn. 1:33-34). Not only does the Son receive the Spirit without measure, but the Father gave all things into His hand (cf. Jn. 5:19-20; 12:49; 13:3; 17:2; Mt. 11:27; 28:18).

Verse 36 certainly fits the character of John the Baptist's preaching as it is recorded in the Synoptic gospels. There his message was, "the axe lieth at the root of the tree . . . hewn down and cast into the fire . . . shall baptize . . . in fire . . . flee from the wrath to come . . . whose fan is in his hand," etc. Here, in verse 36, he intends to warn these quibbling disciples in no uncertain terms that to reject Jesus inevitably brings down the wrath of God upon the disbeliever. The sharp contrasts of the Baptist here between the destinies of the believer and the unbeliever are very similar to the contrast Jesus presented to Nicodemus (3:16-18). John uses the present tense to denote that the one receiving eternal life is one who continually trusts and obeys. One who has an abiding faith has also an ever-present assurance of eternal life.

The only other alternative to accepting Jesus is rejecting Him. With Christ there is no middle-of-the-road policy — men either obey Him or disobey Him. Evidently, there is a plan or a norm which the Son came to manifest, which every man must act in accordance with, or rebelliously reject Him. Believing in Christ, then, entails more than admitting His historicity, and even more than giving intellectual assent to His message and claims. A faith that does not express itself in obedience is a dead and useless faith (cf. Jn. 14:21, 23; 15:10; Jas. 2:26). The gospel of Christ is a gospel demanding obedience, and its commandments are plain enough that "they who run may read." The law of the kingdom of Christ is love. But it is a love which leads to trust, repentance, confession and baptism. These are but the entrance requirements — once received as a citizen by the Lord, the new member must participate and share in the edifying of the whole society of believers to his fullest capacities.

The dreadful sentence upon the disobedient is that even now the wrath of God is potentially abiding upon him. The disobedient does not experience the wrath of God while he yet lives, but when Jesus comes again He will "render vengeance unto all them that know not God and obey not the gospel" (II Thess. 1:8). Then those who have chosen to disobey Christ's terms of entrance into the kingdom will go into eternity to reckon with an all-righteous and perfectly just God. There the unredeemed must bear the eternal and perfect wrath of God all alone. The one who chooses to disobey can blame only himself . . . he has been given the message and the opportunity to accept or reject . . . he brings the wrath of God upon himself.

SPECIAL STUDY NO. 2

Anticipating that there may be some question concerning the paraphrase of 3:16-21 we introduce here Special Study No. 2. This study is interjected in explanation of the substitution of "only-unique" in place of "only begotten" in 3:16, 18. It is hoped that the reader will come to a clearer understanding of the uniqueness and diety of Jesus Christ as a result of this Special Study.

The Study, in its entirety, is from an article by Sheldon V. Shirts entitled, "He Gave the Only Son He Had."

HE GAVE THE ONLY SON HE HAD

THE MEANING OF *monogenes.*

The Greek word under fire is *monogenes.* Originally, Greek words with the common root *gen* carried the basic meaning "to beget." But, as Schmidt proves, many words built upon that basic stem soon lost this early sexual sense. Thus centuries before New Testament days, *genos,* for example, was often used to mean simply a kind of something. So in the New Testament, Jesus parabolically likens the kingdom of heaven to "a net that . . . gathered (fish) of every KIND" (Mt. 13:47), and Paul speaks of "divers KINDS of tongues" and "KINDS of voices" (I Cor. 12:19; 14:10).

Monogenes comes from *monos* (only) and *genos* (kind) — thus, "the only one of its kind," as such authorities as Moulton, Milligan, and Thayer show. Of course, when we speak of human beings, the translation "begotten" makes sense, but the fact remains that that is not the point — the emphasis is upon the person's uniqueness, he is the ONLY one. Thus Plato spoke of *monogenes ouranos* (the only heaven); and Clement of Rome desccribed the legendary bird, the phoenix, as *monogenes,* not that is was the only bird begotten, but the only one of its kind, unique.

LATIN AND SEPTUAGINT USAGE.

Accurately, the earliest Latin translators rendered *monogenes huios* by *filius unicus* (unique son), not by *filius unigenitus* (only-begotten son). It took the dogmatic Arian disputes over Christ's relation to God (318 A.D.) to give first occasion for claiming that Christ was God's "begotten Son," i.e. not a part of creation. And there began the inaccurate Latin rendering of *unigenitus,* (only-begotten).

In the Septuagint, the word occurs eight times, referring to an only child, or to that which was unique or alone (e.g., Psa. 22:20; Judges 11:34; Tobit 3:15). Twice the King James translators render the Hebrew equivalent as "darling," showing that the word *monogenes* acquires a secondary meaning in the fact that what is unique is naturally of special value: an only son is a specially beloved son.

MONOGENES IN LUKE AND HEBREWS.

In the New Testament, *monogenes* appears nine times (always translated "only" in the Revised Standard Version). Only six times does the King James Version have it "only-begotten." If the rendering "only" is so inadequate, why did the King James scholars so translate it three times? An examination of the passages will make it clear. In the story of the widow of Nain, the fact that her dead son had once been begotten was of course true but now of no consequence; the important thing here was that he was her only son! What a pathetic situation! The fact that she is a widow speaks of her past sorrow, but now (Lk. 7:12) the realization that the one and only prop of her life, the stay and hope of her widowhood, had been taken from her, shows realistically her present despair. Surely few greater misfortunes are conceivable than the loss of a widow's ONLY son.

So we can understand the consuming grief of Jairus who fell at Jesus' feet and "besought him to come to his house, for he had an ONLY daughter . . . and she was dying" (Lk. 8:41-42). Likewise, we share the concern of the father of the epileptic boy who cried, "Master, I beg you to look upon my son, for he is my ONLY child" (Lk. 9:38). Can anyone mistake the significance of *monogenes* in these passages? Not even the King James translators could!

But note the strange use of *monogenes* to describe Isaac in Heb. 11:17. Though the King James Version says "only begotten," Abraham obviously had begotten other children (Gen. 25:1, 2). But the point is: Isaac was the ONLY SON OF HIS KIND, as far as God's promise to Abraham was concerned. Thus *monogenes* is justified, and the Revised Standard Version's rendering "only son."

MONOGENES IN JOHN'S WRITING.

To render *monogenes* in John 3:16 as "only" is just as significant, and actually will more clearly reveal the great depth of God's love for us than does the more cumbersome, less accurate expression of the King James Version. For God so loved the world that He gave the ONLY SON HE HAD!

But some insist, "This is not true; John 1:12 says, 'But as many as received him, to them gave he power to become the sons of God . . . ' To call Jesus God's only Son is confusing and false; it strips Him of his divinity and makes Him no more than other men." Then, for a moment, call Him again God's "only begotten," if you must — and then notice that in the next verse, 1:13, all the sons of v. 12 have been "born (Gr. begotten) . . . of God." Constant dilemma greets the one who cannot see beyond the horizons or a single word.

Let us see, with Schaff, in what ways all believers can be called God's children in v. 12 and yet Jesus be God's only son in v. 14: (1) Jesus is the only Son in that there is none like him; they are many; (2) He is the Son eternally; they "become" (v. 12) sons within time; (3) He is the Son by nature; they are made sons by grace and adoption; (4) He is of the same essence with the Father; they are of a different substance. Note that Jesus never unites Himself with us by saying "Our Father." John 20:17 shows most clearly how He distinguishes Himself as the essential Son from all others as only adopted sons: "I am ascending to my Father and your Father, to my God and your God."

NO REFERENCE TO THE VIRGIN BIRTH.

But does not "only begotten" refer to Jesus' virgin birth? Never! In John 1:14 Jesus did not become the Son; He became flesh to manifest Himself as God's eternal Son, Who "in the beginning . . . was with God and . . . was God" (Jn. 1:1). Men became sons of God because the Son of God became man. When "God sent his only Son into the world" (I Jn. 4:9), He did not send one Who became a son only when sent, any more than when God sent forth the Spirit (Gal. 4:6) did He send forth one who became a Spirit only when sent. Jesus has been eternally "in the bosom of the Father" (Jn. 1:18); the Greek even better expresses a relation of closest intimacy and tenderest affection: they are in each other's embrace.

127

THE "ONLY SON" MAKES A BEAUTIFUL PICTURE.

Thus Jesus is not merely the ONLY Son, but the precious beloved Son of God's embrace, and still God gave Him up! Take all the tenderness, forgiveness and love in the relation of an earthly father to his only child, and in that earth-drawn picture you have yet but a faint approach to the fathomless love of God, as He so loved the world that He gave the ONLY SON HE HAD — and what a precious Son — an innocent Son to be slain for the benefit of guilty men — that He might redeem them from eternal condemnation. No clearer picture of the deity of Christ, or the love of God can be seen!

Quiz

1. What great difference between Jesus and himself does John the Baptist point out to his disputing disciples (v. 31)?
2. What has Jesus seen and heard that He bears witness to?
3. How does a person "set his seal" that God is true?
4. Who received the Spirit without measure? Explain!
5. What is the significance of the word obey in verse 36?
6. Which is the best translation — "only-unique Son," or "only begotten Son"?

EXAMINATION
CHAPTERS TWO AND THREE

Multiple Choice

1. The city where Jesus made the water into wine was:
   a. Capernaum
   b. Cana
   c. Chorazin
2. Jesus made the water into:
   a. grape juice
   b. intoxicating wine
   c. we cannot be certain
3. Jesus' brothers were named:
   a. James, Joseph, Judas

b. James, Joseph, Judas, Simon

c. Abraham, Joseph, Levi, Peter

4. During the Feast of Passover, the Jews commemorated:

   a. The passing over of the Death Angel

   b. Their passing over the Jordan River

   c. The death of Pharaoh

5. When Jesus said "Destroy this temple . . ." he refered:

   a. to His physical body

   b. to the Jew's temple

   c. both of the above

6. When Jesus said a man must be "born of water" He meant:

   a. An ocean voyage

   b. born of the Holy Spirit

   c. Baptism

7. The essential idea of "the kingdom of God," is:
   a. The second coming of Christ
   b. The reign of God over the lives of men
   c. A church organization

8. John the Baptist called himself:

   a. The bridegroom

   b. The bride

   c. The friend of the Bridegroom

9. Jesus baptized:

   a. Just His disciples

   b. Many people

   c. No one personally, but representatively through the apostles.

Match These Scriptures

1. "His mother saith unto the servants
2. "Take these things hence:
3. "Destroy this temple
4. "Except one be born anew
5. "And as Moses lifted up the serpent in the wilderness
6. "According to his mercy he saved us
7. "He must increase
8. "He that believeth on the Son hath eternal life
9. "He that believeth on him is not judged
10. "Wherefore if any man is in Christ

a. and in three days I will raise it up."
b. even so must the Son of man be lifted up."
c. but I must decrease."
d. he is a new creature: the old things are passed away; behold, they are become new."
e. but he that obeyeth not the Son shall not see life, but the wrath of God abideth on him."
f. he that believeth not hath been judged already."
g. Whatsoever he saith unto you, do it."
h. through the washing of regeneration and renewing of the Holy Spirit."
i. he cannot see the kingdom of God."
j. make not my Father's house a house of merchandise."

True or False

1. _____ The miracle at the wedding feast was Jesus' first miracle.
2. _____ Jesus used His scourge of cords upon the money-changers.
3. _____ Nicodemus belonged to the sect of the Sadducees.
4. _____ Jesus told Nicodemus there was nothing required of men to enter the kingdom of God.
5. _____ Men judge themselves, in a sense, when they reject the light.

6._____Those who do evil wish to remain ignorant of the true worthlessness of their deeds.
7._____John the Baptist was jealous of Jesus' popularity.

Who said it?

1. "They have no wine."
2. "Every man setteth on first the good wine; and when men have drunk freely, then that which is worse: thou hast kept the good wine until now."
3. "Forty and six years was this temple in building, and wilt thou raise it up in three days?"
4. "How can these things be?"
5. "Rabbi, he that was with thee beyond the Jordan, to whom thou hast borne witness, behold, the same baptizeth and all men come to him."

Describe the location of these:

1. Cana
2. Capernaum
3. The temple
4. Jerusalem
5. Aenon

EXPOSITORY SERMON NO. 3
THE NEW BIRTH
John 3:1-8

Introduction

I Character of Nicodemus
   A. Afraid? probably (Jn. 7:50; 19:39)
   Perhaps sought Jesus when alone — possibly his only free time
   B. At least his mind was honest enough to accept evidence of Jesus' deity.
     1. More than other Pharisees would do
     2. Honest mind necessary to receive any truth
II What was Nicodemus really seeking?
   A. The kingdom of God . . . promised by his prophets
     1. Probably heard John the Baptist and Jesus both preach, "the kingdom of heaven is at hand."

    2. There was a general excitement and expectation (Lk. 3:15)

III What does Jesus really teach Nichodemus?

    A. That the true kingdom of God is spiritual and not physical

    B. That entrance is by spiritual birth, not physical lineage

Discussion

I NECESSITY OF THE NEW BIRTH (v. 3 and 5)

    A. A blow is dealt Nicodemus' religious heritage

        1. A Jew and a Pharisee, yet Jesus implies he has no part in the kingdom of God

    B. Must be "born anew" — regenerated

        1. Generate means to give life.

        2. Without regeneration (spiritually) we are without life (spiritually) SPIRITUALLY DEAD!

        Jesus said as much in 3:18—LIVING DEAD MEN!

    C. Jesus repeats, "Except" and "Ye must" FOR EMPHASIS.

        1. NAME ON CHURCH ROLL, EVEN HOLDING OFFICE DOES NOT GUARANTEE ETERNAL LIFE . . . "YE *MUST* BE BORN ANEW." REGENERATION *IS* NECESSARY

II WHAT IS THE "NEW BIRTH"?

    A. A new birth brings forth a new creature (II Cor. 5:11-17).

    Note the sharp change to a new life in Saul of Tarsus

    B. The old man must die before the new man is born.

        1. "I have been crucified with Christ" etc. (Gal. 1:20)

           a. When Christ lives in us . . . His wants are ours, His loves are ours, His hates are ours.

           b. "I" moves out and Jesus moves in. (Rom. 8:6-9)

           c. Our hearts are filled with fleshly desires like a barrel filled with various things

           We need to empty the barrel and fill it with Christ.

        2. Before we can be saved we must be lost!

           a. Must first accept fact that God has just cause to demand our death because of our disobedience.

           b. WHEN WE VIOLATE GOD'S PERFECT STANDARD, WE JUSTLY DESERVE THE SENTENCE OF PUNISHMENT.

THE GOSPEL OF JOHN

C. Now we are ready to accept LOVE OF GOD manifested in Christ's reconciliation.

III HOW SHALL WE BE BORN AGAIN?

A. Ye must be born of water and Spirit.

1. Both water and Spirit are used without the article "the."

Thus we see that the new birth is a single entity . . . baptism and Spirit one process

2. Compare Titus 3:4-5

B. Spirit operates through the written and spoken Word of God.

1. I Pet. 1:23; Jas. 1:18, 21

a. Spirit came to convict men of sin — done through preaching of apostles. (Jn. 16:8, 13; 17:20)

2. When the seed (Word of God) is shown, it transforms the life.

C. The Spirit gives life (Jn. 6:63).

But, "THE WORDS THAT I HAVE SPOKEN UNTO YOU, THEY ARE SPIRIT AND THEY ARE LIFE."

D. We are:

1. CLEANSED BY THE WORD AND BY THE LAVER OF REGENERATION

2. SANCTIFIED BY THE WORD AND BY BAPTISM

3. LED BY THE SPIRIT (WORD)

4. PURIFIED BY OBEDIENCE TO THE GOSPEL

5. SAVED BY WASHING OF REGENERATION AND OF HOLY SPIRIT

Conclusion

I NOW THE APPLICATION . . . NOW THE DECISION IN REGARD TO NEW BIRTH

A. We know its necessity, what it is, how it shall be done. WE HAVE THE TRUTH, NOW WE MUST OBEY OR REJECT

II Nicodemus stumbled at not being able to see this new birth.

    A. Jesus replied, "If we could not see the wind blow the trees and could not hear it, we would never know it was blowing . . . in like manner, if the Spirit through the Word did not produce reborn men we would never know His presence or working . . ."

        1. MY FRIEND, YOU CAN TELL A REBORN MAN!

        2. THE MIND OF CHRIST WILL MANIFEST ITSELF IN THE PERSON WHO HAS CRUCIFIED SELF AND SEEKS ONLY THE KINGDOM!

III ONE WHO HAS ALLOWED THE WORD OF GOD FREE COURSE IN HIMSELF WILL:

    A. Repent like Zacchaeus (with restitution if necessary)

    B. Confess like Peter and John in Acts

    C. Go anywhere Jesus has commanded, even unto immersion in water . . . although not completely understood

    D. If you will allow him, Jesus will come into your heart and help you live as a Christian
BUT YOU MUST OBEY HIS WORD (Jn. 14:23).

CHAPTER FOUR

This chapter is a gold mine! There are spiritual treasures here to enrich any soul who will search and dig. Take a look at these nuggets — The Humanity of Jesus, The Deity of Jesus, The Universality of the Gospel, Spontaneous Evangelism, True Worship Defined, A Missionary Vision, and other equally precious lessons. Chapter Four is included in the First Year of Public Ministry and is outlined thusly:

WITHDRAWL FROM JUDEA — ARRIVAL IN SAMARIA

Text 4:1-6

1 When therefore the Lord knew that the Pharisees had heard that Jesus was making and baptizing more disciples than John
2 (although Jesus himself baptized not, but his disciples),
3 he left Judea, and departed again into Galilee.
4 And he must needs pass through Samaria.
5 So he cometh to a city of Samaria, called Sychar, near to the

parcel of ground that Jacob gave to his son Joseph;
6 and Jacob's well was there. Jesus therefore, being wearied
with his journey, sat thus by the well. It was about the sixth
hour.

Queries

a. Why would the situation in verses 1-3 cause Jesus to leave Judea?
b. Where is Sychar?
c. What significance is there in Jesus being "wearied"?

Paraphrase

So when the Lord learned that the Pharisees had heard that He was making and immersing more disciples than John the Baptist (although Jesus Himself was not immersing but His disciples were), He left Judea and went away again into Galilee. It was necessary for him to pass through Samaria. He came to a city of Samaria called Sychar, near the plot of ground which Jacob gave to Joseph, his son, and Jacob's well was there. So Jesus, having become tired from His journey, was sitting wearily by the well. It was about six p.m.

Summary

To avoid a premature crisis with the Pharisees, Jesus departs Judea for Galilee, stopping to rest during the journey at Jacob's well near Sychar, a city of Samaria.

Comment

The gospel writer now resumes the chronology of the story where he left it in 3:22-23. He has paused in telling the movements of Jesus to tell of the testimony of John the Baptist, but now he takes up the story of Jesus' travels again.

Beginning with His cleansing of the temple of Jerusalem (Jn. 2:13-22), including a considerable public ministry in the environs of Jerusalem and ending with the Lord's departure into Galilee, a period of approximately eight or nine months have transpired. Jesus arrived in Jerusalem at Passover-time (2:13 — also "harvest-time"). The next notice of time is "yet four months, and then cometh the harvest" (4:35 — which would be four months away from the next Passover-time). Thus we conclude that Jesus spent approximately eight months in Judea — from one Passover-time until about four months before the next Passover-time.

Just prior to the Lord's departure into Galilee, John the Baptist is imprisoned (cf. Mt. 4:12; Mk. 1:14; Lk. 3:19-20). The Baptist's arrest probably also influenced Jesus' decision, as recorded here (4:1-3), to go into Galilee. There are two probable reasons for His change of location: (a) He may have feared a premature death at the hands of the authorities. This would not allow Him to fulfill the earthly ministry which the Father had sent Him to accomplish; (b) or, possibly, He feared a reaction from the multitudes much like that which was to happen later in Galilee (Jn. 6:15). He must yet teach the multitudes of the spiritual nature of His kingdom. Political revolution and bloodshed must be restrained. In His Divine mission a definite time had been appointed for the supreme crisis — He must avoid a premature crisis. So Jesus withdrew from His work of baptizing in the Jordan (somewhere near Jericho) and traveled toward Galilee.

The parenthetical statement of verse 2 is to explain that Jesus did not personally baptize, but is said to have baptized through His agents — the disciples. Compare our comments on John 3:22.

Why does John say Jesus "must needs pass through Samaria"? A brief geographical survey might offer one possible answer. There were three geographical divisions of the land of Palestine in Jesus' day: Galilee in the north, Judea in the south, and Samaria in between (see maps in the back of any Bible).

At first, it would appear to be the natural route of travel to Galilee. If Jesus was in Judea and wanted to reach Galilee, naturally He would have to go through Samaria. But due to an age-old hostility between the Jews and the Samaritans, the usual route of travel between Judea and Galilee was not so. The Jew going north usually crossed to the eastern side of the Jordan river (probably at the Jericho ford) and went up the Jordan Valley to avoid Samaria, and re-crossed the river into Galilee (probably at Bethabara).

There are two possibilities as to why Jesus *must* go through Samaria: (a) it was the shortest route to Galilee, and He was not restricted by the prejudices of the Jews, or (b) He purposely passed through there to "break down barriers" and plant the seed of the gospel that Philip might later reap (Acts 8).

Traveling the Roman road that leads through Samaria, Jesus would come to a fork in the road. At this fork in the road there is a well called Jacob's Well. About one-half mile northwest is the village of Sychar. About the same distance to the west

137

are Mount Gerizim and Mount Ebal, a short distance north of Gerizim, with a natural amphitheatre in between where Joshua stood and shouted the blessings and curses of the Law to the nation assembled on the slopes of these two mountains (cf. Deut. 27:12-13; Josh. 8:33-35). Also in the immediate vicinity is a burial plot, purchased by Jacob but given to his son Joseph, and Joseph subsequently had his bones buried there (cf. Gen. 33:18-19; 48:22; Josh. 24:32).

This location is of great significance in Jewish history. Nearly all archaeologists and scholars of the geography of Palestine agree that Jacob's Well is one place to which we may point with certainty and say, "Jesus sat on these stones." Grooves are worn deep into the stones around the opening of the well where ropes have, for centuries, been let down and pulled up drawing water for thirsty Palestinians.

In verse 6 we meet again the problem of John's method of counting time. This problem was discussed briefly in our comments on John 1:39. There can be little doubt that John counts time by the Roman method (modern method), i.e., from twelve-midnight to twelve-midnight. Some commentators have a problem with the account of the crucifixion. Jesus was crucified at 9 a.m. and died at 3 p.m. John 19:14 describes the trial in progress at the "sixth hour" (6 a.m.). Such an hour (6 a.m.) is *not* too early for sentence to be pronounced and it does *not* leave too long a lapse between sentence and crucifixion as some think. Do not forget the many events that took place between the sentence and crucifixion. Jesus struggled under the burden of the heavy cross probably a mile or more; large crowds pressed on every side slowing progress; He stopped to allow Simon of Cyrene to carry the cross part of the way; He held at least one conversation with some women. Do not forget also that the gospel accounts are fragmentary. After Pilate had pronounced sentence at six a.m., considerably more conversation and discussion may have transpired between Jesus and Pilate, or Jesus and the Sanhedrin.

We are to conclude, until better information comes forth, that John followed the Roman method of counting time. Thus, when Jesus sat by the well "about the sixth hour," it was either 6 a.m. or 6 p.m. The later hour fits the circumstances better.

The significant phrase of verse 6, however, is "Jesus therefore, being wearied with his journey, sat thus by the well." The Gospel of John is "the Gospel of Deity," that is, its primary purpose seems to be to prove the deity of Jesus. But the Fourth Gospel also shows very clearly the humanity of Jesus. He knew exhaustion, thirst, sorrow, joy, temptation; He Who "left an example that we should follow his steps" knew suffering, poverty and opposition, and yet he was without sin. He took the form of a servant and the vessel of human flesh for a number of reasons: (a) that He might become a merciful and faithful High Priest (Heb. 2:17); (b) that He might be able to succor them that are tempted (Heb. 2:18); (c) that He might be touched with our infirmities and give us help in time of need (Heb. 4:15-16); (d) that He might deliver us from the bondage of the fear of death; (Heb. 2:15); (e) and especially that He might condemn sin in the flesh (Rom. 8:3).

Incidentally, this passage shows the writer to have been an eyewitness to what he wrote. The mention of the Lord's posture, and even the hour of day shows the deep impression the events in Samaria must have made on John. Peter and John later enjoyed quite an extensive preaching tour in the land of Samaria (Acts 8:14-25).

Quiz

1. How long was Jesus' first Judean ministry? How do we know?
2. What two possible reasons may be given for His decision to leave Judea and go into Galilee?
3. What are two possible explanations for "He must needs go through Samaria"?
4. Locate Jacob's Well.
5. What time of the day did Jesus stop at the well?
6. Give three reasons for Christ's taking the human form.

JESUS AND THE LIVING WATER

Text 4:7-14

7 There cometh a woman of Samaria to draw water: Jesus saith unto her, Give me to drink.
8 For his disciples were gone away into the city to buy food.
9 The Samaritan woman therefore saith unto him, How is it that thou, being a Jew, asketh drink of me, who am a Samaritan woman? (For Jews have no dealings with Samaritans).
10 Jesus answered and said unto her, If thou knewest the gift of God, and who it is that saith to thee, Give me to drink; thou wouldest have asked of him, and he would have given thee living water.

139

11 The woman saith unto him, Sir, thou hast nothing to draw with, and the well is deep: whence then hast thou that living water?

12 Art thou greater than our father Jacob, who gave us the well, and drank thereof himself, and his sons, and his cattle?

13 Jesus answered and said unto her, Everyone that drinketh of this water shall thirst again:

14 but whosoever drinketh of the water that I shall give him shall never thirst; but the water that I shall give him shall become in him a well of water springing up unto eternal life.

Queries

  a.   What called forth the woman's first question?

  b.   What or Who is the "gift of God"?

  c.   How does the "living water" become a "well of water springing up into eternal life"?

Paraphrase

Presently a woman of Samaria comes all alone to draw water. Jesus says to her, Give me a drink (for His disciples were gone away into the city to buy food). The Samaritan woman asks Him, increduously, How can you, being a Jew, ask me for a drink — I am a Samaritan and a woman also! (This she said because Jews do not use vessels together with Samaritans). Jesus said to her, If you only knew the gift of God and Who it is that is saying to you, Give Me a drink, you would have asked Him and He would have given you living water. The woman replied, Sir, you have no bucket and the well is very deep, where will you get this living water? Surely you do not mean to say that you are greater than our illustrious ancestor Jacob, who never sought any better water than this, either for himself or for his sons or for his cattle!? Jesus answered and said to her, Everyone who drinks this water will grow thirsty again; but whoever shall drink the water that I, Myself, shall give him, he will never, no never, be thirsty again, but to the contrary, the water that I shall give him will become within him a bubbling spring of water welling up unto eternal life.

Summary

Jesus, out of His need for natural water and a woman's need for "living water," teaches His messiahship in Samaria.

Comment

The woman evidently came from the city of Sychar. Every day she would walk half a mile or so to the well, and as far back again carrying her waterpot either on her head or her shoulder. According to the custom, the women of those days met at a certain time of the day at the public watering place to exchange news and "small-talk" as they drew the next day's supply of water. This woman came alone! From subsequent information concerning her adulterous situation we assume she was a social outcast. None of the respectable citizens dared associate with her. She was an outcast — an unclean adulteress — a Samaritan — a woman! How would Jesus approach her? How would He overcome these barriers and reach her without raising more barriers?

The Master Teacher uses His need as an opening to gain her interest. He is tired and thirsty, and He asks her for a drink. It is a natural request, and one which could not raise any barrier. Had His disciples been there, they would have provided for His thirst. But they had gone away into one of Samaritan cities to "market" for food. (The Greek word translated "buy" is from the same word which is often translated "market.")

In verse 9 we see that for Jesus to ask a drink, even to speak to her, was not the ordinary custom of that day. The woman is plainly astonished. She probably recognizes Jesus as a Jew either from His speech or His dress.

Part of her astonishment comes from the fact that Jews did not use the same vessels as Samaritans. They considered the Samaritans as unclean as the Gentiles, and, according to Pharisaic interpretation, they would have to purify themselves ceremonially should they thus defile themselves. If Jesus is to get a drink He will have to drink from her bucket, for He has none of His own. The above interpretation is better than "have no dealings with" and this is evident from the fact that the disciples did go into a Samaritan city and did purchase food from the market-place.

A brief history of Samaria is in order here to show why the Jews considered the Samaritans unclean. When the kingdom of Israel was divided in about 926 B.C. (I Kings 12), the northern kingdom, under Jeroboam, embraced all the territory originally alloted to the ten northern tribes. This kingdom was known as Israel, and encompassed the provinces of Samaria and Galilee. Hoshea, Israel's last king, spurned the powerful nation of Assyria and made a political alliance with Egypt. About the year 722 B.C. the Assyrian king besieged the capitol city and later carried nearly all the people of the northern kingdom away into slavery and captivity ((II Kings 17). A small remnant of the ten tribes was left. The Assyrians, in order to better control the conquered territory, imported foreign peoples into Samaria (II Kings 17:24). The remnant of Jews intermarried with the foreign peoples, and this mixed people was given the name Samaritan.

This heathen mixture worshipped idols. God sent wild beasts, and many Samaritans were slain. They attributed the plague of lions to their failure to know the Law of Jehovah, and they appealed to the king of Assyria for help. He sent them a Jewish priest "to teach them the manner of the God of the land." Although the Samaritan religion was very nearly the same as that handed down by Moses, it was probably tainted with some paganism. This would be one reason for the aversion of the Jew toward the Samaritan.

Approximately 200 years after the captivity of the northern tribes, the kingdom of Judah was taken captive by Babylon. Judah was subsequently allowed to return to her homeland in the days of Ezra and Nehemiah. The first thing the people of Judah did was begin reconstruction of the Temple at Jerusalem. In the fourth chapter of the book of Ezra we are told the Samaritans wanted to join the Jews in rebuilding the Temple. The Samaritans were told with contempt, "You have nothing to do with us in building a house unto our God." The ire of the Samaritans was aroused against the Jew.

Hostility continued and increased between the Jew and the Samaritan. About 409 B.C. Manasseh built a rival temple on Mt. Gerizim. The Samaritans were generally inhospitable toward pilgrims from Galilee going to Jerusalem for the feasts (cf. Lk. 9:52-53), and many of these pilgrims journeyed to the feast by the way of the eastern side of the Jordan valley. The rivalry became so intense that the Samaritans would often set rival fires to perplex and confuse the Jews as they watched for their own signal fires which were to announce the rising of the Passover moon. Someone has written, "The Samaritan was publicly cursed in the synagogues of the Jews . . . and was thus, so far as the Jew could affect his position, excluded from eternal life."

In addition to this centuries-old hostility, no Jew would speak to any woman in public — not even his own wife or daughter. This foolish tradition was carried to such an extreme that some Pharisees would close their eyes when they saw a woman on the city streets. As a result, they often bumped into walls and houses,

and they came to be known as "the bruised and bleeding Pharisees." Thus we can see the woman's astonishment that Jesus
should even speak to her. If He had been a normal Jewish rabbi,
He would have gone home immediately and washed himself
because He had been in her presence.

The Greek idiom of verse 10 gives us an insight into the
thoughts of Jesus. He sees a certain pathos in the woman's situation. He is saying to her, "If you only knew (but you do not)
Who it is . . . He would have given you living water (but He
cannot because you know Him not)." No man can receive the
living water until he "knows" Jesus. Faith comes by hearing,
and the hearing that brings faith comes from the Word of God
(cf. Rom. 10:17; Phil. 3:8-11). Jesus is the source of life, and
we must partake of Him (cf. Jn. 6:53, 63) through His word to
have that life!

Notice how, having gained her sympathy, He gradually raises
her thoughts from the temporal to the spiritual, ever holding her
interest and ever leading (not driving) her into new light.

The woman is a little cynical in her reply. Jesus implies He
can supply her with some sort of perpetual source of water better
than what is in this well. Yet, even the great patriarch Jacob used
this well. Does He insinuate He is greater than their ancestors
(they claimed descent from Joseph and his two sons)?

The water the woman is thinking of (v. 13-14) never completely quenches even the physical thirst. But the water which
Jesus gives completely and perpetually quenches the soul's thirst.
This is what Paul meant when he said, "our inward man is renewed day by day."

The Old Testament is permeated with the idea of God sup-
plying His new people with living water. Jesus was not uttering
a new idea. Of course, the Jews rejected the idea that the
Nazarene could be the "living water," just as they rejected anything connecting Him with the Messiah. Jesus was claiming to
be the fulfillment of these messianic prophecies concerning the
"living water" (cf. Isa. 12:3; 35:7; 44:3; 49:10; 55:1; Psalm
42:1; 36:9; Jer. 2:13; 17:13; Ezek. 47:1-12; Zech. 13:1; 14:8).
Read these references; they are important!

Some commentators do not connect this living water with
the living water of John 7:37-39. But it is improper to disconnect
the two. In 7:37-39 Jesus speaks of the Holy Spirit as the living

water, and adds, "this life-source shall flow out from the believer." Neither passage, 4:13-14 or 7:37-39, is contradictory of the other.

Quiz

1. What were some of the barriers Jesus broke by talking to this woman?
2. Why may we assume that Jews *did* have some dealings with Samaritans?
3. Where did the Samaritan people originate?
4. What was the beginning of hostilities between Jew and Samaritan?
5. Why was Jesus unable to give this woman living water?
6. What was Jesus claiming when He claimed to be able to give living water? Give 5 Old Testament references.
7. What does John 7:37-39 add about the living water?

JESUS SEARCHES OUT A WOMAN'S SECRET

Text 4:15-18

15 The woman saith unto him, Sir, give me this water, that I thirst not, neither come all the way hither to draw.

16 Jesus saith unto her, Go, call thy husband, and come hither.

17 The woman answered and said unto him, I have no husband. Jesus saith unto her, Thou saidst well, I have no husband:

18 for thou hast had five husbands; and he whom thou now hast is not thy husband: this hast thou said truly.

Queries

a. Is the woman's answer sincere?
b. Why does Jesus change the subject?
c. What made the woman say, "I have no husband"?

Paraphrase

The woman said to Him, Sir, give me this living water, that I may never thirst again nor have to come here day after day to draw a new supply of water. Jesus replied, Go call your husband and come here. The woman answered, I have no husband. Jesus then said to her, You have said well, A husband I have not, for you have had five husbands, and the man whom you now have is not your husband. This is indeed a true thing you have said!

144

Summary

The woman fails to comprehend the nature of the living water, and does not realize her need for it. Jesus shows her that she ought to be thirsting for righteousness.

Comment

Is the woman's request (v. 15) sincere, or is it cynical? It is easier to assume that she is sincere. Whatever be her attitude, she has missed the point! She interprets Jesus as speaking of physical water. She has made the same mistake the great crowds made later when Jesus said, "Ye seek me, not because ye saw the signs, but because ye ate of the loaves, and were filled" (Jn. 6:26).

In verse 16 comes the next approach of the Master Teacher. He must use more dramatic and personal means of bringing the woman to an understanding of the living water. First He must make her soul thirsty for this refreshing and revitalizing water. The truth of God reveals two things: (a) our sinful and unrighteous state that causes the honest-hearted to thirst after righteousness; (b) it reveals God, manifested in Jesus, as the Living Water which quenches that thirst (cf. Mt. 5:6; Jn. 6:35; 7:37; Rev. 7:16).

Before men and women can be saved, they must be lost! The man who has not recognized his lost estate cannot be saved. This Samaritan woman must have the full light of God's perfect standard focused upon her immoral life to show her the need for living water. The gospel, of course, can be rejected. When the light of God's truth shines upon good and honest hearts, they will become thirsty and hungry to partake of the nature of God. But the results are different with evil hearts — they are increased in their hardness the longer they reject.

Jesus cannot give the woman of Samaria the living water until she has a thirst for it. Thus Jesus with His omniscient perception forces the woman to see herself as one who needs this vivifying water. Without a word of forewarning, Jesus casts a thunderbolt into the conversation. He says, "Go fetch your husband!"

Verse 17 stands in sharp contrast with the other verses narrating the woman's speech. Before, she had been very eager to converse. Suddenly she becomes very reticent. She speaks (in the Greek) only three words.

145

A few scholars believe the woman to be making a humble confession of her sin rather than seeking to conceal the fact that she was living with a man in an adulterous relationship. The entire narrative, however, seems to point to a studied attempt by the woman to evade the issue. In fact, her very next move was to raise a theological question for dispute concerning the two national religions.

The reply of Jesus (v. 17-18) is very sagacious. He continues to probe. He knows just how to proceed. The construction of the sentence in the original language gives emphasis to the word "husband." It is as if Jesus is saying, "You were correct when you said, 'I do not have a *husband'*." She is living with a man, but he is *not* her husband.

Jesus then proceeds to tell her the story of her life. There are two important blessings this woman receives. Jesus, by His power to search her heart and reveal her past has (a) revealed her sin and made her desirous of righteousness, and (b) manifested, to some extent, His omniscient and divine nature, and thus provided her the way to righteousness.

Quiz

1. How does the woman interpret Jesus' "living water"?
2. What two things does the truth of God reveal?
3. What must a person recognize before one may be saved?
4. How does the woman react when Jesus reveals her sin?
5. What is the significance of Jesus' answer (v. 17-18)?

TRUE WORSHIPPERS OF GOD

Text 4:19-26

19 The woman saith unto him, Sir, I perceive that thou art a prophet.

20 Our fathers worshipped in this mountain; and ye say, that in Jerusalem is the place where men ought to worship.

21 Jesus saith unto her, Woman, believe me, the hour cometh, when neither in this mountain, nor in Jerusalem, shall ye worship the Father.

22 Ye worship that which ye know not: we worship that which we know; for salvation is from the Jews.

23 But the hour cometh, and now is, when the true worshippers

146

shall worship the Father in spirit and truth: for such doth the
Father seek to be his worshippers.
24 God is a Spirit: and they that worship him must worship
in spirit and truth.
25 The woman saith unto him, I know that Messiah cometh (he
that is called Christ): when he is come, he will declare unto
us all things.
26 Jesus saith unto her, I that speak unto thee am he.

Queries

    a. Why did the woman ask about the place of worship?
    b. How is salvation "from the Jews"?
    c. What is worship "in spirit and truth"?

Paraphrase

The woman then said to Him, Sir, I can see that You are a
prophet. Our forefathers worshipped on this mountain, but you
Jews say that in Jerusalem is the place where it is necessary to
worship. Jesus says to her, Woman, believe Me, the hour is
coming when neither on this mountain nor in Jerusalem will you
worship the Father. You Samaritans are worshipping what you
do not know. We are worshipping what we do know, because
salvation is from the Jews. But the hour comes, in fact that
hour has arrived, when the genuine worshippers will worship the
Father in spirit and in truth. For the Father is seeking just such
people as these to be worshippers of Him. God is a Spirit, and
those who worship Him must worship in spirit and truth. The
woman says to Him, I understand that Messiah is coming, the
One called Christ, and when He has come He will declare plainly
to us everything we need to know. Jesus said to her, I, the One
speaking to you, am He!

Summary

Jesus takes a definite side in a religious controversy. The
worship of the Samaritans is condemned because it is contrary
to God's revealed truth. Worship of the One True God must
be in spirit and truth.

Comment

Undoubtedly the woman was visibly shocked. It is charac-
teristically human to try to justify one's sins or change the subject. Notice that this woman does not deny what Jesus has

revealed concerning her life. She realizes that Jesus must have some supernatural power — in fact, she thinks Him to be a prophet!

There are two popular interpretations of the motives behind the woman's interjection of the question about the proper place of worship: (a) some believe the woman to have asked the question because she was intensely interested in the question, while others hold that (b) she was still evading the very embarrassing subject of her sins. When Jesus had before asked her to call her husband she deftly evaded the truth and said, "I have no husband." Thus the second interpretation seems to be the most plausible. It is possible, however, that she would also be interested in the proper place to worship.

By saying, "Our fathers worshipped in this mountain," she evidently refers to the erection of the Samaritan temple on Mt. Gerizim nearly 400 years before her time. However, she may also be referring to the fact that Jacob built altars at Shechem (which was practically on the slopes of Gerizim) (cf. Gen. 33:20). Of course, the Samaritans would be constantly preached to by the Jews that the scriptural place of worship was in the Temple at Jerusalem.

According to the Old Testament Scriptures, which were even then the rule of faith and practice for God's people, there was only ONE place of worship. Moses legislated that there was to be just ONE acceptable altar (cf. Deut. 12:1-14). Later the tribes east of the Jordan (Gad, Reuben and Manasseh) built their own altar, but they made it plain they did not intend to erect an altar upon which to sacrifice (Josh. 22). Still later, in the time of Hezekiah, Judah is reminded of the ONE place to worship God (cf. II Kings 18:22; II Chron. 32:12; Isa. 36:7).

But, according to Jesus in verse 21, the time is coming when it will not be a question of the proper *place*. The time is coming when God will "break down the middle wall of partition," and "abolish . . . the enmity, even the law of commandments contained in ordinances," that all who seek to worship God may "have access in one Spirit unto the Father."

For the present, however, He reminds her (v. 22) that the Samaritan people are worshipping in ignorance. On the other hand, the Jews are worshipping that which they know. This is strikingly true when we realize the Samaritans only recognized the first five books of the Old Testament as authoritative. How could the Samaritans know of the prophetic promises concerning salvation from the Jews through God's suffering Servant? How could they know the devotion and prophecies of the Psalms? That salvation comes exclusively from the Jews is abundantly verified in practically all the prophetical books.

Jesus does not mean to say in verse 23 that at that moment it was permissable to worship God anywhere. He uses the phrase "the hour is coming, and now is," because in His mind the future is already perfected, (cf. also Jn. 5:25; 16:32). In just a few short months He will have fulfilled the Law, and the veil in the Temple will have been rent from top to bottom (Mt. 27:51), and the "hour will have come" when men will no longer be required to worship at ONE place.

What does Jesus mean by worshipping "in spirit and truth"? What has He just been explaining to the woman? It is that (a) the time will soon come when *place* makes no difference and (b) the Samaritans are wrong because they worship in opposition to rvealed truth. Thus, to worship in spirit and truth is (a) to make it a matter of the heart, the will, the spirit and the emotion and not merely a matter of physical atmosphere, and, (b) to worship in accordance with the revealed will of God in the New Testament. Some believers have over-emphasized one or the other, spirit or truth, and such unbalanced worship is wrong. Any worship which is contrary to what is revealed in the New Testament is divisive and disobedient. It is true that mere formalism is as surely an abomination before God.

William Barclay makes the following lucid remarks in his commentary, *The Gospel of John,* Vol. 1, pages 152-154:

"1. A false worship selects what it wishes to know and understand about God, and omits what is does not wish. One of the most dangerous things in the world is a one-sided religion.

"2. A false worship is an ignorant worship . . . In the last analysis religion is never safe until a man can tell, not only what he believes, but why he believes it.

"3. A false worship is a superstitious worship. It is a worship given, not out of a sense of need nor out of any real desire, but basically because a man feels that it might be dangerous not to give it . . . There is too much religion which is a kind of superstitious ritual to avert the possible wrath of the unpredictable gods.

"If God is Spirit, God is not confined to things; . . . if God is Spirit, God is not confined to places; . . . if God is Spirit, a man's gift to God must be gifts of the spirit . . . True and genuine worship is not to come to a certain place; it is not to go through a certain ritual or liturgy; it is not even to bring certain gifts. True worship is when the spirit, the immortal and invisible part of man, speaks to and meets with God, who is immortal and invisible."

God has always yearned for heart-felt worship that is according to truth from His people. He has always abhorred ritualism and formalism, and has sought "willing and obedient" worship (cf. Isaiah, chapter one). Paul says essentially this same thing in Phil. 3:3 and Rom. 2:28-29.

What would a Samaritan know of the Messiah? Josephus, the Jewish historian, seems to indicate there was a vague messianic expectation among the Samaritans (*The Life and Works of Flavius Josephus,* 18:4:1). They were not so far removed from the Jewish nation that they could not be well aware of the general teaching of the Prophets through what little intercourse they had between themselves.

The woman has had her thirst aroused for living water. She wants to know how she may overcome her sin and be cleansed. So, she says, "When Messiah is come, He shall reveal these things to me." She has recognized Jesus as a prophet, but not yet as *The* Prophet — the Messiah.

Jesus, knowing she has now come to a realization of her need and is, in fact, yearning for the One who can supply that need, declares Himself to be the Living Water . . . the Gift of God . . . the Messiah.

What did the woman do? Evidently she did not say anything more to Jesus, but rushed into town, forgetting her water-jar to spread the good news (cf. v. 28).

Quiz

1. What motive do you think the woman had for asking the question about the proper place of worship (v. 20)?
2. Who were correct — according to the Old Testament — the Jews or the Samaritans? Why?
3. Why were the Samaritans worshipping in ignorance?
4. When did the "hour come" that God's people were no longer required to worship in one place?
5. What is worshipping "in spirit and truth"?
6. Name three characteristics of false religion.

SPONTANEOUS EVANGELISM

Text 4:27-30

27 And upon this came his disciples; and they marvelled that he was speaking with a woman; yet no man said, What seekest thou? or, Why speakest thou with her?
28 So the woman left her waterpot, and went away into the city, and saith to the people,
29 Come, see a man, who told me all things that ever I did: can this be the Christ?
30 They went out of the city, and were coming to him.

Queries

    a. Why were the returning disciples reticent?
    b. What was the significance of the forgotten waterpot?

Paraphrase

At this junction His disciples returned from the market, and they were astonished to find Him talking to a woman. However, none of them asked Him, What do you want? or, Why are you talking with her? The woman, forgetting her waterjar, hurried off unto the city and began telling the people, Come, see a Man Who has told me everything that I ever did. You don't think this Man could be the Christ, do you? So the people came out from the city and were coming toward Him in a continual procession.

Summary

The Woman hurries excitedly into the city telling her discovery. The townspeople come immediately in search of a man who may be the Messiah.

Comment

This is one of the first examples of spontaneous evangelism. Perhaps a better title would be "Evangelism by Compulsion." Certainly, as will be discussed later, this woman was "constrained" to tell of the One she had met at the well.

When the disciples returned from market they were taken aback to find Him freely conversing with a woman. The restrictive barriers between men and women were discussed in our comments on 4:9.

151

One noteworthy statement of the gospel writer in verse 27 is the reticence of the disciples to question openly the Master's actions. Either their respect for His wisdom would not allow them to brazenly question Him, or they feared He might upbraid them. The disciples were momentarily interested in eating (v. 31) and not in a long discourse on the emancipation of women. Perhaps this accounts for their silence.

Their conversation having been interrupted by the returning disciples, the woman hastens off to tell the townspeople of her experience (v. 28). In her excitement and soul-gripping conviction she forgets the waterjar sitting on the well-curb, and rushes off down the road toward the city. The verb used by John here, *apheken,* lends itself to the idea that she forgot the vessel. It is the same word which is translated remission, forgiveness, and means a forgetting of our sins by God.

Verse 29 records for us, at least partially, her testimony to the people of the city. We also receive insight into the compelling force that causes her to testify. She had just undergone what some people might call "a religious experience." This experience, as we have commented before (vs. 15-18), consisted in a personal conviction of her sin and a beginning trust in His person as the omniscient One. These two factors were the motivating and compelling force that caused "spontaneous evangelism" in her life. As the apostle Paul said, "Knowing therefore the fear of the Lord, we persuade men," . . . and, "the love of Christ constraineth us . . ." (cf. II Cor. 5:11, 14).

In the concluding phrase of verse 29 the woman puts the question in a hesitant form. As Robertson says, "With a woman's intuition she . . . does not take sides, but piques their couriosity." She is in no social position to make theological decisions and dogmatic conclusions. Who would accept her convictions — a woman who is an outcast of the community! So she deftly plants the seed of couriosity and allows them to form their own conclusions.

The tense of the verb *erchonto* (were coming) in verse 30 is one of John's word pictures. The picture is of a long stream of excited people coming toward Jacob's Well.

Quiz

1. Why do you think the disciples hesitated to question Jesus openly?
2. What caused the woman to leave her water pot?
3. What are two factors which form motivation for spontaneous evangelism?

FIELDS WHITE UNTO HARVEST

Text 4:31-38

31 In the meanwhile the disciples prayed him, saying, Rabbi, eat.
32 But he said unto them, I have meat to eat that ye know not.
33 The disciples therefore said one to another, Hath any man brought him aught to eat?
34 Jesus saith unto them, My meat is to do the will of him that sent me, and to accomplish his work.
35 Say not ye, There are yet four months, and then cometh the harvest? behold, I say unto you, Lift up your eyes, and look on the fields, that they are white already unto harvest.
36 He that reapeth receiveth wages, and gathereth fruit unto life eternal; that he that soweth and he that reapeth may rejoice together.
37 For herein is the saying true, One soweth, and another reapeth.
38 I sent you to reap that whereon ye have not labored: others have labored, and ye are entered into thier labor.

Queries

a. What lesson does Jesus teach the disciples in verses 31-35?
b. Who are "he that reapeth" and "he that soweth"?
c. How may the disciples "reap where they have not labored"?

Paraphrase

In the meantime the disciples continued to beseech him, saying, Master, eat something! But He said to them, I have food to eat which you do not understand. The disciples therefore said among themselves, Has anyone brought Him something to eat?

153

Jesus replied, My food is to do the will of Him who sent Me and to completely fulfill His work. Will you not say that it is yet four months and the harvest comes? Look, I tell you, lift up your eyes and contemplate the fields, that they are white already for harvest. He that reaps receives and gathers fruit unto life eternal, in order that the one sowing and the one reaping may rejoice together. In this way the saying is true, One sows and another reaps. I have sent you to reap a harvest which your labor did not produce. Others have labored and you have entered in to reap the result of their labor.

Summary

Jesus teaches the disciples two lessons: (a) Doing the will of God is spiritual food more satisfying and sustaining than physical food; (b) It is not important whether a disciple be a reaper or a sower — only that he be a laborer in the Lord's field. Both sower and reaper rejoice when the harvest is gathered.

Comment

Jesus sits in silent mediation watching the woman reach the city, and then watching the crowds begin to come. The disciples have set the meal in order. They are hungry and, knowing He must be also, they hesitantly interrupt His meditation, advising Him to eat.

The Master's reply (v. 32) is beyond their perception. Jesus is so engrossed in the great opportunities and apparent victories in Samaria He has only the appetite for a food which the disciples do not comprehend. He is anxious for the crowds to arrive so that He may begin imparting living water to them also. His whole being is so immersed in His mission of saving souls He can think of nothing else.

The disciples either speak loudly enough (v. 33) for Jesus to hear, or He reads their thoughts. Theirs is a natural reaction of Jesus' statement (v. 32). Perhaps they think the woman had left Him something to eat. But Jesus very deliberately explains to them what His food was.

In verse 34 Jesus indicated how completely saturated He was in the will of the Father (cf. Jn. 2:17). We have a saying today illustrative of this. We say, "That person eats and sleeps his occupation." Doing the will of God was the very essence of Jesus' being. He was sustained by it. The Word and will of God was the bread upon which He fed (cf. Mt. 4:4). Barclay points out two blessings in doing the will of God (a) peace, and (b) power. These blessings become obvious when one beholds the perfect peace and victorious power which Christ enjoyed. It is also obvious that He enjoyed these blessings because of His complete submission to, and harmony with, the will of the Father. We shall gain or lose these two blessings in proportion to our unreserved trust in His will (cf. Mt. 26:39; Mk. 14:36; Lk. 22:42; Jn. 5:30; 6:38; 8:29; Heb. 10:7-9). The "accomplishment" of God's work means the fulfillment or completion of the Son's mission upon earth. Jesus, in His atoning death and justifying resurrection, completes and fulfills God's mission for Him (cf. Jn. 17:4; 19:28).

Verse 35 has been the subject of much discussion among Biblical scholars. Was this a proverbial saying quoted by Jesus, or was it actually "yet four months" until the harvest? Nearly all commentators agree that no such proverb has been found to exist. The best interpretation has Jesus implying a question to which He expects the disciples to answer, "Yes." Jesus says to the disciples, "You will probably say that in four months it will be time to harvest, won't you? But I am telling you to open your eyes to the spiritual fields which are ripe *already* for harvest."

Another question of interpreters concerning this verse is "Where does the word *already* belong, to verse 35 or 36?" As R. C. H. Lenski points out, "The contrast is between the attitudes of Christ and the disciples." "You will say yet four months . . . but I say already . . ." Thus, the word *already* rightfully belongs in verse 35.

The spiritual impact of this verse (v. 35) is apparent when we remember Jesus' constant reminder to the disciples of the overabundance of harvest and pathetic lack of laborers. Near the end of His second year of ministry Jesus was "moved with compassion" for the multitudes "because they were distressed and scattered, as sheep not having a shepherd." There, as He traveled among the cities and villages of Galilee, He said to the disciples, "The harvest indeed is plenteous, but the laborers are few. Pray ye therefore the Lord of the harvest, that he send forth laborers into his harvest" (cf. Mt. 9:35-38). This is certainly one prayer the church needs to pray today, but one which is appallingly absent.

Jesus has been deep in thought concerning the opportunities soon to be available for harvesting souls. His next instruction (v. 36) to the disciples is to combat jealously among them as co-laborers in the Lord's fields. They are about to reap a harvest here in Samaria where they had not sown. Others had even sown before Jesus, i.e., the prophets and John the Baptist. In this verse, the emphasis is upon the mutual sharing of the reward by both sower and reaper.

The one reaping receives a reward. What is this reward? The rewards of the spiritual laborer are the souls harvested. Paul's crown and glory were to consist of his converts at the Lord's coming (cf. Phil. 2:14-16; I Thess. 2:19-20). But even Paul reaped at times where others had sown. And, vice-versa, he sowed where others later reaped. In the spiritual realm, both sower and reaper rejoice together at the harvest, for both shared in it. This was John the Baptist's understanding also when he spoke of rejoicing that the Bridegroom had come (cf. Jn. 2:29-30). This was the principle Paul announced in his letter to Corinth, "Paul planted, Apollos watered, but God gave the increase" (I Cor. 3:6-9).

The saying of verse 37 is interpreted in a number of ways. Verses 36, 37, and 38 must all be taken into account in interpreting this saying. The burden of the Lord's teaching is to instruct the reaper not to exalt himself as the one solely responsible for the harvest of souls. There have been sowers doing their work in advance of the reaper. They are equally responsible for the harvest, and they shall be equally rewarded. So in the spiritual sphere it is true: one sows and another reaps where he has not sown, but both rejoice together at the harvest.

What does Jesus mean by the past tense (v. 38), "I *sent* you to reap . . ."? There are two possible answers: (a) Jesus was using prophetic past tenses, i.e., the disciples would soon reap this Samaritan harvest where they had not sown, but Jesus speaks now of their reaping as already past; or (b) He speaks only of their previous reaping when they "made and baptized more disciples than John" (Jn. 4:1-2). They had not sown this earlier harvest of 4:1-2 either, but others, such as the Baptist, had sown, and they reaped.

The first interpretation seems to fit this context better. Jesus had just exhorted His disciples (v. 35) to get a vision of the field which was even at that moment ripe unto harvest. Is not this a form of commissioning, a sending forth? Certainly, the disciples had not labored in these fields, for they had gone away to buy food. But now, as the multitudes approach, and, in the two days to follow, the disciples would act as reapers. Jesus and the woman were the sowers, and the disciples would "enter into their labor." There would be others following these first disciples to reap these same fields (Acts 8:5-7, 14ff). The disciples reaped, but they also sowed seed which those who followed them would reap.

It is true in our day also. The Sunday school teacher sows, and the minister reaps, or the minister sows and the revival evangelist reaps — but both should continually rejoice together in view of the harvest. In the last day, when the. accounts are rendered, it will not be a question of how many talents one possessed — but what he accomplished with the talents he did possess. There will be no asking by Christ whether we were sowers or reapers — only whether we labored or not!

Quiz

1. What was the food which Jesus had to eat?
2. Name two blessings derived from doing the will of God.
3. What contrast does Jesus make by His question concerning the harvest (v. 35)?
4. Matthew................also speaks of "harvest" and "laborers."
5. What is the emphasis of verse 36?
6. How should the past tense "I sent" (v. 38) be interpreted?
7. How is this passage of Scripture (v. 31-38) applicable to Christians today?

REAPING THE HARVEST

Text 4:39-42

39 And from that city many of the Samaritans believed on him because of the word of the woman, who testified, He told me all things that ever I did.

40 So when the Samaritans came unto him, they besought him to abide with them: and he abode there two days.

41 And many more believed because of his word;

42 and they said to the woman, Now we believe, not because of thy speaking: for we have heard for ourselves, and know that this is indeed the Saviour of the world.

Queries

    a. How could the people believe "because of" the woman's testimony?

157

    b. What was the significance of their "hearing for themselves"?

    c. Why do they say "Saviour of the world"?

Paraphrase

And many of the Samaritan people from that city trusted and obeyed Jesus because of the personal witness of the woman who testified, He told me all things which I ever did. When the Samaritans came to Him they begged Him to stay with them. So Jesus remained there two days. And many trusted and obeyed because of His reasoning, and they told the woman, We no longer believe merely through your testimony, but we have heard Him for ourselves and know that this One is truly the Saviour of the world.

Summary

Many of the Samaritans are firmly persuaded that Jesus is the looked-for Saviour, because of both the woman's testimony and Jesus' reasoning with them.

Comment

B. F. Westcott points out the great contrast between these Samaritans and the people of Jerusalem who believed on Him. The Samaritans had, so far as we know, only the testimony of the woman and Christ's reasoning with them for the ground of their faith. On the other hand, the Jerusalem believers had many miracles and signs (Jn. 2:23) upon which to ground their belief. The woman told the townspeople of Jesus' prophetic insight, but they had to trust her testimony, for they had not witnessed the conversation.

Why would they trust her? When one considers her probable reputation, it seems little short of amazing that they would believe her. Doubtless her enthusiasm played a major part in gaining their ears. Furthermore, she would be unlikely to admit that Jesus had prophetically revealed her immoral past, were it not true! But they did not rest their trust in Him solely upon her story, but investigated for themselves. They were like noble Bereans (cf. Acts 17:11).

Verse 40 presents another contrast. Contrast the hospitality of the Samaritans now and the uncharitable attitude of some Samaritans later in the ministry of Jesus (cf. Lk. 9:51-56). Of course, Jesus made disciples only in this one city, and the return trip spoken of in the ninth chapter of Luke may have taken Him through other cities.

One note of interest here is John's taking almost the entire fourth chapter to record only two days' happenings while the timeless events of eternity are grappled with in eighteen short verses of Chapter One!

Some see in the Lord's evangelistic efforts here a contradiction of His later commission to the apostles to "not enter into a city of the Samaritans; but go rather unto the lost sheep of the house of Israel" (Mt. 10:5-6). But the commission of Matthew 10 was: (a) subsequent to the Samaritan event; (b) temporary in nature; (c) cancelled by even later commissions in Matthew 28:19-20 and Acts 1:8. It is also well to remember that Jesus stopped in only one village of the Samaritans, and then only after their continued insistence!

In verse 41, the Samaritans state definitely the cause for their belief — the word of Jesus. The Greek word which has been translated word is *logos,* which may also be translated as discourse of instruction, or expression of reasoning. (See our comments on 1:1-18). In two days' time He had ample opportunity to present His claims and show His fulfillment of the Pentateuch. This incident is illustrative of the principle stated by Paul . . . "Faith comes by hearing and hearing by the word of God" (Rom. 10:17).

Lenski makes a good point in verse 42 by contrasting two kinds of faith: (a) the fledgling's faith based on the testimony of others, and (b) the satisfying faith based on personal investigation and experience. The former is the faith of many children who have been taught by parents and Sunday School teachers; the latter is the type of faith into which the former should grow — a faith which is firmly grounded in one's own personal investigation and contact with Christ and His Word.

Those critics who wish to deny the historicity of the Fourth Gospel claim the Samaritans did not say "we know that this is the Saviour of the world," but that John puts these words into their mouths on his own accord. This is absurd! Jesus told the woman (v. 26) that He was the Messiah. Would not two days be sufficient for Jesus to tell this city of His universal Redeemership? This universality is really the lesson He proceeds to teach the woman in verses 20 through 26! As is usually the case, the destructive critics have failed to read and understand the context!

Quiz

1. How do these Samaritans compare with the believers of Jerusalem (2:23)?
2. Give two reasons to show that Jesus does not contradict His commission of Matt. 10:5-6 by entering a Samaritan city.
3. Would it be possible for the Samaritans to understand Jesus to be a universal Saviour? Explain.

PUBLIC TEACHING IN GALILEE

Text 4:43-45

43 And after the two days he went forth from thence into Galilee.
44 For Jesus himself testified, that a prophet hath no honor in his own country.
45 So when he came into Galilee, the Galileans received him, having seen all the things that he did in Jerusalem at the feast: for they also went unto the feast.

Queries

   a. Why did Jesus say "a prophet hath no honor . . ."?
   b. How did the Galileans receive Him?

Paraphrase

After these two days Jesus went out from Samaria into the province of Galilee. He Himself declared as the reason, A prophet is not famous in his own country. But when He came into Galilee, the Galileans welcomed Him with acclaim, having seen everything that He did in Jerusalem during the Feast of Passover, for they also had attended the Feast.

Summary

Jesus goes to Galilee anticipating an unpretentious arrival, but receives public acclaim.

Comment

In verse 43 the Lord seems to be in a hurry to get to Galilee. With such success in Samaria, He is in danger again of arousing the jealousy of the Pharisees. He proposes to go into Galilee, His home country. The Pharisees were not above following His every movement in order to force the issue, for they later do just that.

Verses 43 and 44 are John's way of resuming the narrative where he left it in 4:1-3. Jesus left Judea originally because His growing popularity was about to bring about a premature collision between Him and the rulers (see our comments on 4:1-3). Add to this the recent success in Samaria, and one begins to understand His determination to go into Galilee. To avoid further antagonizing the rulers, He departs for His own country where He anticipates a quiet arrival, for no prophet is overly-honored in His own country.

He will not always seek to avoid this clash, however, for when the appointed time comes for Him to fulfill all things, He will "steadfastly set His face to go to Jerusalem," and force the issue with the jealously blind leaders there.

When Jesus arrived in Galilee, however, the people welcomed Him openly (v. 45). They had been to the Passover (2:23) and seen the many signs He did there. Again we see the contrast between the Galileans and the Samaritans. Those of Samaria eagerly welcomed Jesus into their homes, although they had been given no signs; the Galileans received Him primarily because He was a "wonder-worker" (cf. 4:48 also).

So Jesus now embarks on a public ministry in Galilee. The ministry which follows, however, seems to speak of a "guarded revelation of Himself" as compared with the open declaration of Himself in Samaria as "the Messiah — the Saviour of the world." This Galilean ministry will last approximately sixteen months. There will be only one interruption — a brief trip to Jerusalem for a Passover feast recorded in John 5. It is a ministry almost completely left out of John's gospel except for John 4:43-54 and 6:1-7:10. But this early Galilean ministry is reported extensively by the Synoptic Gospels (cf. Mt. chapters 4-14; Mk. 1-6; Lk. 4-9). See Map No. 3, page 170.

Quiz

1. Why did Jesus go into Galilee?
2. What does He mean by saying "a prophet hath no honor in his own country?"
3. Why was Jesus popular in Galilee?
4. How long is the Galilean ministry to last?
5. What portion of the great Galilean ministry is reported by John?

HEALING A NOBLEMAN'S SON AT CAPERNAUM

Text 4:46-54

46 He came therefore again unto Cana of Galilee, where he made the water wine. And there was a certain nobleman, whose son was sick at Capernaum.

47 When he heard that Jesus was come out of Judea into Galilee, he went unto him, and besought him that he would come down, and heal his son; for he was at the point of death.

48 Jesus therefore said unto him, Except ye see signs and wonders, ye will in no wise believe.

49 The nobleman saith unto him, Sir, come down ere my child die.

50 Jesus saith unto him, Go thy way; thy son liveth. The man believed the word that Jesus spake unto him, and he went his way.

51 And as he was now going down, his servants met him, saying that his son lived.

52 So he inquired of them the hour when he began to amend. They said therefore unto him, Yesterday at the seventh hour the fever left him.

53 So the father knew that it was at that hour in which Jesus said unto him, Thy son liveth: and himself believed, and his whole house.

54 This is again the second sign that Jesus did, having come out of Judea into Galilee.

Queries

    a. Why would this nobleman think Jesus could heal his son?

    b. What degree of faith did this man display?

    c. What is the significance of Jesus' manner of healing here?

Paraphrase

So Jesus came again to Cana of Galilee where He had made the water into wine. Now there was a certain royal official whose son was desperately ill in Capernaum. This official, hearing that Jesus had come from Judea back into Galilee, went to Him and begged Him to come down to Capernaum and heal his son, for the boy was at the point of death. Jesus said to the man, Unless you Galileans see signs and wonders you will never believe. But

162

the official said to Him, Sir, please come down at once before my little boy dies. Jesus replied to him, Go your way, your son lives! The man trusted what Jesus had said to him and began his journey home. But while he was still on his way home, his servants met him and said, Your little boy lives! So he immediately inquired of them the time when his son began to improve. They answered, Yesterday evening, about seven, the fever left him. Then the father knew that it was at that very hour when Jesus had said to him, Your son lives. Then the nobleman and his entire household believed on Jesus. This is the second sign which Jesus did after He had come from Judea into Galilee.

Summary

A desperate father seeks the Man of Whom it is rumored, that He is a miracle-worker. Jesus fans the spark of faith within this man and heals his little boy. This, incidentally, is His second miracle in Galilee.

Comment

Why would Jesus go to Cana? (a) He had friends there. Perhaps the same family who invited Him to the wedding feast (2:1-2) had opened their home to Him now; (b) Cana was the home of Nathanael (21:2); (c) There would be better opportunity to preach there first since He had already performed one great miracle there.

Jesus seems to have been in Cana a day or so before the nobleman came, at least long enough for the royal officer to learn of His whereabouts and come seeking Him. The word translated nobleman is *basilikos* (related to *basileus* which means king) and means an official of the King's court. This royal official lived at Capernaum about twenty miles distant from Cana over mountain terrain.

News of the Nazarene's arrival back in Cana, where He had once made water into wine, would spread swiftly from village to village. This nobleman of Capernaum heard that Jesus had come to Galilee and went away from his son's bedside seeking the miracle-worker. The courtier may have already spent great sums on physicians to no avail (cf. Lk. 8:43). His son was "at the very point of death."

What would cause this man to go to Jesus? (a) First, his desperate situation. What parent cannot sympathize with him? (b) All of Galilee would be filled with the reports of Jesus' amazing miracles performed at Cana and Jerusalem. It is not impossible for this officer to have been at the feast in Jerusalem himself when Jesus performed many miracles (2:23).

It is uncharitable to say the man had no faith to begin with, yet his faith is imperfect at the start. He is persuaded that Jesus can heal only if He come to his son's bedside.

Verse 48 shows again the Lord's perfect method of fanning the tiniest spark of faith into a reckless, burning trust. Jesus replies seemingly unconcerned, "Unless you Galileans see signs and wonders you will never believe." As one commentator points out, however, Jesus is not so unconcerned and unsympathetic as it may seem. He has a way of testing men and women to determine the sincerity of their faith. He tested the Syro-Phoenician woman severely. Had this royal official turned away in exasperation and indignation, his faith would have been shown to be superficial, not able to stand testing. Notice the plural "ye" in verse 48. Jesus addresses the thrill-seeking crowds as well as the nobleman. Theirs indeed does turn out to be a superficial, pleasure-seeking faith.

But the nobleman will not be denied. He cries out to Jesus with the clutching intensity of a drowning man. The Nazarene is his last hope. "Come down ere my child dies!"

What faith is exemplified in the man's action! It must be evident from this incident that faith without implicit obedience is dead, useless and no faith at all. Jesus' words of verse 50 are a mighty test of the nobleman's faith. The Nazarene bade him "Go thy way, thy son liveth." This certainly shows that faith means both trust and obedience. The man believed Jesus and started immediately for home.

The incidental mention of "as he was . . . going down" shows the author of the Fourth Gospel to be familiar with the topography. Cana is approximately 2850 feet above normal sea level. Capernaum is on the north-west shore of the Sea of Galilee which is 682 feet below sea level. The man would truly be "going down" to Capernaum.

Verse 52 raises again the question of John's method of counting time. We must remember, however, he here reports the words of the servants. Since they were probably Jewish, this mention of time might be the Jewish seventh hour, which would mean the boy was healed at 1:00 p.m. the day before. The Jews counted their new day as beginning after sunset. It would take the man at least eight hours to walk the short, though mountainous, 20 miles. He would then, according to Jewish reckoning, be near Capernaum the next day, although shortly after sunset. John could also have used the Roman method of time. Had Jesus pronounced the word of healing at 7:00 p.m., the nobleman would not near Capernaum until early the next morning, approximately 3:00 a.m.

As he approached the city, his servants ran to meet him and excitedly related to him the strangely instantaneous recovery of the young lad. The joyous father's faith took another leap forward. This man had found another King and had surrendered to His service. He related the wonderful story of Jesus to his family, and they too surrendered to Him. We would like to hear more about this nobleman. How difficult it must have been to maintain a Christian witness in the court of Herod! How would his Jewish associates receive his testimony concerning Jesus of Nazareth? But John is not writing a story of men, but a history of the Son of God.

There are four exemplary traits in this nobleman which all men would do well to copy: (a) He did not let position, pride or effort prevent him from coming to seek Christ's aid; (b) He stood the test of his faith; (c) He showed the reckless type of faith (not ignorant) which Jesus desires — the only way to receive the full benefit of the promises of God's Word is to believe in Jesus unreservedly; (d) He became a witness for the Lord.

There are number of facts which make this a notable miracle: (a) it was a cure performed at a distance from the sick child; (b) it was performed for a distinguished officer of the king's court; (c) Jesus said no peculiar "healing formula"; (d) the child evidently did not have any faith in Jesus; (e) the child was at the point of death.

Modern faith-healers are not known for any such miracles. Today's "healers" insist that faith is an established condition for healing. Search the Gospels as you will, and you will find only one time in thirty-one instances of healing where the Lord required faith (cf. Mt. 9:28). In nine cases of healing there is no evidence at all of faith; in four instances faith is very unlikely; in four other healings performed by Jesus there is no faith possible! (cf. Lk. 7:11-17; Jn. 5:2-13; Jn. 11:1-46; Mt. 9:18-26).

Others have attacked this miracle upon the grounds that it was not a miracle at all but Jesus was merely giving the father a reassuring word, like any modern physician, that his son would "pull through." But John definitely states that it is a miracle.

Quiz

1. Give three reasons for Jesus' going first to Cana.
2. Can you locate Cana and Capernaum on the map of Palestine?
3. What was the degree of illness of the son?
4. Why did Jesus answer as He did in verse 48?
5. List four traits of the nobleman worthy of practicing.
6. Give four reasons why this is a notable miracle.

EXPOSITORY SERMON NO. 4
John, Chapter 4

"YOU CAN BE A SOUL WINNER"

Introduction

I THERE IS NO QUESTION THAT EVERY CHRISTIAN MUST BE SOUL WINNER.
Plainly commanded (Mt. 28:18-20; John 15:1-6).

II REALIZATION OF DUTY NOT THE PROBLEM
Some realize, but are downright lazy and indifferent.
These will have blood of many souls on their heads (Ezek. 18 and 30).
B. Most Christians lack confidence or courage.
"Me, a personal witness . . . I just couldn't . . . How?"
C. Every Christian who really wants to can be a soul winner.
There is nothing in the New Testament that says you cannot get a decision, hear a person's confession of Christ, and baptize him yourself!

III JESUS THE PERFECT EXAMPLE OF A SOUL WINNER IN JOHN 4
A. He had a deep LOVE FOR THE SOULS OF MEN.
B. He was PREPARED.
C. He was UNSELFISH.

Discussion

I HE LOVED THE SOULS OF MEN AND WOMEN.
A. Not just "interested in people" . . . but having an OUTGOING LOVE
B. He let nothing stand in His way of speaking a word to her soul.
1. Not hunger, not race, not social barriers

2. WE LET MANY THINGS STAND IN OUR WAY.
   a. How many outcasts of society have gone to Christless graves because we loved our reputation more than their souls? . . . JESUS WENT INTO THE HOMES OF TRAITORS, PROSTITUTES, INSANE, BEGGERS, ETC.
   b. How many of the upper class have died without the Lord because we have been ashamed to witness (Rom. 1:16)?
C. Jesus found a way to begin witnessing.
   1. How does one start?
   2. Jesus said to the woman at the well, "Give me a drink."
      To Mary and Martha He used the subject of their beloved Brother's recent death!
   3. Paul in Athens mentioned the city's idols
   4. Most parents can be reached through their children

II CHRIST WAS PREPARED
A. Unpreparedness is the major reason people lack confidence.
   WE MUST DRILL ON THE SCRIPTURE REFERENCES TO THE PLAN OF SALVATION
   It is shocking the number of long-time Christians who do not know where to find these Scriptures!
B. He knew His prospect (by divine insight).
   1. We must get to know people.
      a. Their fears (of water, etc.), their beliefs
      b. Must build up and encourage, not tear down what little faith some do have
      c. Must win people's confidence and trust
      d. Must, many times, dissolve barriers others erect
   2. Jesus knew how to keep on the subject
C. He knew His message
   1. The woman tried to bring up old family traditions
   2. Jesus did not compromise the truth
   3. He did not argue, but always came back to her personal responsibility!
   4. Peter said, "BE READY ALWAYS TO GIVE ANSWER TO EVERY MAN THAT ASKETH THEE CONCERNING THE HOPE THAT IS WITHIN THEE."

We need to learn by heart these basic things:

a. How to show the Bible as the word of God, infallible

b. How to show the New Testament as the Book for Christians

c. How to show the Scriptures explaining the plan of salvation

d. How to show that this is the only gospel (Gal. 1:8-9)

e. How to show that Christ demands unity in essentials of all who profess belief in Him.

HE HAD A MESSAGE WHICH HE KNEW MEN NEEDED MORE THAN THEY NEEDED EVEN FOOD AND CLOTHING, AND HE WAS CONSUMED WITH A DESIRE TO GIVE THEM THIS WORD.

III HE WAS UNSELFISH IN HIS VISION OF THE LOST

A. This holds many Christians back from witnessing.

B. His vision encompassed the world.

What will the Lord say about expensive church buildings while millions are going into their building simply out of pride? The church should have adequate space and up-to-date facilities, but there must be good stewardship here as well as anywhere else.

C. He was not jealous

1. Told His disciples:

a. They would reap where they hadn't sown.

b. They would sow and others would reap.

2. Many a Christian has sown, never seeing results, and as a result has ceased to sow.

MUCH OF EVERY PREACHER'S REAPING IN ANY CHURCH IS DUE TO SOWING BY BIBLE SCHOOL TEACHERS, ELDERS AND OTHER MEMBERS.

IF ONE SOWER DOES NOT SEE RESULTS, OTHERS WILL . . . LET US REJOICE TOGETHER!

3. Paul said he rejoiced over men preaching the gospel even if they tried to defame him and take honor away from him . . . still they were converting people to Christ (Phil. 1:15-19).

4. Few people get more jealous than preachers and church members.

THERE IS NO ROOM FOR SELFISHNESS, JEALOUSY OR DESPAIR IN CHRISTIAN SOUL WINNING . . . THE LORD KNOWS HOW TO REWARD HIS FAITHFUL SOLDIERS. SOME MAY GO UNNOTICED BY ANYONE ELSE IN THIS WORLD, BUT THE LORD KNOWS HIS OWN, AND THEIR WORKS OF LOVE!

Conclusion

I THERE ARE TWO KINDS OF REWARD
    A. Heavenly reward not able to be expressed in human language says Paul (II Cor. 12:2-4)
    B. Neither can we know fully the terrors of Hell!

II THERE WAS A MAN WHO DECIDED TO BE A SOUL WINNER . . . ALAS, TOO LATE!
    A. Parable of Lazarus and rich man . . . "just let me go tell my brothers."
    B. We must work the works of God while it is day, for the night comes when no man can work.
    C. Paul said, "knowing the fear of the Lord, we persuade men."

III JESUS NEVER MADE UP ANYONE'S MIND FOR THEM.
He presented the glad tidings, and he presented the only alternative. THEN HE LET MEN AND WOMEN MAKE THEIR OWN DECISION. *WHAT IS YOUR DECISION?*

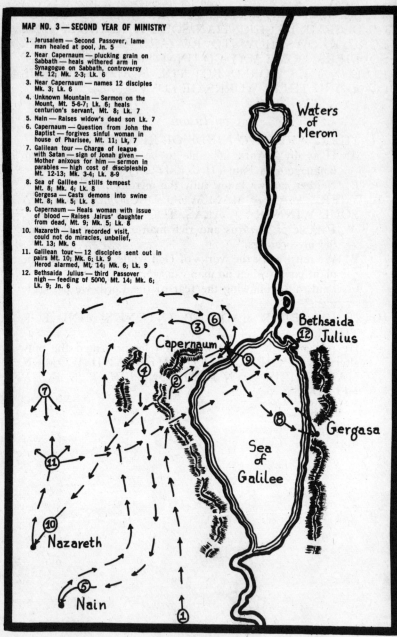

MAP NO. 3 — SECOND YEAR OF MINISTRY

1. Jerusalem — Second Passover, lame man healed at pool, Jn. 5
2. Near Capernaum — plucking grain on Sabbath — heals withered arm in Synagogue on Sabbath, controversy Mt. 12; Mk. 2-3; Lk. 6
3. Near Capernaum — names 12 disciples Mk. 3; Lk. 6
4. Unknown Mountain — Sermon on the Mount, Mt. 5-6-7; Lk. 6; heals centurion's servant, Mt. 8; Lk. 7
5. Nain — Raises widow's dead son Lk. 7
6. Capernaum — Question from John the Baptist — forgives sinful woman in house of Pharisee, Mt. 11; Lk. 7
7. Galilean tour — Charge of league with Satan — sign of Jonah given — Mother anixous for him — sermon in parables — high cost of discipleship Mt. 12-13; Mk. 3-4; Lk. 8-9
8. Sea of Galilee — stills tempest Mt. 8; Mk. 4; Lk. 8 Gergesa — Casts demons into swine Mt. 8; Mk. 5; Lk. 8
9. Capernaum — Heals woman with issue of blood — Raises Jairus' daughter from dead, Mt. 9; Mk. 5; Lk. 8
10. Nazareth — last recorded visit, could not do miracles, unbelief, Mt. 13; Mk. 6
11. Galilean tour — 12 disciples sent out in pairs Mt. 10; Mk. 6; Lk. 9 Herod alarmed, Mt. 14; Mk. 6; Lk. 9
12. Bethsaida Julius — third Passover nigh — feeding of 5000, Mt. 14; Mk. 6; Lk. 9; Jn. 6

Waters of Merom

Bethsaida Julius

Capernaum

Gergasa

Sea of Galilee

Nazareth

Nain

CHAPTER FIVE

This chapter is the really great chapter on the deity of Jesus. Here He brings to testify undeniable witnesses to His Sonship. In this chapter we also see the first of open controversy on the part of the Jewish rulers. In connection with this we have included a Special Study on "Controversies and Objections in Jesus' Ministry," by Seth Wilson at the end of this chapter.

Between the incidents in Cana of Galilee (chapter 4) and His return to Jerusalem for the unnamed feast of 5:1, Jesus carried on a considerable ministry in Galilee. He returned to His home town Nazareth, preached in the synagogue, and was rejected (Lk. 4) ; He called the four fishermen the second time and healed many (Mt. 4; Mk. 1; Lk. 5) ; He made a Galilean tour among great crowds (Mt. 4; Mk. 1; Lk. 5) ; He healed a leper (Mt. 8) ; a paralytic (Mt. 9) ; called Matthew (Mt. 9) ; and ran into controversies about eating and fasting (Mt. 9; Mk. 2; Lk. 5). See Map No. 3 page 170.

We outline the fifth chapter of John as follows:

II The Word Manifested to the Jews and Their Rejection of Him. 1:19-12:50 (cont'd)

    C. Public Ministry — Second Year 5:1-47

        1. Open controversy begins
            a. A helpless man healed 5:1-9
            b. Sabbath controversy 5:10-18

        2. Jesus claims deity
            a. The deity stated 5:19-23
            b. Powers inherent in that deity 5:24-29

        3. Jesus gives evidence for His deity
            a. Jesus' own witness 5:30-32
            b. John the Baptist's witness 5:33-35
            c. The Father's witness 5:36-38
            d. The witness of the Scriptures 5:39-47

A HELPLESS MAN HEALED

Text 5:1-9

1 After these things there was a feast of the Jews; and Jesus went up to Jerusalem.
2 Now there is in Jerusalem by the sheep gate a pool, which is called in Hebrew Bethesda, having five porches.
3 In these lay a multitude of them that were sick, blind, halt, withered.
5 And a certain man was there, who had been thirty and eight years in his infirmity.
6 When Jesus saw him lying, and knew that he had been now a long time in that case, he saith unto him, Wouldest thou be made whole?
7 The sick man answered him, Sir, I have no man, when the water is troubled, to put me into the pool: but while I am coming, another steppeth down before me.
8 Jesus saith unto him, Arise, take up thy bed, and walk.
9 And straightway the man was made whole, and took up his bed and walked. Now it was the sabbath on that day.

Queries

a. Why were the people gathered at this pool?
b. Why would Jesus ask such an obvious question?
c. What did the man mean by "when the water is troubled"?

Paraphrase

After a considerable ministry in Galilee, there was the (Passover) feast of the Jews, and Jesus went up to Jerusalem. Now there is a pool in Jerusalem near the sheep gate which is called in Hebrew, Bethesda, having five covered porches. In these porches lay great crowds of sick people, some blind, some crippled and some shrunken and emaciated. There was a certain man there having had a lingering illness for thirty-eight years. Jesus, seeing him lying there, and knowing that for a long time he had been an invalid, said to him, Do you want to be made healthy? The sick man answered, Sir, I have no one to put me into the pool when the water is troubled, and when I try by myself to get down to the pool another person steps down to it before me. Jesus said to him, Arise! take up your pallet and walk. Immediately the man became well, and took up his pallet and walked. But that day was a Sabbath day!

Summary

Jesus heals a helpless man who was hopelessly ill and manifests His deity. But it was performed on the Sabbath, and the Jews will attack Him for breaking the Sabbath.

Comment

What feast is this? There is great diversity of opinion among scholars. Andrews, Hendriksen, and Foster, among others, hold that it is probably the Passover. It cannot be Purim, for Jesus would hardly celebrate such a riotous, unspiritual festival as Purim. Furthermore, Purim came sometime in February and would not allow sufficient time for the early ministry in Galilee. Jesus arrived in Galilee in December (four months before harvest). The feasts of Tabernacles and of Dedication are ruled out because they come in October and December respectively. Were this feast either of these two, it would allow only four or six months for the later great Galilean ministry. It is extremely improbable that all the events which transpired in this great Galilean ministry took place in only four to six months. Between the two feasts (John 5 and John 6), Jesus traveled extensively in Galilee. He returned to Capernaum from Jerusalem, went into the mountains and delivered the Sermon on the Mount, healed the Centurion's servant, went to Nain, returned to Capernaum, toured the cities and villages of Galilee, crossed the Sea of Galilee to Gergesa, recrossed the sea, went to Nazareth, toured again the cities and villages of Galilee, and finally crossed the sea to Bethsaida for the sermon on the Bread of Life after feeding the five thousands. See Map No. 3, page 170, for an outline of this great Galilean ministry.

This feast could be either Passover or Pentecost (50 days after Passover), but hardly any of the other feasts will fit the chronology. Passover makes more allowance for the subsequent ministry in Galilee. As R. C. Foster says, "The indentification of the feast is a decisive factor in determining the length of Jesus' ministry. If it was the Passover, then there are four Passovers in the ministry of Jesus which must have lasted through three years and a fraction."

Verse two also poses its problems: (a) There is no word in the original for the word gate. Literally, this verse would be translated, ". . . there is in Jerusalem by the (place or thing) belonging to the sheep, a pool . . ." Some have surmised the *probatikos* (place belonging to the sheep) to be a sheep-gate, others a sheep-market, still others a sheep-pool. It is difficult to determine just what John speaks of when he says "the place belonging to the sheep." Most scholars claim that sheep-gate is the meaning, since Nehemiah 3:32 and 12:39 mentions a sheep-gate. This gate would depend for its location upon the location of the pool of Bethesda. (b) Various names have been given this pool. The word for pool comes from *kolumbethra,* and means a pool large enough to swim in. Some manuscripts have Bethesda (House of Mercy), some have Bethzatha (House of the Olive), and others have Bethsaida. Bethesda fits the evident use made of

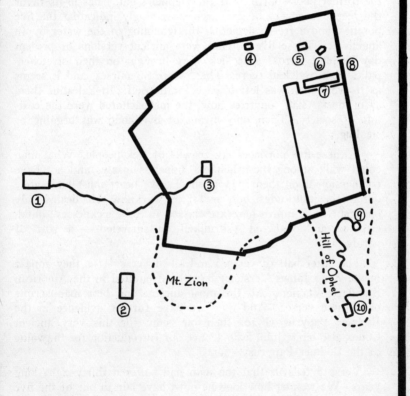

POOLS OF JERUSALEM

1. Upper Gihon
2. Lower Gihon
3. Pool of Hezeklah
4. Jeremiah's Pool
5. Pool of Lady Mary (Bethesda?)
6. Church of St. Anne
7. Pool of Israel
8. St. Stephen's Gate
9. Virgin's Pool (Bethesda?)
10. Pool of Siloam
11. Job's Well

Mt. Zion

Hill of Ophel

Fig. No. 1

this pool. Certain archaeologists locate the pool just inside the gate of St. Stephen (on the east wall, just north of the temple area); Robertson and Foster claim Bethesda to be none other than the Virgin's Pool. See Figure No. 1, page 175. The reason for associating Bethesda with the Virgin's Pool is that the latter periodically bubbles over from a natural spring, which also forms a sort of natural syphon. It is called "the Gusher." The Virgin's Pool is south of the Temple, on the east side of the Hill of Ophel. The bubbling nature of the Virgin's Pool might account for the man's description in verse 7. On the other hand, the former pool (north, near St. Stephen's gate) has in its favor the recent discovery of five arches seemingly indicating the five porches, and a fresco depicting the troubling of the water by an angel. (c) These five porches were ancient versions of present day hospital wards. The sick were brought on their stretcher-pallet beds and laid there. There were no nurses, and it seems as if every man was left to care for himself. In Palestine then, as in most Asian countries now, the incapacitated were the cast-offs of society. Their only means of livelihood was begging or stealing.

In these five porticoes lay crowds of sick people. What man could walk among these helpless, hopeless masses and not have compassion upon them? How the Lord's heart must have gone out to the multitudes, but, as far as we know, He healed only one man. The infirm here are classed in three sicknesses; blind, crippled and withered (shrunken or shriveled — a sort of paralysis).

The latter half of verse 3 and all of verse 4 (as they appear in the King James Version) have been omitted in the American Standard Version. All the most ancient and best manuscripts omit these verses. And now we have further evidence in the Bodmer Papyrus II for their omission, for this very ancient Codex also omits John 5:3b-4. See our Introduction for the value of the Bodmer Papyrus.

Verse 5 tells us that the man had suffered thirty-eight long years. We wonder how long he must have lain in one of the five porches trying to get someone to help him down to the pool. How would he survive? What a bitter cup to drink! Some commentators guess that the man's infirmity was due to "youthful excesses" (cf. v. 14). We wonder why Jesus healed only one man from such a multitude. We can only guess, but the severe hopelessness and helplessness of the case offers Jesus an opportunity to demonstrate His great power.

Singling out this man, Jesus asks him a most obvious question. We are told that Jesus knew the man had been a long time infirm. John does not tell us how He knew, but what need is there to conjecture when He Himself knew "what was in man." Could He not know this by reason of His omniscient nature? Jesus' question to the man is probably to call the attention of the crowd to the miracle He is about to perform. The Lord's question was also to arouse hope in the heart of the man, but the man is resigned to hopelessness. The man's answer seems to say, "Sir, it is not a question of whether I want to be healed or not, but it is a question of opportunity or inopportunity."

Although verses 3b and 4 seem to be the invention of some scribe who inserted them in late manuscripts, verse 7 tells us the water was disturbed in some manner. The man felt there was some therapeutic value in the bubbling water. This should present no problem, for today we have our "whirlpool baths," and our mineral springs, etc. This invalid's problem was that no one would help him into the pool. The word he used for put is *ballo*, and usually means to throw. Perhaps the man means he has no one to take him, even roughly if need be, and roll him off his pallet into the pool. Whatever be the case it is plain that the man expresses no faith. As Lenski says, "Here is a plain instance where the miracle precedes the faith . . ."

It is strange to some commentators that Jesus would heal anyone without some evidence of faith. What of the widow's son at Nain — of Lazarus — of Jairus' daughter? After Jesus commanded the man, "Get up, pick up your pallet and walk," verse 9 informs us the man was made whole immediately. John's use of the particular adverb "straightway" seems to indicate his desire to emphasize the immediacy of the miracle. Note also the completeness of the cure. An invalid who had not walked in thirty-eight years arises to walk at once. There is no experimenting, no learning all over to walk again.

The last phrase of verse 9, "Now it was the Sabbath on that day," is very significant. Surely Jesus knew of the absurdly strict Sabbath laws of the Pharisees. Why then would He open Himself to controversy by commanding this man to carry his bed on the Sabbath? We should like to quote here a paragraph from R. C. Foster's *Studies in the Life of Christ,* Vol. 1, page 246.

"Why did Jesus heal the man on the Sabbath day, if He knew it would bring such bitter criticism upon Him? Jesus made a deliberate choice in the whole matter as to the man and the time, for He approached the man, and He commanded the man to take up his bed and carry it home, even though He knew that the sight of this man carrying such a burden through the Sabbath day crowds which thronged the temple would create controversy. The difference in the methods of Jesus is most pronounced: in Galilee, where such intense excitement prevailed over His ministry that it threatened to get out of hand, He counseled a leper to tell no one of his cure; here in Jerusalem which was so full of hostility on the part of leaders that even the people who favored Him only dared to talk of Him in whispers, Jesus boldly threw down the gauntlet to the cold and callous unbelief of the leaders by sending this man right through their midst on the Sabbath day carrying his bed in proof of the miracle. Moreover, Jesus did not attempt to hide behind the man when the storm of criticism arose. The man evidently acted in harmony with the will of Jesus when he immediately reported to the Pharisees who had cured him. This completed the testimony of the man to them concerning the miracle."

In addition to the external evidence (omission in oldest manuscripts), there are three internal reasons for rejecting the spurious verses 3b and 4: (a) Miracles of the Bible are always connected inseparably with the gospel message. Neither Jesus nor the apostles healed primarily to relieve suffering. As R. C. Foster points out, the best way to show the unscriptural nature of modern faith-healers is to point to the fact that there are a great number of religious sects claiming to heal — yet they teach absolutely contradictory doctrines. If their so-called miracles are genuine, they make God the author of division, confusion, and thus a liar. Miraculous healing by the waters of a pool, without a gospel message, is unscriptural. (b) If people had actually been healed by the pool, then only the rich and the strongest would have been able to obtain. This also contradicts the tenor of Scripture. (c) Again Foster points out, "Four hundred years of silence concerning miracles since the close of the Old Testament emphasizes the miracles of Jesus." Not even the great man who came in the "spirit and power of Elijah" worked miracles. If miracles were being worked by a pool of water before and during Jesus' ministry, this emphasis is lost.

Quiz

1. What feast of the Jews is referred to in 5:1? Give reasons for your answer.

2. What does the identification of this feast have to do with Jesus' ministry?

3. Which pool of Jerusalem today is more likely to be the pool of Bethesda?

4. Give 4 reasons why verses 3b and 4 are not a part of the inspired record of John.

5. What measure of faith in Jesus Christ did this man have before his healing?

6. Why did Jesus choose the Sabbath day to perform this miracle?

SABBATH CONTROVERSY

Text 5:10-18

10 So the Jews said unto him that was cured, It is the sabbath, and it is not lawful for thee to take up thy bed.

11 But he answered them, He that made me whole, the same said unto me, Take up thy bed, and walk.

12 They asked him, Who is the man that said unto thee, Take up thy bed, and walk?

13 But he that was healed knew not who it was; for Jesus had conveyed himself away, a multitude being in the place.

14 Afterward Jesus findeth him in the temple, and said unto him, Behold, thou art made whole: sin no more, lest a worse thing befall thee.

15 The man went away, and told the Jews that it was Jesus who made him whole.

16 And for this cause the Jews persecuted Jesus, because he did these things on the sabbath.

17 But Jesus answered them, My Father worketh even until now, and I work.

18 For this cause therefore the Jews sought the more to kill him, because he not only brake the sabbath, but also called God his own Father, making himself equal with God.

Queries

a. Why did the Jews ask the man about his Healer?

b. What prompted the man to tell the Jews that Jesus healed him?

c. What does Jesus mean by the word working in verse 17?

Paraphrase

But the Jews told the man that had been healed over and over again, Today is the Sabbath day and it is not permissable according to law for you to take up your stretcher. The man answered, The Man Who made me well, that Man spoke authoritatively and told me, Lift up your stretcher and walk. The Jews asked him, Just Who is this fellow Who told you to take up your stretcher and walk? But the man did not know Who his benefactor was, for Jesus had quietly slipped away unnoticed because there was a great crowd there. Afterwards Jesus finds the man in the temple and says to him, Look! You are well, stop sinning lest a worse thing come upon you. The man went away and said to the Jews, It is Jesus of Nazareth who made me well! Now because of this the Jews stalked Jesus to persecute Him because He was doing these things on the Sabbath. But Jesus replied, My Father is working even now on the Sabbath and therefore I also am working. On account of this the Jews were more determined to kill Him because He not only violated the Sabbath traditions but He also said God was His own unique Father, making Himself equal with God.

Summary

The Jews discover that Jesus healed the man and also commanded the man to break their Sabbath traditions. They increase their hate and determination to kill Jesus, for He has made Himself equal with Jehovah God.

Comment

Sabbath laws are legislated in Exodus 20:10; 23:12; 31:12-17; Jer. 17:21 (cf. also Neh. 13:15). An example of punishment for Sabbath breaking is found in Num. 15:32-36. Rabbinical tradition said one who inadvertently carried a burden on the Sabbath could sacrifice for his sin. But wilful disobedience brought interdict and death by stoning. These Jews cared not a bit that the man had been relieved of his long and helpless condition. As we

have commented before (3:1), the Pharisees had added manifold
and ridiculously impractical regulations to Sabbath-keeping laws.
Their purpose, of course, was to make a system of meritorious
law-keeping, hoping thereby to attain righteousness. Mercy and
love upon a hopelessly ill man was beside the point with them —
someone had broken the Sabbath traditions and he must be pun-
ished. Jesus told the Pharisees later that they neglected the
essential matters of the Law such as justice, and mercy, and faith
(cf. Mt. 23:23-24).

The man did not even so much as know Jesus' name. But
verse 11 gives us insight into the man's attitude. The Jews have
attacked him for violating the Sabbath, but the man points out
to the Jews that the Man who healed him had told him to take
up his bed. It is not that the man is seeking to lay the blame on
Jesus, but he thinks the Jews ought to see that if a Man was able
to miraculously heal him, that same Man ought to be able to give
commands concerning the Sabbath!

Contemptuously, in verse 12, the Jews asked the man, "Just
Who is this fellow that told you to pick up your bed?" The Jews
undoubtedly knew who the "Healer" was. They probably asked
His name to get legal testimony to use against Him later. Who
else was traversing Palestine healing the sick and restoring sight
to the blind? The rulers of the Jews were not above reverting to
deceit!

But the man could not answer (v. 13), for Jesus had silently
glided from the midst of the great multitude gathered there. The
word *exeneusen* comes from a Greek word which means to swim,
glide, float. The crowd was the reason for Jesus' departure. The
Lord's action here certainly shows that His primary mission was
higher than the mere healing of every infirm body. Notice also
from this instance that Jesus is able to heal even when the person
does not know Him as Christ.

The present tense of the verb *finds* in verse 14 seems to indicate that Jesus was looking for the man. Now we see His higher
purpose for this man — the healing of the man's soul. Most
commentators think this verse indicates the man's illness was
due to his previous sinful life. All sickness, however, is not the
result of personal sin; but much sickness can be logically and
scientifically traced to indulgence and immorality. Jesus uses
the present tense again (continued action tense) when He says
"Do not continue sinning." If this man now wilfully continues

in sin something worse than thirty-eight years of infirmity will befall him — he will be lost forever in the abyss of Hell to suffer eternal and excruciating punishment.

There are two views as to the man's running to the Jews upon discovering Jesus' name: (a) The man sought to clear himself with the authorities. He felt if Jesus had the power to heal, He also had authority to issue commands to break the Sabbath traditions. The man may have been referring the Jews to Jesus in all innocence. He could not defend his actions, but Jesus could! (b) He was ignorant of their intense hatred and determination to kill Jesus and unwittingly betrayed Jesus. Whatever the situation, the man's actions must have conformed to the purposes of Jesus for He did not chastize the man.

The antagonism of the Jews toward Jesus really began in 2:13, and was fanned by His increasing popularity in 4:1. But now it turns into a white-hot hate. They stalk Him like wild beasts of prey (indicated by the verb *ediokon*). Henceforth they will pursue His every move, seeking occasion to trap Him and do away with Him (cf. Mk. 2:23-3:2).

Jesus' answer (v. 17) definitely shows His recognition of Sonship early. In performing this work of mercy on the Sabbath, He is merely doing what His very own Father-God is continuing to do each day of the week (Sabbath included). The Father causes the rain to fall, the sun to shine and the grain to grow on the Sabbath as well as on Monday or Friday. Jesus, being equally a part of the Godhead, works also on the Sabbath. What a strange paradoxical contrast! The Jews, by placing legalistic prohibitions against work on the Sabbath, put a heavy yoke of meritorious work upon the necks of the people which they were not able to bear. Jesus, on the other hand, by doing works of mercy and love, found the genuine rest and peace in doing the will of the Father! As the Pharisees understood it, man was created to be a keeper of Sabbath laws — Jesus knew the truth that the Sabbath was made for man (cf. Mk. 2:27).

Give the Jews credit for more intellectual honesty than some of our modern "scholars." The Jews at least understood Jesus' claim of equality with God, and they saw the alternatives. Either Jesus was telling truth and must be worshipped as God, or He was a blasphemer worthy of death. Some of our modern "Doctors of Divinity" would have us believe Jesus' claims for equality with God to be a philosophy evolving from the second century church.

The word *equal* in this verse comes from the Greek word *isos*. The Anglicized form of this word is used in the English language as a prefix meaning equal. Thus, an isosceles triangle is a triangle with two equal sides. Paul used the same word *(isos)* in Philippians 2:6 where Jesus, "existing in the form of God, counted not the being on an equality with God a thing to be grasped . . ."

Quiz

1. What does the Law of Moses legislate concerning the Sabbath?
2. Why would the man think Jesus had authority to command him to take up his bed on the Sabbath?
3. What was Jesus' higher purpose in seeking the man in the temple?
4. How does the Father "work until now"?
5. What is the difference between Jesus' view of the Sabbath and the view of the Jews?

THE DEITY STATED

Text 5:19-23

19 Jesus therefore answered and said unto them, Verily, verily, I say unto you, The Son can do nothing of himself, but what he seeth the Father doing: for what things so ever he doeth, these the Son also doeth in like manner.

20 For the Father loveth the Son, and showeth him all things that himself doeth: and greater works than these will he show him, that ye may marvel.

21 For as the Father raiseth the dead and giveth them life, even so the Son also giveth life to whom he will.

22 For neither doth the Father judge any man, but he hath given all judgment unto the Son;

23 that all may honor the Son, even as they honor the Father. He that honoreth not the Son honoreth not the Father that sent him.

Queries

a. What are the "greater works" of verse 20?
b. To whom does the Son give life?
c. What is the significance of honoring the Son?

183

Paraphrase

So Jesus answered the Jews, saying, I tell you truly, The Son is not able to do anything of His Own accord, but He does only those things which He sees the Father doing; for whatever the Father is doing, these things also the Son is doing in like manner. The Father loves the Son and discloses to the Son everything which He Himself is doing; and the Father will disclose greater works than these which you have just seen. He will disclose these greater works to the Son in order that you may be caused to wonder. Just as the Father raises the dead and makes them live, so also the Son gives life to whomever He wills. Furthermore, the Father judges no one; but He has given all the prerogatives of judgment unto the Son in order that all men may honor and worship the Son just as they honor and worship the Father. The man who does not honor and worship the Son does not honor and worship the Father Who sent the Son.

Summary

Jesus claims equality with the Father, and bases His claim upon His power to give life and His authority to judge.

Comment

Jesus' answer to the Jews' accusation that He makes Himself equal to God is "Yes, absolutely yes." His answer is a tremendously daring claim that He does exactly what God does. He said much the same in 5:30; 7:28; 8:28; 14:10, and already implied it in 5:17. Unless He sees the Father doing something, He does not do it. Although He is on earth, Jesus is aware constantly of what the Father wishes to have done, and He fulfills only what is the Father's will (cf. Mt. 11:27; Jn. 8:29). Whatever Jesus does emanates from the Father. When, therefore, the Jews attacked Him for breaking their Sabbath traditions, they were in reality declaring war on God. Notice here that the Son sees all that the Father does; in the next verse (v. 20), the Father shows the Son all that He is doing. There is absolute harmony and oneness.

Verse 20 shows the active part of the Father in this relationship. The Father is not passive — He does not merely allow Jesus to discover what He can of the Father's will, but the Father discloses His will to the Son. Jesus then tells His enemies of the greater works the Father will show them. If the Jews are astonished at the healing of a helpless invalid, they will be caused to wonder even more at the greater works to come. What are these greater works? Some think (a) Jesus refers only to the general resurrection and judgment; (b) others, that He speaks of specific resurrections, e.g., Lazarus, the widow's son, etc., plus the final resurrection of all and the judgment; (c) still others, that He refers to the raising of the spiritually dead, the raising of the bodily dead, and the judgment. The last interpretation seems to be more compatible with the entire context. It is interesting to note the promise of Jesus to the disciples (Jn. 14:12) that they shall do even greater works than Christ in His earthly ministry. Did not their tremendously fruitful labors in giving life to dead souls overshadow the Lord's restoring life to mortal bodies? How can making dead souls live be greater than restoring life to mortal bodies? When Christ seeks to give life to the spiritually dead, they are able to exercise their wills and reject life. But in the final bodily resurrection, *all* will be fitted with bodies in which to spend eternity whether they desire them or not — the saved unto eternal bliss, the disobedient to eternal condemnation.

The emphasis of verse 21 is on ascribing to Jesus equal power with God to "make alive" (as the source of life). The Israelites ascribed to Jehovah's being the source of life, especially having the power to raise the dead (cf. Deut. 32:39; I Sam. 2:6). Jesus is simply claiming again to be equal with Jehovah God. The emphasis of this verse is not on any particular resurrection of the dead, but upon the astounding claims of Jesus. Not only has Jesus the power to give life, but He also exercises the prerogative of arbitrary choice. He will give life to whomsoever He desires. In the light of the entire New Testament revelation we know that Jesus desires to give spiritual life to all who trust and obey Him. It is not the Lord's will that stands in the way of any man's eternal destiny, but man's own stubborn will (cf. Jn. 5:40).

The Father has also relegated to the Son all the prerogatives of judgment (cf. Jn. 3:17; Mt. 25:31-46). If the Son has authority to establish the church, to legislate its terms of entrance and its sustaining ordinances, He necessarily judges all who refuse His church. All who are not receiving life through His kingdom are necessarily condemned by their refusal (cf. Jn. 3:18).

Verse 23 seems to be the climax to this particular context. First, there is the statement that the Father and Son are equal in Person; second, the claim substantiated by equality of works; now, the result — equality of honor. To honor is to do homage to, to reverence, to worship. Jesus is God! This was pointedly directed toward the unbelieving Jews, but every professing Christian ought to etch these words upon his heart! Any person professing to follow the One True God must also reckon with this very plain demand. This *must* be the test of every religious profession and practice, whether by individuals or organizations. Any that do not honor Jesus Christ as Lord are dishonoring God, and are condemned by this verse. Those who do not worship Jesus Christ do not worship God at all. Jesus Christ is ALL or nothing! He cannot be followed as a mere human teacher, nor esteemed even as a prophet commissioned by God . . . He must be exalted and worshipped as Creator, Redeemer and Judge.

Quiz

1. How does Jesus claim deity here?
2. Give three interpretations of "greater works" (v. 20).
3. How is making dead souls live greater than restoring life to physical bodies?
4. Name two prerogatives which the Father has given to the Son.
5. Does any person honor God if he does not worship Jesus?
6. Can a Christian conscientiously belong to any organization which refuses to honor Jesus Christ as Lord?
7. Explain your answers to questions 5 and 6.

POWERS INHERENT IN THAT DEITY

Text 5:24-29

24 Verily, verily, I say unto you, He that heareth my word, and believeth him that sent me, hath eternal life, and cometh not into judgment, but hath passed out of death into life.

25 Verily, verily, I say unto you, The hour cometh, and now is, when the dead shall hear the voice of the Son of God; and they that hear shall live.

26 For as the Father hath life in himself, even so gave he to the Son also to have life in himself:

27 and he gave him authority to execute judgment, because he is a son of man.

28 Marvel not at this: for the hour cometh, in which all that are in the tombs shall hear his voice,

29 and shall come forth; they have done good, unto the resurrection of life; and they that have done evil, unto the resurrection of judgment.

Queries

a. Will the believer be exempt from appearing at the judgment?
b. How many resurrections are spoken of here?
c. What is meant by "he is a son of man"?

Paraphrase

I tell you truly, The one who hears and obeys my Word and trusts and obeys the Father who sent me, does even now possess eternal life. Such a one will not incur the penalty or sentence of judgment, but he has already been translated out of the state of eternal separation from God into the glorious state of eternal life with God. Again, I tell you truly, the time is coming and has already arrived when the spiritually dead shall hear and obey the voice of the Son of God, and those who hear and obey shall be made spiritually alive. For even as the Father is the eternal source of Life, so He has also given to the Son to be the eternal source of Life. The Father has given the Son authority to execute judgment because He is partaking of human nature. You should not be amazed at these claims, for the time is coming when all those who are in their graves shall hear His voice and they shall come forth; those that have done good unto the resurrection of eternal life with God, and those that have done worthlessly or uselessly unto a resurrection for sentence and condemnation.

Summary

Jesus claims power to give eternal life to any who believe. He further claims power to resurrect and judge the dead — both believer and non-believer. The believer will live eternally present with God; the unbeliever will be condemned to eternal banishment from God.

Comment

Those who will hear Jesus' teaching and obey His Word (14:15) may have eternal life. Although Jesus does not use the word obey here, obedience is implied in the word *akouo* (hear). If one truly hears Jesus, one will obey His voice (cf. Jn. 10:14, 16, 27). The one who believes in Jesus must also accept His deity

— that He came forth from the eternal Father. He was sent from God in a unique manner. He was, in fact, God incarnate.

There are tremendous implications in this verse (24). The man who trusts in Jesus enough to keep His Word will not come into condemnation. In other words, the Christian is even now in a state of eternal life. He is restricted, to be sure, having to dwell in an earthly tabernacle (cf. II Cor. 5:1-8; Phil. 1:21-24), but he enjoys a present salvation. The believer (from the moment of his acceptance of the gospel) passes out of the state of a living death (Jn. 3:18) into a present condition of eternal life restricted only by flesh, time and space. But when this mortal shall have been changed, he will put on immortality and incorruption (cf. I Cor. 15:42-58). The man who persists in unbelief is, even while physically alive, in a condition of separation (death) from God, and this condition, persisted in beyond physical death, becomes permanently fixed (Lk. 16:26).

This verse excuses no one, not even the sanctified, from the general resurrection and appearance before the judgment seat of Christ. All of God's creatures will be there (cf. II Cor. 5:9-10; Rom. 14:10; Acts 17:30-31; Rev. 20:11-15, etc.) Saved and unsaved alike will be there, but the saved will be clothed in Christ's righteousness and under no sentence of condemnation (Rev. 3:5, 18; Rom. 8:1).

The reader of this section of Scripture must be careful, for Jesus speaks of a spiritual resurrection as well as a bodily resurrection. Many scholars take the spiritual regeneration (Titus 3:5; Jn. 3:1-8, etc.) or the new birth to be the first resurrection, and the future resurrection of the body to be the second resurrection.

How is it possible for a man to be dead while physically alive? What is a spiritual resurrection? Notice that the prodigal son was said to have been dead when separated or alienated from his father, but alive upon his repentance and return to the father's house (Lk. 15:32). The Gentiles were said to have been dead while living in an unregenerate condition (Eph. 2:1; 5:14) but made alive in Christ. Thus, the one who has sinned (and all have sinned, Rom. 3:23) has incurred the sentence of God upon sin, which is death or separation from God Who is the only source of life. The sinner is, in reality, dead — alienated from God, (cf. Isa. 59:2; Ezek. 18:4, 20; Rom. 6:23). But, as Jesus says in verses 24 and 25, the time has come that all who are spiritually dead may hear His voice, obey it and be quickened (made alive)

188

from the dead. Notice the following comparison:
First Resurrection (Spiritual)

John 5:24

Time has come when the dead shall hear the voice
of the Son of God . . . and live and not come into
condemnation.

Revelation 20:5b-6

This is the first resurrection. Blessed is he that hath
part in the first resurrection; over these the second
death hath no power.

Second Resurrection (General, Bodily)

John 5:28

Time is coming when all who are in tombs will
hear His voice and come out — the good unto
resurrection of life — evil unto resurrection of
condemnation.

Revelation 20:13-15

And the sea gave up the dead that were in it; and
death and Hades gave up the dead that were in
them: and they were judged every man according
to their works. And death and Hades were cast
into the lake of fire. This is the second death, even
the lake of fire. And if any was not found written
in the book of life, he was cast into the lake of fire.

Verse 26 is a continuation of the preceding thought. Just as
the Father is inherently the source of all life, so also is the Son.
The Son has been sent to reveal the way of life eternal. Incidentally, in so doing He demonstrated Himself also, through
miracles, to be the source and regulator of all that is alive in the
physical creation.

Verse 27 has been the subject of various interpretations.
There is no disagreement over the fact that Jesus is spoken of
as "a son of man," or that Jesus has the authority to judge. But
the commentators cannot agree upon the meaning behind . . .
"he is *a* son of man." The absence of the definite article (the)
before "son" perplexes them. The verse does not say "because
he is *the* son of man." Below are the three main interpretations:
(a) Jesus has been given the authority to judge because He is a
son of man — "son of man" being a Messianic title (cf. Dan.

189

7:13; Mt. 12:8; Mk. 8:31; Lk. 21:27; Rev. 1:13, etc.). This would be synonymous with *"the* Son of man." (b) Jesus has been given the authority to judge because He appeared in human form, presented the gospel, and necessarily judges all who reject His message. By his appearance among men in man's form, men were caused to stumble and to think His claims absurd. Thus He judges because He is a son of man. "The eternal love condemns no one because he is a sinner; . . . it leaves it to men to judge themselves through rejection of the Saviour who is presented to them." Expositor's Greek Testament. (c) Jesus has been given the authority to judge because He was born man and partook of man's nature, was tempted as man, yet without sin, suffered the limitations and weaknesses of flesh, and is able therefore to judge justly and mercifully. The last interpretation harmonizes more perfectly with other New Testament teachings (cf. Phil. 2:9-11; Heb. 2:13-18; 4:14-16). If our High Priest must be taken from among men, so must our Judge (cf. Heb. 5:1-10).

Jesus speaks next (v. 28) of the universal resurrection of saved and unsaved — the bodily resurrection where departed souls will be reunited with new bodies. He not only has power to supply spiritual life and authority to judge, but He also claims power to raise the actual dead unto new bodies fitted for eternity. The Jews were told to stop marvelling that He claimed to be able to impart spiritual life and to judge, for the day would come when He would raise their dead ancestors by the power of His voice. When that day comes, they will no longer reject His claims — then every knee shall bow and every tongue shall confess that Jesus is Lord to the glory of the Father (cf. Phil. 2:10-11) — but too late for some!

Then (v. 29) will *all* men be given a body prepared for their eternal destination. Then will the saints be pronounced "not guilty" because they have appropriated to themselves the atoning blood of Jesus. Then they will be dwelling in God's eternal tabernacle (cf. Rev. 21:1-4).

It is interesting to note the word evil is the Greek word *phaula* which means worthless, vain, useless, and not necessarily "immoral" or "vile." The saved are those who have, by faith, done righteous and profitable works of truth. The condemned are those who have, by unbelief, done worthless, vain and unprofitable works of darkness. How *careful* one must be to occupy himself with works that are profitable and glorifying unto God! Even "worthless" and "idle" words will be judged (cf. Mt. 12:36).

The Greek word *krisis* (judgment) can mean either the activity or process of judgment, or the condemnation and punishment that follows the process. It is evident from the light of other Scriptures that the word means punishment in both verses 24 and 29, for while the saints will appear before the judgment seat of God, they will not suffer the punishment.

The Bible reveals that the judgment will be:

  a. Universal (Rom. 14:10; II Cor. 5:10, etc.).
  b. Individual (Rom. 14:12; II Cor. 5:10, etc.).
  c. According to the New Testament (Jn. 12:48; Rom. 2:2, 16).
  d. According to man's works (Rom. 2:6; II Cor. 5:10; Rev. 20:12, 13).
  e. As certain as the resurrection of Christ (Acts 17:31).

Quiz

1. How does the believer enjoy a present salvation?
2. How is it possible for a man to be "dead" while physically alive?
3. What are the first and second resurrections?
4. State briefly three interpretations of "because he is a son of man."
5. Which resurrection does Jesus refer to in verse 28-29?
6. What is another definition of "evil" as used here?
7. Name at least 5 characteristics of the future judgment.

JESUS' OWN WITNESS

Text 5:30-32

30 I can of myself do nothing: as I hear, I judge: and my judgment is righteous; because I seek not mine own will, but the will of him that sent me.
31 If I bear witness of myself, my witness is not true.
32 It is another that beareth witness of me; and I know that the witness which he witnesseth of me is true.

Queries

  a. What makes Jesus' judgment righteous?
  b. Why would Jesus' witness of Himself not be true?

191

Paraphrase

I am not able to act strictly from My Own will, but as I hear directly from the Father, so I decide and act, because I have no desire to please Myself; My only aim is to act according to the will of the Father Who sent Me. So if I testify to Myself and My Own glory, apart from the Father, then My testimony is untrue. There is Another Who is testifying concerning Me, and I know that His testimony is true.

Summary

Jesus and the Father are absolutely One, and thus Jesus' judgment is righteous. He is therefore bound to testify to His own deity, or be untrue.

Comment

Jesus, in verse 30, re-states the fact of His oneness with the Father, as He had previously declared it in verse 19. The reason His judgment is righteous (just, infallible, perfect) is that He sees what the Father does, and the Father shows Him all things. As Wescott points out, Jesus' judgment is absolutely just because He has no regard for His own will in any judgment, but He abides altogether within the will of the Father. Human judges often do not know how to judge justly. They may at times seek their own will or let their emotions rule instead of that which is just and right. Not so with the Son. He is omnisicient.

There are a number of interpretations for verse 31: (a) The sentence should be interrogatively punctuated . . . "If I bear witness concerning Myself, My witness is not true?" (b) "If I should testify to My Own deity without other witnesses, My testimony would not be according to Mosaic law, therefore, I adduce the following witnesses . . ." (the Father, John the Baptist, the Scriptures, etc.). (c) "If I bear witness to Myself, My witness is not true in your estimation.

It is more in harmony with the context, however, to assume that Jesus is making another claim to Oneness with the Father — in a negative sense . . . "If I should testify to Myself as doing these works independently of God I would be a liar, for I can of Myself do nothing, etc. . . ." The Jews had given indication that they expected Him to disclaim any equality with God (cf. 5:17-18), but this He could not do and remain true!

192

John 5:31 and 8:14 have been ridiculed for years by un-thinking critics as "contradictions in the Bible." The critics, as usual, take Jesus' words out of context and interpret them, hav-ing already decided beforehand what He says. A careful study of the two passages *in their respective contexts* will show that on both occasions He affirmed exactly the same thing from opposite angles.

5:31

My witness is untrue if given independently of God.

8:14

My witness to Myself is true because I and the
Father are One in knowledge and will.

In verse 32 Jesus is expressing His confidence in the witness of Another. This other One is even His Father, God. Jesus briefly introduces the Father as His witness here, and later (v. 36-37) elucidates. Jesus will rest His case upon the testimony of the Father, which the Father is continuing to witness through signs and wonders. When the Father bears witness to Jesus' deity, there can be no question — one can only accept the testi-mony, or reject it and judge oneself.

Quiz

1. Why is Jesus' judgment absolutely just?
2. How should verse 31 be interpreted?
3. Does John 5:31 contradict John 8:14? Explain.
4. What is the significance of verse 32?

JOHN THE BAPTIST'S WITNESS

Text 5:33-35

33 Ye have sent unto John, and he hath borne witness unto the truth.

34 But the witness which I receive is not from man: howbeit I say these things, that ye may be saved.

35 He was the lamp that burneth and shineth; and ye were willing to rejoice for a season in his light.

Queries

    a. Why does He not receive witness from man?
    b. How did they rejoice in the Baptist's light?

193

Paraphrase

You yourselves have sent unto John, and he has testified the truth concerning me. Although I am not dependent upon mere man for witness, I am telling you these things in order that you might accept John's witness and be saved. John was the lamp that was burning and shining to guide you to the Way, and you were willing for a time to bask yourselves in his light.

Summary

Since they stumble at His self-witnessing, He refers them to John the Baptist's witness that they might be led to accept Him.

Comment

They had, indeed, sent unto John asking him of his preaching (1-19), and John confessed to the truth (1:20, 26, 29, 35, 36, etc.) that Jesus was the Son of God. John also testified that Jesus and the Father were one (3:31-36).

On the other hand, Jesus did not need any mortal to take the witness stand on His behalf. He could call upon divine witness. Yet, because of the hardness of their hearts and their spiritual blindness, He urged them to consider John's witness. The Baptist's witness was true, and they had shown some interest in his message at first (v. 35b).

Barclay gives an interesting analogous comparison of John the Baptist and a lamp: (a) A lamp bears a borrowed light. It is not the source of light, but is lit. (b) John's message was warm — not coldly intellectual or ritualistic. (c) John had light — light guides — he guided men to repent in preparation for the coming King and His kingdom. (d) A lamp burns itself out. John decreased while Jesus increased — the true witness for God burns himself out in the service of God.

The emphasis upon the attracting nature of the lamp is in this passage also. The Jews flocked to John the Baptist in the beginning of his ministry, just as insects flock to a lamp (cf. Mt. 3:5; 21:26; Mk. 1:5; 6:20; Lk. 3:15). They rejoiced in his message (of the coming Messiah) until that light turned upon them and revealed their worldliness and sin. They were also attracted to John because of his eccentric and spectacular mode of dress, life, and the presentation of his message. The spectacular in John's ministry soon lost its drawing attraction, however, when he boldly challenged the nation to "bring forth fruits worthy of repentance," and they rejected him (cf. Mk. 6:19; Lk. 7:24-35). There are people like that in every age. As long as a preacher will make himself or the gospel into a spectacle they will "rejoice for a season in his light" (the spectacle), but once the light illumines their unworthiness and pricks their consciences by openly denouncing their sins, they haughtily reject both the preacher and the message (cf. II Tim. 4:1-4).

Quiz

1. Where is the record of the Baptist's witness to Jesus?
2. Why did Jesus call their attention to the witness of John?
3. How is John "the lamp burning and shining"?
4. How did the Jews "rejoice in his light" for only a "season"?

THE FATHER'S WITNESS

Text 5:36-38

**36 But the witness which I have is greater than that of John; for the works which the Father hath given me to accomplish, the very works that I do, bear witness of me, that the Father hath sent me.
37 And the Father that sent me, he hath borne witness of me. Ye have neither heard his voice at any time, nor seen his form.
38 And ye have not his word abiding in you: for whom he sent, him ye believe not.**

Queries

  a. What works did Jesus accomplish (v. 36)?
  b. Why had they not heard the Father's voice nor seen His form?
  c. How does the Word of God abide in a person (v. 38)?

Paraphrase

But I have continually the witness of One Who is greater than John the Baptist, for the miraculous works which the Father has given unto Me to complete, these very works which I am doing are bearing witness concerning Me that the Father has sent Me. And the Father Who sent Me has Himself testified concerning Me. You have never at any time heard His voice nor perceived what He is like; and because you do not believe and obey

195

Him Whom the Father has sent, you do not have the Father's life-giving Word dwelling within you.

Summary

The miracles of Jesus and the testimony of the Father are now introduced as the "greater witness". Rejection of Jesus by the Jews gives evidence of their ignorance of God. Furthermore, by rejecting Him they show their hearts to be bereft of God's Word.

Comment

The miracles of Jesus are undeniable evidence for His deity. Nicodemus could not deny them (Jn. 3:2); Jesus' own brothers admitted them as factual (Jn. 7:3); and the Jewish rulers could not deny the miracles of the apostles (Acts 4:16). But they would not accept Jesus as the Son of God. This is a strange dilemma! Jesus said that the very miracles He *was then doing* (present tense — continuing action) were testifying on behalf of His Sonship. He undoubtedly had in mind especially the lame man just healed by the pool of Bethesda.

The Son had previously introduced the Father as a witness (v. 32). Following that, He introduced two very obvious witnesses (John the Baptist and His own miracles) to ease their animosity against His claiming the Father as a witness. The Jews should have accepted these obvious witnesses.

Verse 37 is a connecting verse. By this verse the witness of the Father is inseparably connected with both Jesus' miracles (v. 36) and the Scriptures (vs. 38-39). But what does Jesus mean by "Ye have neither heard His voice at any time, nor seen his form"? It is evident that He does not mean literal failure to hear and see, for some had heard His voice at Jesus' baptism (cf. Mt. 3:17; Mk. 1:11; Lk. 3:22) on the Mount of Transfiguration (cf. Mt. 17:5-6; Mk. 9:7; Lk. 9:35) and in the Temple area (Jn. 12:28). Jesus is referring to spiritual hearing and spiritual perception (cf. I Jn. 4:12).

Their failure to hear and see God has also special connection with their refusal to hear and discern Jesus as God incarnate (v. 38): "In Him dwelleth all the fulness of the Godhead bodily" (Col. 2:9; cf. also Jn. 1:14; II Cor. 4:4; 5:19; Heb. 1:3). Had God's revelation by types, shadows, prophecies and promises (Old Testament) gained possession of their hearts, they would have readily accepted Jesus as Emmanuel (God with us). It is significant that Jesus makes acceptance of Himself the condition of the indwelling of God's Word. Except a man accept Jesus as the Son of the living God he has no part with God's Word — neither its commands nor its promises (cf. I Jn. 4:15; 5:1, 9:12).

Quiz

1. Give three Scripture references to show that miracles of Jesus cannot be denied as factual.
2. In what two ways has the Father witnessed concerning Jesus?
3. In what sense had the Jews not heard or seen the Father?
4. Why did God's Word not abide in the Jews?

THE WITNESS OF THE SCRIPTURES

Text 5:39-47

39 Ye search the scriptures, because ye think that in them ye have eternal life; and these are they which bear witness of me; **40** and ye will not come to me, that ye may have life. **41** I receive not glory from men. **42** But I know you, that ye have not the love of God in yourselves. **43** I am come in my Father's name, and ye receive me not: if another shall come in his own name, him ye will receive. **44** How can ye believe, who receive glory one of another, and the glory that cometh from the only God ye seek not? **45** Think not that I will accuse you to the Father: there is one that accuseth you, even Moses, on whom ye have set your hope. **46** For if ye believed Moses, ye would believe me; for he wrote of me. **47** But if ye believe not his writings, how shall ye believe my words?

Queries

a. Why did the Jews search the Scriptures?
b. Why would Jesus not accuse them?
c. Where did Moses write concerning Jesus?

Paraphrase

You are searching the Scriptures because you think you have eternal life through searching them; and these very Scriptures which you search so diligently are testifying of Me. But still, you are not willing to come unto Me so that you might have eternal

197

life. The glory of men is not My motive in making these claims
to deity, but I know you do not receive Me because you do not
have the love of God in your hearts. I have come with the
authority and nature of My Father, and you do not receive me,
but if another come in his own authority and seeking the glory
of men, you will accept him. How is it possible for you to believe,
seeing that you are always seeking approval from one another,
and not the approval of the only true God? Do not think that I
will accuse you before the Father, for Moses, the very person
upon whom you have built your hopes, he is the one accusing
you. If you really believed Moses you would believe in Me, for
he wrote concerning Me. But if you do not believe what Moses
wrote concerning Me in the Scriptures, how can you believe what
I say?

Summary

The incomparable and irrefutable witness of the Scriptures
is called to testify to the deity of Jesus. This same testimony
also produces judgment upon the unbelieving Jew.

Comment

The Greek verb *eraunte* (search) of verse 39 may be interpreted two ways. It may be either in the indicative mood (mood
of stating a fact) or in the imperative mood (mood of command).
The verb has been translated both "Ye are searching the scriptures . . ." and "Search the scriptures . . ." The context, however calls for the indicative mood rather than the imperative
for the following reasons: (a) They were searching the Scriptures for a reason, e.g., "because ye think, etc. . . ." which would
preclude the necessity for a command for them to search the
scriptures. (b) Jesus is basing His whole argument as to their
unbelief on their perverted use of the Scriptures. (c) The practice of the Jews at that time was to study each word minutely,
and to build absurd mystical and allegorical interpretations around
these word studies.

With all their diligent searching, their tedious allegorical
interpretations, and their rote memorization of the Law, the
Jews rejected the Messiah when He came to them. There are
at least two reasons for this: (a) Their minds were made up as
to what the Messiah must be before they read the Scriptures.
Then they read the prophecies and perverted them to conform
to their prejudiced ideals. (b) They were Bibliolatrists (Bible

worshippers) : they worshipped the words of the Bible. The Bible should NOT be worshipped. Jesus Christ is the Way, the Truth and the Life — the Bible is merely the INSPIRED RECORD of God's revelation. The true function of the Scripture is expressed by Jesus Himself, "These are they which testify concerning me." Only when we have the Scriptures in our minds and written on our hearts (cf. Heb. 8:10) — only when they bring us into a personal relationship of trust and obedience to the Person of Christ do we have life from them. Entrance into the promises of God's Word comes by the free gift of God, but only to those who have become sons of God through the adoption covenant recorded in the New Testament, i.e., the plan of salvation.

Verse 40 very definitely shows salvation to be more than a passive acceptance of a "soverign, irresistable grace" of God. Jesus affirms the free will of man. Man is partially responsible for his own eternal destiny (cf. Jn. 7:17; 8:44).

Jesus rebuked the Jews for their superstitious and fruitless searching of the Scriptures in verses 39-40. The Jews then probably reasoned: "He is angry because we did not give Him our praise and approval for healing on the Sabbath." Jesus anticipates their reasoning and answers, "I receive not the glory of men." What the Lord is saying is this, "I am not making these claims to deity and doing these works for ambition's sake (to win the applause of men). I am claiming deity and showing you your error because I want to save you" (cf. Jn. 5:34). The statement of verse 41 does not mean that we should refuse to praise the name of Christ. Christ's *motive* in doing His works and making His claims was not selfish glory-seeking, but deep self-sacrificing love. This very sacrificial motive, however, earned for Him exaltation from God and praise from men (cf. Phil. 2:5-11).

What was the real reason for their failure to acknowledge Him as the Messiah? It was not that He was a praise-seeker. The real reason was their lack of the love of God in their hearts (cf. I Jn. 2:5; 4:7-9; Rom. 5:5-8). They had no real spiritual knowledge of God or love for God's will and purpose; thus it was impossible for them to recognize the presence of God in Christ.

Verse 43 shows the correctness of the statement of verse 42 (complete lack of fellowship of the Jews with God's will). Jesus

came in the effulgence of God's glory and was the very image
of His substance, but they rejected Him. If a mortal comes
in his own authority, patterning his programs after their desires,
they will receive him. Jesus may have had in mind all the false
Christs and insurrectionists who came before Him, and would
come after Him (cf. Acts 5:36-37). The worldling offers men a
comparatively easy and glorious path to fame or satisfaction.
Jesus offers only the strait (confined) and humiliating road to
satisfaction.

"The root of their unbelief was their earthly idea of glory,
what they could win or bestow. This incapacitated them from
seeing the glory of Christ, which was divine and heavenly, which
men could not give or remove" (The Expositor's Greek Testament). According to verse 44 the Jews made the praise and glory
of men their goal and standard. So long as they sought only the
praise of men and measured themselves by human comparisons
it was impossible for them to believe (cf. II Cor. 10:12) . . .
they were, by such action, "without understanding". In order to
trust in the mercy of God and believe His promises one must
need to believe in God. One can only *need* to believe in God when
one has compared himself with God and has seen his lost estate.
The next step one must take is to desire the approval, or praise,
of God and His salvation. The Jews were not interested in God's
approval (cf. Mt. 6:1ff; Mt. 23:5; Jn. 12:43).

Jesus says in verse 45, "Do not complacently suppose that in
rejecting Me you have done away with the possibility of being
accused before God! The very Moses in whom you base your
hopes will accuse you through his writings, for he prophecied of
My deity which you have rejected". The Greek word *kategoreso*
has been translated accuse here. It is a composite of *kata*
(against) and *agoreuo* (speak in the public assembly), hence,
bring a public accusation against. We have the English word
categorize from this word.

Jesus would not need to condemn or accuse them for their
rejection of Him, since the prophecied Messiah of the Pentateuch
would cause their esteemed Moses to condemn them. In spite of
their claiming to be the disciples of Moses (Jn. 9:28), they did
not believe his writings.

Verse 46 is another of the numerous places where Jesus bears
witness to the fact that Moses was the author of some portion of
the Scriptures, and further that Moses prophecied concerning the

Christ. In other instances, Jesus establishes Moses as the author of the Pentateuch (cf. Lk. 24:44).

If they had believed Moses they would have believed Him (v. 46). The converse is now given — if they believe not the words Moses has written how shall they believe the words of Jesus? If they could not believe Moses' words, and seek the approval of God — how could they believe the words of Christ which came to them without the recommendation of use and age?

That which had been the greatest advantage and privilege of the Jew (cf. Rom. 3:1-4) became their accuser and condemner (cf. Rom. 2:1-29). Knowledge carries with it responsibility. The greater one's privilege or position is, the greater is the responsibility and condemnation for failure (Jas. 3:1).

Quiz

1. Is Jesus commanding them to search the Scriptures, or merely stating the fact that they do so, in verse 39?
2. Give two reasons why the Jews could not come to Jesus even though they searched the Scriptures diligently.
3. How does verse 40 refute the doctrine of "irresistable grace"?
4. In what way does Christ *not* seek the praise of men?
5. Why do they receive one who comes in his own name, but not Jesus Who came in the name of the Father?
6. How does Moses accuse the Jews?
7. Give two Scripture references which show "the greater the position, the greater the responsibility".

SPECIAL STUDY NO. 3

Christianity stands or falls with the deity of Jesus. The Fourth Gospel is vigorously attacked by hostile critics because it so plainly declares the deity of Jesus of Nazareth. The unbeliever assumes that once he has destroyed the historicity of John's Gospel, he has destroyed the deity of Jesus, since the remainder of the New Testament (according to the unbelieving critic) makes no such claims as the Gospel of John.

We introduce here a term paper written by Miss LaDonna Woods, student at Ozark Bible College. Her paper is a very comprehensive and well-organized compilation of facts gathered from many sources. The author gratefully acknowledges Miss Wood's permission to reproduce the study. The reader will notice that Christ's deity is asserted and substantiated throughout the entire New Testament.

201

THE GOSPEL OF JOHN
THE DEITY OF JESUS
by LaDonna Woods

I. CLAIMS OF JESUS

I. "The Son of Man"

This was Jesus' favorite name for Himself. It occurs about seventy times in the Gospels: Matthew, 30 times; Mark, 5 times; Luke, 25 times; John, 10 times.

It was used in Daniel 7:13, 14, 27 as name for the coming Messiah. Jesus' adoption of it is thought to have been equivalent to a claim of Messiahship.

He also carried this title with Him to heaven (Acts 7:56).

II. "The Son of God"

Jesus called Himself the Son of God in John 5:25. John tells us in John 5:18 that the Jews sought to kill Him because he not only broke the Sabbath, but also called God His own Father, making himself equal with God. Three times Jesus categorically said, "I am the Son of God": Mark 14:61-62; John 9:35-37; 10:36.

III. Expressions of Himself that can be predicated only of deity:

A. "I am the Way the Truth and the Life" (John 14:6).

B. "I am the door; by Me if any man enter in he shall be saved and shall go in and out, and shall find pasture" (John 10:9).

C. "No man can come unto the Father but by Me" (John 14:6).

D. "I am the Bread of Life" (John 6:35, 38).

E. "I am the Life" (John 11:25;14:6).

F. "I am the Resurrection" (John 11:25).

G. "He that believes on Me shall never Die" (John 11:26).

H. "I am the Messiah" (John 4:25-26).

I. "Before Abraham was I am" (John 8:58).

J. "Father, glorify Me with the glory I had with Thee before the world was" (John 17:5). (a clear declaration of His pre-incarnate existence).

K. "He that has seen Me has seen the Father" (John 14:9).

L. "I and the Father are one" (John 10:30).

M. "All power on earth and in heaven has been given unto me" (Mt. 28:18).

N. "I am with you always, even unto the end of the world" (Mt. 28:20).

O. "I am the Light of the world" (Jn. 8:12).

P. "I am the good Shepherd" (Jn. 10:11).

Q. "You are of this world; I am not of this world. You are from beneath; I am from above" (Jn. 8:23).

R. "Your father Abraham rejoiced to see my day, and he saw it and was glad" (Jn. 8:56).

S. "Moses wrote of Me" (Jn. 5:46).

T. "The Father, He has borne witness of Me" (Jn. 5:37).

U. "Except you believe that I am He, you shall die in your sins" (Jn. 8:24).

V. "Blessed are your eyes, for I say unto you many kings and prophets desired to see the things that you see, but did not see them, and to hear the things which you hear, but did not hear them" (Lk. 10:23-24).

W. "The queen of Sheba came from the ends of the earth to hear the wisdom of Solomon. A greater than Solomon is here. The Ninevites repented at the preaching of Jonah. Here is a greater than Jonah" (Mt. 12:41-42).

Who else could have said such things about himself? Only God incarnate! Of whom else could we say them? None except the Son of the living God. Let us now consider what the apostles had to say concerning the deity of Jesus.

II. THE APOSTLES' CLAIMS CONCERNING CHRIST
I. Peter

When at Caesarea Philippi Jesus asked His disciples who men said that He was, Peter answered and said unto Him, "Thou art the Christ, the Son of the living God" (Mt. 16:13-20). This is told also in Mark 8:27-29 and Luke 9:18-20.

It had been some three years since Peter had first accepted Jesus as the Messiah (Jn. 1:41-42). A year later he called Him Lord (Lk. 5:8). Half a year later he called Him the holy One of God (Jn. 6:68-69). Now, after two and one-half years of association with Jesus he expresses his conviction in the deity of Jesus.

The Rock (Mt. 16:18) on which Christ would build His church is not Peter, but the truth which Peter confessed, that Jesus is the Son of God. The deity of Jesus is the foundation upon which the church rests, the fundamental creed of Christendom.

II. John
A. Jesus was in the beginning.

THE GOSPEL OF JOHN

In John 1:1-3 we are reminded of the opening words of Genesis. Jesus is called God and Creator. John is very positive that Jesus was a personality existing from eternity, and that He had a hand in the creation of the universe. In John 17:5 Jesus is quoted as referring to the "glory He had with the Father before the world was."

Jesus is also called the Word in John 1:1; that is, Jesus was God's expression of Himself to mankind. Jesus was God. Jesus was like God. Jesus was God's message to mankind.

B. Jesus is the Light of the world.

John tells us this in John 1:4-13; 8:12; 9:5 and 12:46. This is one of the keynotes in John's thought about Jesus (cf. I John 1:5-7). It means that Jesus, as Light of the world, is the One who makes clear the meaning and destiny of human existence.

C. The Incarnation (John 1:14-18).

God became a man in order to win man to Himself. God could have made man with an instinct to do His will; but He chose rather to give man the power to decide for himself his attitude toward his Creator. But God is a spirit; and man is hedged in by the limitations of a material body, and has scant conception of what a Spirit is. So the Creator came to His creatures in the form of one of them to give them an idea of the kind of being He is. God is like Jesus. Jesus is like God.

III. Jesus is called the Son of God by:
A. Mark (1:1)
B. John (3:16, 18; 20:31)
C. John the Baptist (Jn. 1:34)
D. Nathanael (Jn. 1:49)
E. Peter (Mt. 16:16)
F. Martha (Jn. 11:27)
G. The Disciples (Mt. 14:33)
H. Gabriel (Lk. 1:32-35)

These are the claims of some of Jesus' apostles and disciples concerning His deity. Let us take a general look at the Scriptures.

NAMES AND TITLES APPLIED BY THE SCRIPTURES TO CHRIST

The Christ, the Messiah, Saviour, Redeemer, Wonderful Counsellor, Faithful Witness, the Word of God, the Truth, the Light of the World, the Way, the Good Shepherd, Mediator, Deliverer, the Great High Priest, the Author and Perfector of our Faith, the Captain of our Salvation, Our Advocate, the Son of God, the Son of Man, God, the Holy One of God, only begotten Son, Mighty God, the image of God, everlasting Father, Lord, Lord of All, Lord of Glory, Lord of Lords, blessed and only Potentate, King of Israel, King of Kings, Ruler of the kings of the Earth, Prince of Life, Prince of Peace, the Son of David, the Branch, David, Root and Offspring of David, the Bright and Morning Star, Immanuel, the second Adam, the Lamb of God, the Lion of the tribe of Judah, the Alpha and the Omega, the First and the Last, the Beginning and the End, the beginning of the creation of God, the First born of all creation, the Amen.

Only Jesus could be rightfully named all these names. It is not enough, however, for one just to be called these names, for they merely claim deity. We must have proof if we are to trust in Jesus as divine. This proof is found in the fulfillment by Jesus of the Old Testament prophecies, in the amazing character of Jesus, in the miracles which Jesus performed, in His resurrection and in His ascension.

III. PROPHECIES OF THE OLD TESTAMENT, AND THEIR FULFILLMENT IN JESUS CHRIST

The complete story of Jesus' life: its main features, events, and accompanying incidents, even in minutest detail, is plainly foretold in the Old Testament Scriptures.

I Birth

A. Prophecy that a Messiah was to come:

1. Jesus accepted the Old Testament prophecies which declared the absolute deity of the coming Messiah, as referring to Himself. "Therefore the Lord Himself shall give you a sign; Behold a virgin shall conceive, and bear a son, and shall call his name Immanuel" (Isa. 7:14). This is a clear statement of the birth of Christ. It also plainly says that the Son born of this virgin should be called Immanuel, literally, God with us.

2. "For unto us a child is born, unto us a son is given: and the government shall be upon his shoulder: and his name shall be called Wonderful, Counsellor, the Mighty God, the everlasting Father, the Prince of Peace" (Isa. 9:6). The names of this child are the names of deity! The child to be born, the Son to be

given, was to be very God, as clearly deity as God the Father Himself, and in fact, a very manifestation of the Father.

B. Genesis 3:15 — The Seed of Woman
   1. The Deliverer from sin must be:
      a. Of the seed of woman
      b. Temporarily hindered
      c. Finally victorious
   2. Paul writes, "but when the fulness of time came, God sent forth his Son, born of woman" (Gal. 4:4, 5).

C. The Deity of Christ is substantiated by the virgin birth.
   1. It was prophesied that the Christ would be born of a virgin. (Isa. 7:14).
   2. Matthew 1:20, 21 is the fulfillment of this prophecy.

D. It was prophesied that He would be born in Bethlehem. Micah 5:2 — fulfilled Matthew 2:6; Luke 2:4-7 (cf. John 7:42).

E. It was prophesied that He was to be of David's family.
   1. Old Testament
      a. II Sam. 7:12-16; Psa. 89:3-4; 110:1; Gen. 49:8-10
   2. New Testament
      a. Matt. 1:1, Rev. 22:16; Rom. 1:3

II His Life

A. Prophesied that He would sojourn in Egypt
   1. Hosea 11:1 — fulfilled Matt. 2:13-15

B. Prophesied that Jesus would live at Nazareth
   1. Isa. 11:1; Jer. 23:5; Zech. 3:8 — fulfilled Matt. 2:23; Lk. 4:16

C. Jesus' Ministry
   1. Prophesied that He would proclaim a jubilee to the world. Isa. 61:1 — fulfilled Lk. 4:16-21
   2. Prophesied His ministry to be one of healing. Isa. 53:4 — fulfilled Matt. 8:14-17
   3. Prophesied He would teach by parables. Isa. 6:9-10; Psa. 78:2 — fulfilled Matt. 13:14-35
   4. Prophesied He would be rejected by the rulers.
      a. Psa. 69:4; 118:22 — fulfilled Matt. 21:42; Mk. 12:10, 11; Lk. 20:17; Acts 4:11-12; I Pet. 2:4
      b. Isa. 53:1 — fulfilled Jn. 12:37-41; 15:25 (cf. Psa. 35:19; 119:4).

III His Death in Prophecy
  A. Prophesied that He would be betrayed by a friend for thirty pieces of silver.
    1. Zech. 11 :12-13; Psa. 41 :9 — fulfilled Matt. 27 :9-10; John 13 :18.
  B. Prophesied that He would be given vinegar and gall.
    1. Psa. 69 :21 — fulfilled Matt. 27 :34; John 19 :29
  C. Prophesied that they would cast lots for His garments.
    1. Psa. 22 :18 — fulfilled John 19 :24
  D. Even His dying words were foretold.
    1. Psa. 22; Psa. 33 :5 — fulfilled Matt. 27 :46
  E. Prophesied that not a bone of His body would be broken.
    1. Ex. 12 :46; Num. 9 :12; Psa. 34 :20 — fulfilled Jn. 19 :36
  F. Prophesied that His side would be pierced.
    1. Zech. 12 :10; Psa. 22 :16 — fulfilled Jn. 19 :37

IV His Burial in Prophecy
  A. It was prophesied that He would be buried by a rich man. Isa. 53 :9; Matt. 27 :57-60 (The fact is stated in Matthew, but the prophecy is not quoted).

V His Resurrection in Prophecy
  A. Prophesied that He would rise from the dead the third day: Matt. 12 :40, Lk. 24 :46. No particular passage is quoted from the Old Testament for this, but Jesus likens His burial and resurrection to Jonah's entombment in the belly of the whale.
  B. That He would rise from the dead as prophesied is Peter's application of Psalm 16 :8ff in his sermon in Acts 2 :25-32 (cf. also Acts 13 :33-35 and Psa. 2).
  C. Jesus said, "it is *written*, that the Christ should suffer, and rise again from the dead the third day" (Lk. 24 :46).

Christ is the theme of the Bible (Jn. 5 :39; Heb. 10 :7). He is the Word of God (Jn. 1 :1-18; Rev. 19 :13), and the Bible is the Word of God (Heb. 4 :13). He is the Word incarnate, and the Bible is the Word written.

He is the theme of the whole Bible. Not only in the New Testament but in the Old Testament as well, He is the central figure. Throughout the Book "the testimony of Jesus is the spirit of prophecy" (Rev. 19 :10). In I Peter 1 :10-11 it is declared that the sufferings of Christ and the glory that shall follow constitute the theme of the Old Testament writers.

We have already seen some of the prophecies concerning Christ in the Psalms that were completely fulfilled. There are many more references to the prophetic nature of the Psalms yet in the New Testament.

When Christ was talking to His apostles after His resurrection, He definitely mentioned the Psalms (Lk. 24:44). There are many references to the Second Psalm in the New Testament, and their application to our Lord is clear:

1. Psalms 2:1-13 is applied to Christ in Acts 4:23-26; 27-28.

2. Psalms 2:7: "I will tell of the decree Jehovah said unto me, Thou art my son." In Acts 13:35 the same words are applied to Christ: "Thou art my Son; this day have I begotten thee." That the Lord Jesus is the One spoken of here is shown by the New Testament references to this verse. In Hebrews 1:4, 5, His superiority to the angels is deduced from the fact that to none of the angels did God ever say, "Thou art my Son"; and in Hebrews 5:5, it is declared specifically that the words of this seventh verse of the Second Psalm refers to Christ. "This day have I begotten thee" — The day referred to here is the day of His resurrection, as is seen by Paul's words in Acts 13:32, 33 declaring the "glad tidings, how that the promise which was made unto the fathers, God hath fulfilled the same unto us their children, in that he hath raised up Jesus again; as it is also written in the second psalm, Thou art my Son, this day have I begotten thee." On that day He became the first begotten from the dead. Others had been raised from the dead, but in their case it was only resuscitation of the natural body; He was the first to come forth with an immortal and glorified body.

3. Psalms 22, 23 and 24 are all Shepherd Psalms: In the New Testament our Lord is presented as a Shepherd in three ways: (1) In John 10 He is the Good Shepherd giving His life for the sheep (Jn. 10:11); (2) In Hebrews 13:20 He is the Great Shepherd, "brought again from the dead . . . through the blood of the everlasting covenant," Who is now in resurrection power and glory caring for His flock; (3) In I Peter 5:4 He is the Chief Shepherd who will one day appear to reward His undershepherds and take immediate charge of His sheep. All these relationships are set forth in the three Shepherd Psalms: (1) In Psalm 22 the Good Shepherd lays down His life for His sheep; (2) In Psalm 23 the Great Shepherd is leading His sheep and caring for them; (3) In Psalm 24 He is the King of glory, in His appearing at the end of the age.

THE GOSPEL OF JOHN

We have seen how the prophecies of the Old Testament fulfilled in Christ show that He truly is the promised One, the Messiah. Let us now look at the character of Jesus while He was here among men. Even though He came as a man we can see from a study of His earthly life that He was divine, the One sent forth from God.

IV. CHRIST'S UNPARALLELED CHARACTER
(John 18:19-40)

I Challenge of a Perfect Life
  A. He prayed for forgiveness of His murderers Lk. 23:34
  B. He laid down His life for the unrighteous. Rom. 5:8
II His enemies find no fault in Him
  A. Pilate said, "Behold, the man, I find no fault in him." Jn. 19:4, 5, 6.
  B. Bovee said, "Even if we should reject all other miracles of the Christ, yet we have the miracle of Christ Himself."
III Characteristics of an Ideal Man
  A. He was a man of strength, not a weakling (Mt. 4:1-10) Jesus withstood the temptation of Satan. Even Samson, a physical giant, could not do that.
  B. Jesus was a man of power, not an incompetent (Jn. 18:1-11)
    1. As a man alone against a great mob of people who were sent to take Him, He caused the mob to fall to the ground when he said, "I am He."
  C. Jesus was a man of courage, not a coward (Lk. 9:51-56)
    1. Knowing that a horrible death awaited Him at Jerusalem, he "set his face steadfastly to go to Jerusalem."
  D. Jesus was a man of compassion (Jn. 11:30-36).
    1. Men sometimes look upon tears from the eyes of men as a sign of weakness, but they most certainly are not. Severity, harshness, coldness, are not signs of real manhood. Tears reveal a heart. A powerful man without a heart is more liable to be a menace than a blessing. The coward may be brazen, but a courageous man may yet be tender to the point of tears. Jesus' tears for the suffering but enhance Him as the Man of men.

E. Jesus was a man of forgiveness (Lk. 23:23-38)
   1. Could we only experience Christ's humiliation when
      He was mocked, jostled, lied about, spat upon, thorn-
      crowned, and then nailed to the cross to die in the
      most excruciating agony, actually praying in the midst
      of His agony for the forgiveness of those who were
      cursing, mocking and taunting Him, we should have
      some idea of the degree of forgiving grace which
      He possessed. There is none to equal it! (cf. I Pet.
      2:21-25)

From these instances alone we have the picture of One who
perfectly fulfills every characteristic of the ideal man. He is the
one and only such fulfillment the world has ever known!

Such a man as this would be able to do great wonders. Jesus
did do many miracles while He was here on this earth in the form
of man. Let us look at some of these miracles.

V. MIRACLES OF JESUS

Jesus said, "The works which the Father has given me to do,
the very works that I do, bear witness of me" (Jn. 5:36).

Aside from supernatural manifestations such as angelic an-
nouncements, virgin birth, the star that guided the Magi, Jesus
passing through hostile mobs, cleansing the temple, His transfiguration, soldiers falling, darkness at the crucifixion, the tombs
opened, the earthquake, Jesus' resurrection, angel appearances,
there are recorded thirty-five miracles which Jesus wrought.
Below are a few of the more outstanding ones:

A. Bodily Cures
   1. Healing the nobleman's son at a distance (Jn. 4:41-59)
   2. Healing a leper (Mt. 8:2-4; Mk. 1:40-45; Lk. 5:12-15)
   3. Healing the lame man at the pool (Jn. 5:2-9)
   4. Many others!

B. Miracles over the forces of nature
   1. Turning the water into wine (Jn. 2:1-11)
   2. The draught of fishes near Capernaum (Lk. 5:1-11)
   3. Stilling the tempest (Mt. 8:23-27; Mk. 4:35-41; Lk. 8:22-
      25)
   4. Feeding the five thousand (Mt. 14:13-21; Mk. 6:34-44;
      Lk. 9:11-17; Jn. 6:1-14)
   5. Walking on the water (Mt. 14:22-33; Mk. 6:45-52, Jn.
      6:19)

6. Jesus feeds the four thousand (Mt. 15:32-39; Mk. 8:1-9)
C. Cures of Demoniacs
   1. One healed in a synagogue (Mk. 1:21-28)
   2. Blind and dumb one healed (Mt. 12:22; Lk. 11:14)
   3. Syro-Phoenician woman's daughter healed (Mt. 15:21-28; Mk. 7:24-30)
D. Three raised from the dead
   1. Jairus' daughter (Mt. 9:18-26; Mk. 5:22-43; Lk. 8:41-56)
   2. Widow's son at Nain (Lk. 7:11-15)
   3. Lazarus (Jn. 11:1-44)
E. Other Miracles
   1. John 2:23
   2. Matthew 4:24
   3. Matthew 15:30-31
   4. John 21:25
F. Purpose of the Miracles

Jesus' miracles imply an exercise of creative power — a life-giving source. They were a part of God's way of authenticating Jesus' mission. Jesus said that if He had not done the works that no other ever did, they would not have had sin (Jn. 15:24) thus indicating that He regarded His miracles as proof that He was from God. Then, too, His miracles were the natural expression of His sympathy for suffering humanity (Mk. 2:10; Jn. 5:36; 14:11-12).

We could not leave this study of the deity of Jesus without discussing how His resurrection and ascension definitely show forth His deity.

V. THE RESURRECTION OF JESUS

It is absolutely certain that the apostles of Christ, and the first teachers of Christianity asserted the fact of Jesus' resurrection (every recorded sermon in the book of Acts mentions His resurrection as its basis, plus all the mention of it in the Epistles).

Should the question arise whether the things told of Christ be the very things which the apostles and first preachers delivered concerning Him, we must rely upon the evidence we possess of the genuineness of the Scriptures. On the subject of the resurrection we need no such discussion, for such a doubt cannot be entertained. The only points we could discuss on this subject is whether the apostles knowingly published a falsehood or whether they were themselves deceived; whether either of these suppositions be possible. It is very unlikely that the first supposition is true. The nature of the undertaking, and of the men; the extreme unlikelihood that such men should engage in such a measure as a scheme; their personal toils and dangers and sufferings in the cause; their appropriation of their whole time to the object; their zeal and earnestness, their sincerity, relives any suspicion of imposture.

Some would like to resolve the conduct of the apostles into misguided enthusiasm; which would class the evidence of Christ's resurrection with the numerous stories of the apparitions of dead men. There are many circumstances found in the Bible which destroy this hypothesis completely.

It was not one person who saw Jesus after His resurrection, but many; they saw Him not only separately, but together, not only by night, but by day, not at a distance but near, not once but several times; they not only saw Him, but touched Him, conversed with Him, ate with Him and examined His person to satisfy their doubts.

These facts are recorded in the Bible. Here are the appearances Jesus made after His resurrection:
1. To Mary Magdalene (Mk. 16:9-10)
2. To the other women (Mt. 28:9-10)
3. To two disciples on the way to Emmaus (Mk. 16:12-13; Lk. 24:13-32)
4. To Peter (Lk. 24:34)
5. To the eleven (Mk. 16:14; Lk. 24:36; Jn. 20:19)
6. To the eleven (Jn. 20:26-31 — Thomas present)
7. To the seven (Jn. 21)
8. To the eleven (and 500 at once?) (Mt. 28:16-20)
9. To James (I Cor. 15:7)
10. Ascension (Mk. 16:19; Lk. 24:44; Acts 1:6-11)

In I Corinthians 15:5-8 and Acts 9:1-9 we learn that Jesus also appeared, twenty-seven years after the Resurrection, to the arch-enemy of the church, Saul of Tarsus!

The statement in Acts 1:3, "showed himself alive by many proofs by the space of forty days, speaking things concerning the kingdom of God," along with similar statements in Acts 10:41 and 13:31, implies the possibility that He may have made many appearances besides those recorded and that His post-resurrection ministry may have been more extensive than we know.

With all these accounts, the writings of five different men, plus the conversion of the most determined and feared persecutor of Christianity, how could anyone doubt that Jesus did rise from the dead and did show Himself alive to eyewitnesses? We know such testimony would stand up in any court of any nation as evidence to establish the fact beyond a reasonable doubt! If any person persists in rejecting the resurrection of Jesus Christ from the dead, he rejects the historic evidence and testimony which, *above all other history,* meets the test of sound canons of credibility. Such a person could not believe any history!

VII. THE ASCENSION OF JESUS

The final miraculous event in Jesus' life as a man here on earth occurred forty days after His resurrection. After His resurrection, Jesus appeared unto His apostles, teaching them things concerning the kingdom of God. He gave to them the Great Commission to go into all parts of the world and preach the gospel, and also the promise of the Holy Spirit. On the final day, as they were all assembled together on the Mount of Olives, Jesus "was taken up; and a cloud received him out of their sight" (Acts 1:9). As the apostles stood watching, two men in white apparel appeared and told the apostles that Jesus would one day come again in like manner as they beheld Him going (Acts 1:1-11).

We do know that Jesus returned to His heavenly glory. Stephen tells us, as he is being stoned for preaching the deity of Jesus, "Behold, I see the heavens opened, and the Son of man standing on the right hand of God" (Acts 7:56).

VIII. CONCLUSION

We have set forth the names and titles which ascribe deity unto Jesus of Nazareth. It is not enough, however, to accept these claims unsubstantiated.

We then proceed to prove the deity of Jesus of Nazareth by: (1) fulfillment of Old Testament prophecies in His Person; (2) the undeniable perfect character of Jesus; (3) the miracles He actually performed; (4) His own bodily resurrection foretold by Himself as proof for His claims to be the Son of God; (5) His ascension to the right hand of God.

The resurrection and the ascension of Jesus would have been stupendous events to behold. Yet we will one day witness just as great an event — the day when Jesus comes again. Those who have believed and trusted Jesus — those who have obeyed Him and remained faithful shall be caught up with Him to be with Him forever. We must remain strong in our faith, never doubting.

We must believe that the Bible is the inspired Word of God. If we believe this, then we will believe in the deity of Jesus, for we know that this is the central theme of the entire Bible.

SPECIAL STUDY NO. 4

The earthly ministry of the Lord of Glory was fraught with controversy and objection. It is surprising to some to discover this fact. It is even more surprising to recognize that Jesus actually performed some of His miracles (such as the one in John 5) to touch off controversy.

Again, we are indebted to Seth Wilson, Dean of Ozark Bible College. He has compiled all the research and has graciously permitted us to introduce it here as Special Study No. 4.

The ministry of Jesus, judged by modern standards, would appear unsuccessful, ill-prosecuted and certainly not an ideally peaceful ministry.

Notice that controversy began almost immediately at the commencement of His public ministry. The controversy, however, did not intensify and cause determinate conclusions by the Jews until the Second Year of His ministry (John 5).

CONTROVERSIES AND OBJECTIONS IN JESUS' MINISTRY
by Seth Wilson

FIRST PASSOVER Cleansing of temple in Jerusalem (John 2). Jewish officials challenge His authority to do it:

Does Nicodemus' coming at night indicate that Jesus was a controversial figure? (John 3)

Beginning of Galilean Ministry, 8-9 months after first Passover at Nazareth; sermon in Synagogue, pushed to the cliff Luke 4:23-30

At Capernaum; paralytic forgiven; scribes and Pharisees thought it blasphemy (Mt. 9:2-8; Mk. 2:1-12; Lk. 5:18-26). (Note Pharisees following from Jerusalem)

At Matthew's house; feast with publicans and sinners; Pharisees object (Mt. 9:10-13; Mk. 2:15-17; Lk. 5:29-32).

Objection implied in the question of John the Baptist's disciples about fasting (Mt. 9:14-17; Mk. 2:18-22; Lk. 5:33-39).

THE GOSPEL OF JOHN

SECOND PASSOVER

At pool in Jerusalem; heals lame man on Sabbath; first definite effort of Jews to kill Him (Jn. 5, esp. v. 18).

In grain fields; 2nd Sabbath controversy - - - over plucking grain (Mt. 12:1-8; Mk. 2:23-38; Lk. 6:1-5).

In Synagogue; 3rd Sabbath controversy; heals man with the withered hand (Mt. 12:9-14; Mk. 3:1-6; Lk. 6:6-11).

In house of Simon the Pharisee; Simon's mental objections to Jesus' letting sinful woman touch Him (Lk. 7:36-50).

At Capernaum; very busy with great crowds; dumb demoniac healed; Pharisees claim He is possessed by Beelzebub (Mt. 12:22-37; Mk. 3:22-30); His family attempts to interfere, seeming to object to the strenuousness of His ministry (Mt. 12:46-50).

East side of Galilean sea, land of Gadarenes; casts out demons; people ask Him to leave (Mt. 8:43; Mk. 5:17; Lk. 8:37).

At Nazareth, last visit recorded; general unbelief and rejection (Mt. 13:54-58; Mk. 6:1-6).

THIRD PASSOVER NEAR

Fed 5000; sermon on Bread of Life at Capernaum; "This is a hard saying, who can receive it?" They forsook Him (John 6).

General Condition:

John 7:1 — the Jews seek to kill Him.

Capernaum: Jerusalem Pharisees publicly criticize Jesus for His disciple's eating with unwashed hands (Mt. 15:1-20; Mk. 7:1-23).

At Magadan; Pharisees and Sadducees demand a sign from heaven (Mt. 15:39; 16:1-4; Mk. 8:10-12).

At Caesarea Philippi; Peter objects to the first plain prediction of Jesus' death (Mt. 16:21-26; Mk. 8:31-38; Lk. 9:22-26).

At Capernaum; Jesus' unbelieving brothers object to His staying in seclusion, and urge Him to go to the Feast of Tabernacles (Jn. 7:3-9).

FEAST OF TABERNACLES (Six months before His death)

Jerusalem during the Feast; the rulers seek to kill Him (Jn. 7:14-24). They seek to arrest Him (Jn. 7:30). Disputing over their freedom and fatherhood (Jn. 8:-31-47). They accuse Jesus of being a Samaritan and

215

having a demon, and object to the promise that believers will never see death, they take up stones to stone Him (Jn. 8:48-59).

Jerusalem; man born blind healed on the Sabbath. The healed man is excommunicated . . . brief exchange between Jesus and Pharisees on blindness and guilt (Jn. 9:1-41). Dispute among the Jews about the sermon on the Good Shepherd (Jn. 10:19-21).

Judea; dumb demoniac healed and Jesus again accused of demon possession Lk. 11:14-26.

Dining in house of Pharisee; Jesus does not wash His hands, Pharisees astonished . . . they press Him hard to catch something for which to accuse Him (Lk. 11:37-54).

In a Synagogue on Sabbath; healing a bent woman; ruler of synagogue indignant (Lk. 13:11-17).

FEAST OF DEDICATION

Jerusalem; Jesus tells Jews "I and the Father are one." They take up stones to stone Him. They accuse Him of blasphemy and try again to arrest Him (Jn. 10:34-39).

DEPARTURE TO PEREA (Three months before His death)

In Perea; Herod seeks to kill Jesus (Lk. 13:31-35).

In home of Pharisee on Sabbath; man with dropsy healed. Jesus accused of unlawful action (Lk. 14:1-6).

Publicans and sinners come to Jesus; Pharisees murmur (Lk. 14).

Teaching in Perea; Pharisees scoff at Him (Lk. 16).

After raising Lazarus from dead; priests and Pharisees seek to put Jesus and Lazarus both to death (Jn. 11:43-54).

Last Journey to Jerusalem; Pharisees test Him with question about divorce (Mt. 19:1-9; Mk. 10:1-12).

At Jericho; Zacchaeus receives Jesus, the people sneer (Lk. 19:1-10).

Few days before Passover; chief priests demand anyone knowing where Jesus is must inform so they may arrest Him (Jn. 11:55-57).

Feast in Bethany; Judas objects to Mary's anointing Jesus as being wasteful (Mt. 26:6-13; Mk. 14:3-9; Jn. 12:1-8).

THE GOSPEL OF JOHN

Crowds praising Him; Pharisees say, "Teacher rebuke thy disciples" (Lk. 19:37-40).

Next day (Monday); cleanses Temple again. (Mt. 21:12-17; Mk. 11:15-19; Lk. 19:45-58).

Healing in the Temple; children praise; priests and scribes object (Mt. 21:14ff).

Next day (Tuesday) in Temple; Jesus' authority challenged by priests (Mt. 21:23-27; Mk. 11:27-33; Lk. 20:1-8). A trap question about tribute to Caesar (Mt. 22:15-22; Mk. 12:13-17; Lk. 20:20-26).
The Sadducees' question about marrage in ressurection. The Lawyer's question about the greatest commandment. Jesus' question about David's son being David's Lord (Mt. 22:23-46; Mk. 12:18-37; Lk. 20:27-44).
Disciples warned against the Pharisees and their hypocrisies (Matthew 23).

Last Tuesday or Wednesday; Reflections about the coming of the Greeks to Jesus; many believe but will not confess for fear of the Jews (Jn. 12:20-50).

Thursday night; Trials before Annas, Caiaphas, Sanhedrin, Pilate, Herod, Pilate. Mockings and charges at the trials and at the Crucifixion.

EXPOSITORY SERMON NO. 5
JESUS, THE SON OF GOD

John 5:1-47

Introduction

I BEGAN WITH CONTROVERSY OVER HEALING ON SABBATH

A. Set the scene
  1. Feast, pool, man ill 38 years, is healed
  2. Pharisaic rules for Sabbath-keeping
  3. Possibility that Jesus deliberately aroused controversy to bring about a demonstration of His deity
B. Importance of John 5
  This sin-sick world needs to be encouraged:
  1. that Jesus is the Christ, the manifestation of God in the flesh

217

2. that with a conviction of this absolute truth we can become new creatures

II JESUS' SERMON FALLS NATURALLY INTO THREE DIVISIONS:
  A. His equality with God — the prerogatives of deity
  B. The witnesses to His deity
  C. The causes of unbelief in His deity

Discussion

I JESUS' EQUALITY WITH GOD — PREROGATIVES OF DEITY
  A. He and the Father One (5:17-20) in:
    1. Intimate love
    2. Knowledge of wills
    3. Purposes for mankind
       Father works deeds of providential mercy on Sabbath, so also did Jesus
  B. Son has authority to raise the dead (v. 24-29)
    1. Spiritually
    2. Physically
  C. Son given authority to judge (v. 22-23)
    1. Imagine Pharisees taken aback at this statement, they who would soon arrest and judge Him
    2. Many today judge Jesus
       a. Imposter
       b. Good man
       c. BUT ALL SHALL STAND BEFORE HIM TO BE JUDGED
    3. Judgment given Him that all may honor Him as God
       a. Jesus claims right to be worshipped by men
       b. Any who deny deity of Jesus dishonor God

II WITNESSES TO THE DEITY OF JESUS
  A. John the Baptist (v. 33-35)
    1. That he (John) was not the Christ
    2. That he (John) was the forerunner
    3. That Jesus was the Lamb of God
    4. That the bodily presence of the Spirit was manifested as descending upon Jesus
    5. Jews rejoiced over John's great announcements of the coming Messiah, but when he focused truth on their sins, they killed him

6. Remember when Jews questioned Jesus' authority to cleanse temple?
   a. He asked them concerning John's baptism
   b. They recognized John as a prophet, but rejected his message of repentance and baptism because they loved the glory of men.
   RELIGIOUS LEADERS TODAY KNOW THAT THE NEW TESTAMENT PLAN OF SALVATION IS GOD'S WAY, BUT WILL NOT OBEY FOR THE SAME REASON

B. Witness of the Father through miracles (v. 36-38)
   1. Nicodemus, a Pharisee, admitted fact of miracles and Jesus' commission from God (John 3:2)
   2. Rulers later had to admit apostles worked miracles (Acts 4:16-17)
      a. They could not deny the fact, so they persecuted
   3. There is more than sufficient testimony to support the factuality of miracles of Jesus
      a. Testimony of conversions of thousands after being told of these miracles
      b. Testimony of preachers who sacrificed lives to preach resurrection of Jesus
      c. Testimony of Paul, former murderer of Christians
      d. These miracles of Christ "were not done in a corner."

C. Witness of the Scriptures (39-40)
   1. They were studying the Scriptures — and there was a way to eternal life indicated in the Old Testament.
      a. Faith in and obedience to the Messiah when He should come (cf. Deut. 18:15)
      b. See also Psalms 2, 22, and Isa. 53.
   2. Details of Jesus' life prophecied — fulfilled to minutest detail

III CAUSE OF UNBELIEF IN HIS DEITY
A. Jews had not love of God in them
   1. They wanted to glorify the Messiah temporally, BUT DID NOT WANT TO SUBMIT THEIR WILLS TO HIM . . . THEIR DEEDS AND THEIR MOTIVES
   2. Men today deny deity of Jesus in the same manner
      a. Have love of self, not love of God in them

b. Will not let Christ captivate their thoughts
B. They wrested the Scriptures (v. 45-47)
  1. They regarded Jesus as an accuser
    a. Cited their devotion to Moses
  2. They believed only so much of the Scriptures as suited their prejudiced ideas of the Messiah
    a. But Moses will be their accuser, for he wrote of the Messiah and demanded they hearken unto Him
  3. Many today who fail to obey commands of the New Testament really rejecting the Scriptures which they claim to reverence.

Conclusion

I NOTICE PERFECT ONENESS OF WILLS OF FATHER AND SON
We need to recognize that in oneness with Lord's will is our own happiness
  1. John 15:10-11
  2. John 13:17
  3. Jesus had perfect, absolute joy in abiding in the Father's will
  4. He told us His secret of peace, happiness and joy; remaining in the Father's will
II NOTICE THE FACTUAL EVIDENCE TO ESTABLISH JESUS' DEITY
  A. John the Baptist — an eyewitness to the descent of the Spirit upon Jesus
  B. Miracles of Jesus — the greatest of which is resurrection
  C. The Old Testament Scriptures — fulfilled prophecy
III NOTICE WHERE YOU STAND TODAY ON THIS MATTER OF JESUS' DEITY
  A. With the Pharisees?
  They loved self — did not want Him to rule in their hearts
  B. With the disciples?
  "To whom shall we go? Thou hast the words of eternal life" (John 6:68-69).

CHAPTER SIX

Inasmuch as the events of Chapter Six are coincident with the third Passover feast of Jesus' public ministry, we outline this chapter as the beginning of the third and final year of public ministry. Wescott summarizes the chapter as containing "the whole essence of the Lord's Galilean ministry." It decisively contrasts the true and false conceptions of the Messianic kingship; Christ's concept is universal and spiritual; the people's concept is local and material.

All four Gospels record the miracles of feeding the five thousand and walking on the sea. To afford the reader a more comprehensive view of the events we have reproduced a harmony of all four accounts taken from *The Gospels; The Unification of the Four Gospels,* by Thomas G. Deitz, published by Eerdmans.

The three discourses of this sixth chapter have been sorely perverted by the advocates of Transubstantiation, Consubstantiation and Sacramentalism. The serious Bible student would do well to abide by the Lord's own interpretation of these discourses on the "Bread of Life" as He gives it in verse 63.

We have outlined chapter six as follows:

II The Word Manifested to the Jews and Their Rejection of Him. 1:19-12:50 (cont.)
D. Public Ministry — Beginning of Third Year 6:1 - 12:50
1. The Bread of Life 6:1-71
a. Miracle of the loaves and fishes 6:1-13
b. Reaction of the multitudes 6:14-15
c. Walking upon the sea 6:16-21
d. The Mistaken search, 6:22-29
e. The Bread of Life I, 6:30-40
f. The Bread of Life II, 6:41-51
g. The Bread of Life III, 6:52-59
h. The Bread of Life explained, 6:60-65
i. The Twelve, their finest hour 6:66-71

THE UNIFICATION OF THE FOUR GOSPELS
by Thomas Deitz

The following harmony is a conflation of all four Gospel accounts (Matthew, Mark, Luke and John) of the two miracles; feeding of the five thousand and walking on the sea:

"After these things Jesus went away to the other side of the sea of Galilee, which is the sea of Tiberias. And a great multitude followed him, because they beheld the signs which he did on them that were sick. And Jesus went up into the mountain, and there he sat with his disciples. Now the passover, the feast of the Jews, was at hand. And the apostles gather themselves together unto Jesus; and they told him all things, whatsoever they had done, and whatsoever they had taught. And he saith unto them, Come ye yourselves apart into a desert place, and rest a while. For there were many coming and going, and they had no leisure so much as to eat. And he took them. And they went away in the boat to a city called Bethsaida to a desert place apart. And the people saw them going, and many knew them, and they ran together there on foot from all the cities, and outwent them.

Jesus therefore lifting up his eyes, and seeing that a great multitude cometh unto him, had compassion on them and he welcomed them, and spake to them of the kingdom of God, and began to teach them many things, And them that had need of healing he cured, because they were as sheep not having a shepherd.

And the day began to wear away; and the twelve came, and said unto him, The day is now far spent, Send the multitude away, that they may go into the villages and country round about, and lodge, and get provisions: for we are here in a desert place. Jesus saith unto Philip, Whence are we to buy bread, that these may eat? And this he said to prove him: for he himself knew what he would do. Philip answered him, Two hundred shillings' worth of bread is not sufficient for them, that every one may take a little; But Jesus said unto them, They have no need to go away; give ye them to eat. How many loaves have ye? Go and see. One of his disciples, Andrew, Simon Peter's brother, saith unto him, There is a lad here, who hath five barley loaves, and two fishes: but what are these among so many? Now there was much grass in the place, And he commanded them that all should sit down by companies upon the grass. And they sat down in ranks, by hundreds and by fifties. And he took the five loaves

222

and the two fishes, and looking up to heaven, he blessed, and brake the loaves; and he gave to the disciples to set before them; and the two fishes divided he among them all. And they all ate, and were filled. And when they were filled, he saith unto his disciples, Gather up the broken pieces which remain over, that nothing be lost. And they took up broken pieces, twelve basketfuls, and also of the fishes which remained over unto them that had eaten. And they that did eat were about five thousand men, besides women and children.

When therefore the people saw the sign which he did, they said, This is of a truth the prophet that cometh into the world.

And straightway he constrained his disciples to enter into the boat, perceiving that they were about to come and take him by force, to make him king, and to go before him unto the other side of Bethsaida, while he himself sendeth the multitude away. And after he had sent the multitudes away, he went up into the mountain apart to pray: and when even was come, he was there alone.

And when evening came, his disciples went down unto the sea; and they entered into a boat, and were going over the sea unto Capernaum. And it was now dark, and Jesus had not yet come to them. And the sea was rising by reason of a great wind that blew. When therefore they had rowed about five and twenty or thirty furlongs, the boat was in the midst of the sea and he alone on the land. And seeing them distressed in rowing, for the wind was contrary unto them, about the fourth watch of the night he cometh unto them, walking on the sea; and he would have passed by them; but they, when they saw him walking on the sea, supposed that it was a ghost, and cried out; for they all saw him, and were troubled. But he straightway spake with them, and saith unto them, Be of good cheer; it is I; be not afraid. And Peter answered him and said, Lord, if it be thou, bid me come unto thee upon the waters. And he said, Come. And Peter went down from the boat, and walked upon the waters, to come to Jesus. But when he saw the wind, he was afraid; and beginning to sink, he cried out, saying, Lord, save me. And immediately Jesus stretched forth his hand, and took hold of him, and saith unto him, O thou of little faith, wherefore didst thou doubt? They were willing therefore to receive him unto them into the boat, and the wind ceased. And they were sore amazed in themselves; for they understood not concerning the loaves, but their

heart was hardened. And they that were in the boat worshipped
him, saying, Of a truth thou are the Son of God.

And when they had crossed over, they came to the land unto
Gennesaret, wither they were going, and moored to the shore.
And when they were come out of the boat, straightway the people
knew him, and ran round about that whole region, and began to
carry about on their beds those that were sick, where they heard
he was. And wheresoever he entered, into villages, or into cities,
or into the country, they laid the sick in the marketplaces, and
besought him that they might touch if it were but the border of
his garment: and as many as touched him were made whole."

MIRACLE OF THE LOAVES AND FISHES

Text 6:1-13

1 After these things Jesus went away to the other side of the
sea of Galilee, which is the sea of Tiberias.
2 And a great multitude followed him, because they beheld the
signs which he did on them that were sick.
3 And Jesus went up into the mountain, and there he sat with
his disciples.
4 Now the passover, the feast of the Jews, was at hand.
5 Jesus therefore lifting up his eyes, and seeing that a great
multitude cometh unto him, saith unto Philip, Whence are we
to buy bread, that these may eat?
6 And this he said to prove him: for he himself knew what
he would do.
7 Philip answered him, Two hundred shillings' worth of bread
is not sufficient for them, that every one may take a little.
8 One of his disciples, Andrew, Simon Peter's brother, saith
unto him,
9 There is a lad here, who hath five barley loaves, and two
fishes: but what are these among so many?
10 Jesus said, Make the people sit down. Now there was much
grass in the place. So the men sat down, in number about five
thousand.
11 Jesus therefore took the loaves; and having given thanks,
he distributed to them that were set down; likewise also of the
fishes as much as they would.
12 And when they were filled, he saith unto his disciples,
Gather up the broken pieces which remain over, that nothing
be lost.

13 So they gathered them up, and filled twelve baskets with broken pieces from the five barley loaves, which remained over unto them that had eaten.

Queries

a. What are Jesus' reasons for feeding this multitude?
b. Which passover is at hand?
c. Why did Jesus command the left-overs to be gathered up?

Paraphrase

After the interval of a year of increasingly popular ministry in Galilee, Jesus went across the Sea of Galilee (the Sea of Tiberias) to the eastern side. A great multitude was following Him because they were seeing the miracles which He was performing upon those who were sick. Jesus went up the hillside and there He sat down with His disciples. Now the Passover, the feast of the Jews, was at hand. Jesus looked up, therefore, and seeing that a great multitude was coming unto Him, said to Philip, Where are we to purchase food that these people may eat? This He said to test Philip, for He Himself knew what He was about to do. Philip answered Him, A year's wages would not buy enough bread that everyone may receive even a small portion. But one of His disciples, Andrew — Simon Peter's brother, says to Him, There is a lad here who has five barley loaves and two small fish, but what are these among so many? Jesus said, Make all the people to sit down. Now there was much grass in that place and the men therefore (about five thousand in number) sat down. Jesus took the loaves, when He had given thanks, and He distributed to the people who were sitting down; likewise He distributed the small fish, as much as the people wanted. When they were all full, He said to His disciples, Gather up the fragments that are left over so that nothing may be wasted. So they gathered them up and they filled twelve hand-baskets with fragments left over by those who had eaten from the five barley loaves.

Summary

Jesus tests the faith and spirituality of a great throng of about fifteen thousand people, plus His twelve disciples, by providing a miraculous meal for all present.

Comment

John's indefinite note of time in verse 1 cannot be construed to mean the events of Chapter Six must follow immediately the events of Chapter Five. A whole year's ministry intervenes between chapters 5 and 6 including such events as:

1. Controversies about the Sabbath in Capernaum; Mt. 12; Mk. 2; Lk. 6
2. Sermon on the Mount; Mt. 5, 6, 7
3. Raising Widow of Nain's Son; Lk. 7
4. Healing demoniac at Gergesa; Mt. 8; Mk. 5; Lk. 8
5. Second visit to Nazareth; Mt. 13; Mk. 6
6. Twelve sent in pairs to preach; Mt. 10; Mk. 6; Lk. 9
7. Herod desires to have Jesus visit him; Mt. 14; Mk. 6; Lk. 9

See Map No. 3 page No. 170 for the Second Year, the popular year, of public ministry.

There are at least four things which led Jesus to seek retirement in a "desert (uninhabited) place," beyond the Sea of Galilee:

a. The news of the death of John the Baptist
b. The sudden, and probably evil, interest of Herod
c. The return of the Twelve from intense evangelistic labors
d. The great multitudes pressing upon Him continually

Jesus saw the tide of crisis mounting, and He wanted time alone with the Twelve to prepare them and Himself for the coming climax of His ministry (v. 60-71). He thus took the disciples in a boat to the eastern side of the Sea of Galilee to a city called Bethsaida Julias (cf. Lk. 9:10; also Map No. 4, page No. 266). This city was at the northeast corner of the Sea of Tiberias. The sea of Galilee had many names:

a. Sea of Chinnereth (Nu. 34:11; Deut. 3:17; Josh. 13:27).
b. Sea of Chinnereth (Josh. 12:3; I Kings 15:20).
c. Lake of Gennesaret (Lk. 5:1).
d. Sea of Tiberias (Jn. 6:1).

Mark 6:32-33 pictures for us the great Passover crowds catching a glimpse of Jesus and His Twelve disciples, and recognizing Him as the great Galilean miracle Worker. Upon which, more than fifteen thousand people began running along the northern seashore, and arrived ahead of Jesus at the eastern side of the sea.

Enthusiasm was high. It was Passover time, the great deliverance festival of all Jewry. A miracle-working Prophet had arisen
in Galilee — He might even be *the* long-awaited hoped-for Prophet
"like unto Moses" (Deut. 18:15).

He seems to have eluded the vast throngs momentarily as He
goes up into the hillside and sits down with His disciples. Rest
was the primary motive, but secondarily, perhaps, He wanted to
give the Twelve a "birds-eye-view" of the great mass of people,
preliminary to His test questions.

The mention of the feast and its specific name, Passover, is
primarily to give a note of time. It may also be given in explanation of the great throngs of people. This is undoubtedly the
third Passover in Jesus' ministry — 2:13; 5:1; 6:4, and the
fourth, 13:1.

Many commentators see a problem in verse 5, and its parallels
in the Synoptics. They cannot harmonize the fact that Matthew
and Luke, and especially Mark, say that the crowd arrived first
(cf. Mt. 14:13-14; Mk. 6:33-34; Lk. 9:11), while John says
Jesus arrived first. R. C. Foster, in his *Syllabus of the Life of
Christ* Harmonizes the difficulty in this manner:

*"Mark 6:33-34 explicitly affirms that the crowd outran the
boat,* and when Jesus and the apostles disembarked they found
the crowd. Such a multitude — men, women, children; young
and old; sturdy, and sick or crippled — would be strung out for
miles by such a race. The vigorous ones outran the boat; Jesus
saw the situation and picked a natural amphitheatre on the mountain side. By the time the weak stragglers arrived and the multitudes fully assembled, Jesus was seated with His disciples prepared to teach and heal. The accounts are wonderfully *independent* and *harmonious."*

The Synoptics also include the Lord's tender compassion as
He beheld the great crowds coming toward Him. They were "as
sheep not having a shepherd" (Mk. 6:34). They were not being
led in spiritual paths by the religious leaders of the day. Jesus
took this opportunity to heal many and teach them concerning
the kingdom of God (cf. Lk. 9:11).

As the day began to "wear away" (Lk. 9:12), the Twelve
came to Jesus, asking Him to stop teaching and to dismiss the multitudes that they might go into the villages and obtain food. But
Jesus proposed an astounding question, intended to elicit an affirmation of faith and trust in His omnipotence. He turned to
Philip with the question, "Whence are we to buy bread that these

may eat?" Why question *Philip?* As a matter of fact, there is no conclusive answer. The Lord was testing Philip's faith, but He was also testing the faith of the other eleven. It is manifestly ridiculous to grasp at only one or two incidents of Philip's life and give him a "matter-of-fact" personality.

Jesus questioned Philip directly, but the entire group indirectly (cf. Mt. 14:16; Mk. 6:36). He needed no help for this situation, for He knew all along what He was going to do. His questions to the disciples were test questions. It is amazing that not one of them could remember the previous miracles, e.g., raising the widow's son from a funeral bier; casting legions of demons out of a man; and even earlier and more appropriate, the changing of water into wine at Cana. Could they not even remember these and suggest that Jesus exercise His miraculous prerogatives to provide food? Perhaps their faith was staggered at the vision of fifteen thousand people.

Philip's answer in verse 7 was one, as Godet puts it, "of good common sense, but not of faith." Many followers of Christ since Philip have followed the road of "good common sense," allowing multitudes to go unfed by the true Bread of Life, when they should have taken the stand of daring-yet-trusting faith.

The "two hundred shillings" would be equivalent to nearly a year's wages! One shilling, or denarius, represented one day's wages. A year's wages would not purchase enough bread that each of the more than fifteen thousand might have even a very small amount! The situation was an impossible one in the eyes of Philip and the others.

There seems to be a considerable lapse of time between verses 7 and 8, for the Synoptics report Jesus as sending the disciples into the crowd to gather all the available food (cf. Mk. 6:36). They found a lad with barley loaves and two small fish. Andrew then stepped forward with the find, but he too, sees the situation to be impossible.

As Hendriksen points out, numerous sermons have been preached on the lad here, but John focuses our attention on the Lord of lords, not the lad.

The loaves were probably somewhat like American hamburger buns, only thinner and harder, while the fishes were probably small, sardine-like fish processed into pickled delicacies. Pickled fish from Galilee were renouned throughout the Empire.

Jesus then, verse 10, prepared the mass of people for the coming repast. He commanded that the people be made to assume the customary position (half-way reclining) for eating. Mark adds (6:39-40) very picturesquely that they "reclined, garden beds, after garden beds (row after row of people in many colored costumes), by hundreds and fifties." Foster comments, "The lanes of green grass and the solid groups of people dressed in the gay colors of the East looked just like a flower garden . . ."

There are two apparent reasons for this seating in companies:

a. That there might be orderliness, no greediness and elbowing, nor confusion of any sort.

b. Probably to test the faith of the multitudes.

John says there were about five thousand men. Matthew 14:21 adds, "besides women and children." The Greek word which has been translated "number" is *arithmon,* and we have our English word "arithmetic" from it.

As was His customary practice, Jesus gave thanks before the meal. Then He distributed bread and fish to the assembled multitude. Immediately the curiosity seekers ask, "Where and how did the actual miracle take place?" Matthew 14:19 states that Jesus distributed to the disciples, and the disciples to the crowds. This is as descriptive as the Gospel writers become. All four are amazingly brief — certain indication of the guidance of the Holy Spirit. The Scriptures never place emphasis upon the mechanics of miracles, but upon their factuality and completeness. Every person there had as much as he could eat and some, it seems, took more than they could use, for there were broken fragments left over.

And so it is, in verse 12, that Jesus sends the disciples back among the rows of men and women to gather up the leftover fragments. What a lesson for the poor stewardship of present day followers of Jesus! The Lord not only taught good stewardship, but He also practiced it! The Creator of all abundance guarded against waste. Certainly it behooves us as dependent recipients of God's providential care to exercise good stewardship, and to guard against waste.

The disciples gathered up (v. 13) twelve *kophinos* (stout wicker baskets) full. These baskets were bottle-shaped, and no Jew ever travelled without his *kophinos.* By carrying his own food along with him he was not forced to shop in markets and touch (ceremonially) unclean persons and objects, and thus be forced to go through the tedious rites of purification overly much. Furthermore, the ceremonial cleanness of his food itself could be assured since he could carry it from his own table.

An interesting story is told in connection with this miracle. A Sunday School teacher was trying to convince her class of youngsters that there was no actual miracle performed by Jesus here at the sea of Galilee. "Children," she said, "you must realize that Jesus didn't actually provide bread and fish for the people to eat. They were really filled by His teaching." A small lad revealed heaven-sought faith when he said, "But what about the twelve baskets left over, Teacher?"

Quiz

1. How many of the Gospel writers record this miracle?
2. Is there an interval of time between chapters 5 and 6? If so, how much?
3. What did Jesus do and teach before providing food for the vast multitude (cf. Mk. 6:34)?
4. What sort of answer did Philip give Jesus?
5. How much bread is two hundred shillings worth?
6. Approximately how many people were fed?
7. What lesson is taught in this miracle regarding stewardship?

REACTION OF THE MULTITUDES

Text 6:14-15

14 **When therefore the people saw the sign which he did, they said, This is of a truth the prophet that cometh into the world.** 15 **Jesus therefore perceiving that they were about to come and take him by force, to make him king, withdrew again into the mountain himself alone.**

Queries

   a. Who is the prophet the people are looking for?
   b. Why would they resort to force?

Paraphrase

When the people saw the miracle which Jesus performed, they began saying, This is surely the Prophet who is to come into the world. Jesus knowing, therefore, that the people were about to come and seize Him in order that they might forcibly make Him king, withdrew again unto the mountain, Himself alone.

230

Summary

Enthusiasm grips the multitude. Jesus reads their hearts and sees their materialistic determination to violently force Him to be king.

Comment

When the people saw the sign and had satiated their hunger they immediately concluded, "This must surely be the promised Messiah-Prophet." All in the same day they had heard him speak of the kingdom of God on earth; many of them had seen and experienced His miraculous healing, and everyone had witnessed and partaken of the abundance of miraculously provided food. Some would recall His first sermon in Nazareth where He promised "release to the captives, recovering of sight to the blind and liberty to the bruised."

Because of their carnal attitude, the miracle merely confirmed them in their false Messianic hopes, for they "interpreted it as a sign and pledge of the highest temporal prosperity under His rule . . ."

Goaded by visions of temporal glory and prosperity, the multitude decided to seize Him by force, if necessary, and proceed triumpantly to Jerusalem and the Passover. As before, Jesus read their hearts and knew beforehand what they were about to do.

The Synoptics tell us that Jesus first sent the Twelve away in a boat toward the western shore of the sea. Then, by the majesty and authority of His countenance and voice, He dismissed the multitudes, which were already showing signs of taking Him, and went farther into the mountain and began to pray (cf. Mt. 14:23; Mk. 6:45). Jesus prayed for about eight or nine hours. The carnal attitude of the people sorely distressed and tempted Him to avoid the cross. He also wanted to pray that the Twelve not become saturated with this materialistic vision of Israel's Saviour.

Quiz

1. Can you name three things the people had experienced which would cause them to be so enthusiastic?
2. How did Jesus take charge of the situation?
3. How long was Jesus in prayer?
4. Why and for whom would Jesus need to pray?

231

WALKING UPON THE SEA

Text 6:16-21

16 And when evening came, his disciples went down unto the sea;

17 and they entered into a boat, and were going over the sea unto Capernaum. And it was now dark, and Jesus had not yet come to them.

18 And the sea was rising by reason of a great wind that blew.

19 When therefore they had rowed about five and twenty or thirty furlongs, they beheld Jesus walking on the sea, and drawing nigh unto the boat: and they were afraid.

20 But he saith unto them, It is I: be not afraid.

21 They were willing therefore to receive him into the boat: and straightway the boat was at the land whither they were going.

Queries

   a. Why was Jesus not with the disciples?
   b. Why were the disciples afraid?
   c. How did the boat get to land "straightway"?

Paraphrase

Late in the evening His disciples went down to the sea. And they took a boat and began to cross the sea toward Capernaum. As they were going, it became dark and still Jesus had not yet come to them. The sea then began to rise and become exceedingly rough because of a violent wind that was blowing. When they had rowed about three or four miles they saw Jesus walking on the water and coming toward the boat, and they were terrified. But Jesus said do not be afraid, It is I, Myself. Then they were willing for Him to come into the boat, and immediately the boat reached the shore toward which they had been rowing.

Summary

Jesus again manifiests Himself as Lord of nature by walking on a storm-tossed sea. The disciples are overawed by this manifestation of the supernatural.

Comment

It was late evening, near dark, when the disciples finally embarked in a boat and began rowing for the western shore. They seemed to have been in no hurry to leave Jesus. He had to constrain them earlier to leave Him (cf. Mk. 6:45).

As they rowed darkness enveloped them and the winds began to blow violently and the waves pitched and tossed furiously. Travellers have described the storms on the Galilean Sea as storms of a most violent nature. The sea is surrounded on all sides by mountains, which makes the sea appear as the bottom of a huge bowl. When the winds begin to sweep down into the bowl-like hole, violent sea storms are the result.

They left the eastern shore about dusk, six or seven in the evening, and now it was about three or four a.m. the next morning (fourth watch, Mt. 14:25). Their progress was so slow that they had rowed only about 3 miles (25 or 30 furlongs) in approximately nine hours.

They were just about midway between the shores, for the Sea of Galilee is approximately six miles wide. Mark (Mk. 6:47-50) tells us that Jesus saw their predicament and came to them walking on the sea. Jesus wished to pass them by, but when they saw Him they thought they were seeing a ghost and they literally shrieked in terror. Before we smile at the superstitious fears of the disciples, let us consider what we would have felt and said had we been in the boat with them.

When Jesus came close enough to be recognized He shouted, "Do not be afraid, it is I, Myself." Matthew records the next incident — Peter's attempt to walk to Jesus on the water (Mt. 14:28-31).

It is worthy of note here to see the independence of the accounts of this miracle:

a. Matthew alone mentions Peter's attempt to walk on the water (Mt. 14:28-31).

b. Mark alone mentions Jesus seeing their distress while still on the mountain (Mk. 6:47-48).

c. John alone mentions that it was dark (6:18) that they had rowed about 3 or 4 miles (6:19), and that the boat arrived "straightway" where they were going (6:21).

The infidelic theories of the liberal and radical scholars claim the Gospel writers were not inspired to write independent accounts, but copied from one another. *But the facts say differently* — they wrote independently of one another.

Upon recognizing the figure and hearing His voice, the twelve were very glad to let Him come into the boat. Matthew again tells us that when He and Peter entered the boat the disciples worshipped Jesus (Mt. 14:33).

The "straightway" of verse 21 may mean either:

a. The sea was calmed and the boat was rowed quickly to their destination, or,

b. A miraculous immediate arrival of the boat at its destination was effected.

Mark (Mk. 6:53-56) shows us where they were going. They had started for Capernaum (6:17), but driven by sea and wind, they eventually landed at the plain of Gennesaret (cf. Map No. 4, page 267). Here the people ran to Him from all the region round about, carrying their sick to Him. "As many as touched Him were made whole."

Quiz

1. How did the violence of the storm affect the progress of the disciples in the boat?
2. How did Jesus know of their predicament?
3. What did the disciples do when they saw Jesus coming toward them?
4. What did Peter do when he recognized the Lord?
5. Name the three incidents reported independently by Matthew, Mark and John.
6. Where did the disciples and Jesus finally put to shore?

THE MISTAKEN SEARCH

Text 6:22-29

22 On the morrow the multitude that stood on the other side of the sea saw that there was no other boat there, save one, and that Jesus entered not with his disciples into the boat, but that his disciples went away alone

23 (howbeit there came boats from Tiberias nigh unto the place where they ate the bread after the Lord had given thanks):

24 when the multitude therefore saw that Jesus was not there, neither his disciples, they themselves got into the boats, and came to Capernaum, seeking Jesus.

234

25 And when they found him on the other side of the sea, they said unto him, Rabbi, when camest thou hither?
26 Jesus answered them and said, Verily, verily, I say unto you, Ye seek me, not because ye saw signs, but because ye ate of the loaves, and were filled.
27 Work not for the food which perisheth, but for the food which abideth unto eternal life, which the Son of man shall give unto you: for him the Father, even God, hath sealed.
28 They said therefore unto him, What must we do, that we may work the works of God?
29 Jesus answered and said unto them, This is the work of God, that ye believe on him whom he hath sent.

Queries

a. What is the significance of the parenthetical statement of verse 23?
b. How has God sealed the Son of man?
c. How can belief be a work?

Paraphrase

The next day the multitude that remained on the other side of the sea realized that there was only one boat there, and that Jesus had not embarked in it with His disciples, but that His disciples had gone away by themselves (howbeit there were some boats, driven from Tiberias by the storm near to the place where they ate the bread and fish after the Lord had given thanks); and when the multitude saw that neither Jesus nor His disciples were there, they got into the boats from Tiberias and came to Capernaum seeking Jesus. When they found Jesus on the western side of the sea, they said to Him, Teacher, when did You come here? Jesus answered them, saying, I tell you most truly, you have been searching for Me not because you saw signs of deity in My miracles, but because you ate of the loaves and were satiated like cattle. Stop working for the temporal food, but work for the food which endures continually unto eternal life. The Son of man will give you this food, for God the Father has confirmed His deity and has put His seal of endorsement upon Him by the signs and miracles which He does. They said therefore to Him, What are we to do that we may be working the ordinances and laws of God? Jesus answered them, This is the work which God requires of you, that you trust and obey Him Whom God has sent.

Summary

The crowd, in their search the day following the miracle of the feeding, found Jesus and the disciples both gone. They crossed the sea in search of the miraculous meal-providing Prophet. The multitudes found Jesus only to hear Him accuse them of carnal motives in their search.

Comment

Where such a multitude found lodging during the stormy night we do not know. Perhaps the storm was localized upon the sea only and the great crowds slept under the stars. The next morning the people noticed three things:

a. Only one boat remained (however, boats from Tiberias appeared later).

b. Jesus had not entered the boat with His disciples the night before, yet Jesus was nowhere to be found.

c. The disciples had gone away alone and had not returned.

Evidently, some of the people did not go away when Jesus dismissed them. Perhaps the storm caused many to remain until it should pass.

Mention of the boats (v. 23) from Tiberias is interesting. Tiberias, of course, was a city on the western shore of the sea. The boats were probably blown across the sea during the storm since the wind was blowing from west to east, or, contrary to the direction the disciples were rowing. The multitude presumed Jesus to have gone away in the night in one of these boats.

When they realized that Jesus was not there, and that the disciples had not returned for Him, they got into the boats from Tiberias and began to search for Jesus. This multitude was determined to find Him and carry out their original plan to make Him king. Further, they did not wish to lose a "meal-ticket." The Jews, except for the rich, spent every waking moment toiling for the barest necessities — many were starving.

Finding Jesus on the western side of the sea, they began to question Him, "Teacher, when did You come over here? We were looking for You on the other side; how did You get over here?"

The Lord, with His omnisicient and infinite discernment, reveals (v. 26) the carnal motivation behind their searching. They saw the miracles, but they did not see them as signs of His deity and the spiritual nature of His kingdom. They saw in the

THE GOSPEL OF JOHN   6:27-28

miracles, rather, an era of sensory prosperity — "easy street" for Israel.

The multitudes sought Jesus because they had had their hunger satisfied. Like beasts of the field, they sought only to satisfy their physical desires — they walked by taste and sight, not by faith! In fact, the Greek word *echortasthete* here translated "were filled" means, literally, "to give fodder to animals." They could not think of their souls for thinking of their stomachs. Some think it strange that these people, having heard Jesus speak of the kingdom of God and seen Him work the miracles of the previous day, should still have a materialistic attitude. It is even *more strange* that millions of men and women of the twentieth century in America should be obsessed with gaining only material values because:

a. We have in the completed New Testament a better testimony to the deity of Jesus and the spiritual nature of His kingdom — better even than the knowledge of the eyewitnesses.

b. We enjoy more freedom to search out and adhere to what is truth than the people of that day, for they were beset by religious intolerance and persecution.

c. We are not sorely pressed with the burden of providing just the basic necessities as were most of the Jewish people.

Millions surely need the admonition of Jesus in Matthew 6:19-34 especially, "But seek ye first his kingdom, and his righteousness; and all these things shall be added unto you" (Mt. 6:33).

Jesus tells the people (v. 27) they are spending their best energies on that which is temporal (cf. Isa. 55:1ff). Physical food satisfies only physical hunger. But man is also created with a hunger for spiritual satisfaction (cf. Mt. 5:6) which only spiritual food can satisfy. There are at least four things for which men hunger in the realm of the spiritual:

a. Righteousness and justification before God

b. The ultimate truth

c. Life beyond the grave

d. True unselfish love

Christ alone can supply satisfaction to the hungry spirits of men. He will show (John 6:30-65) what the true spiritual food is. For the present, He makes it plain that God has sealed Him to be the source of spiritual life. The word sealed means that God sent Him, and confirmed His commission through signs and miracles. In Bible times the seal on a document was the sign of authority. If a document was impressed with King's seal, it was to be obeyed just as explicitly as any verbal order of the King. These Jews should have recognized the impressed seal of Jehovah-God in the miracles of Jesus and should have sought the spiritual kingdom which Jesus taught.

The people of Palestine, so long accustomed to the Pharisaic system of meritorious works, immediately seized upon Jesus' words and eagerly desired to know what works they might do to enjoy their illusioned era of material plenty. They expected Jesus to begin laying down rules and regulations by which they might earn prosperity.

In verse 29 Jesus reconciles all the teachings of the New Testament on faith and works. Westcott says, "This simple formula contains the complete solution of the relation of faith and works." But how is faith a *work?* Here are the answers of some highly respected and conservative scholars:

a. ". . . the work of faith is the work of receiving the gift of God." (Hendriksen)

b. "It is a true work as answering to man's will, but it issues in that which is not work." (Westcott)

c. "Faith means a certain relationship with God . . . a relationship in which we give God the trust and the obedience and the submission which naturally arise from this new relationship." (Barclay)

Faith, then, becomes a work when man submits his will to the revealed will of God and acts in accord with the commandments of the will of God. What better explanation can we find of the relationship between faith and works than that of James 2:20-26: Saving faith must be manifiested by obedience to the commands of God through His Son, even Jesus Christ!

Quiz

1. How would boats get from Tiberias to the eastern side of the sea?
2. What did the multitudes see in the miracle of the loaves?
3. In what manner did Jesus describe their desire to be fed?
4. Why is it strange that 20th century people should be obsessed with material ideals? Give three answers.
5. Name four things men hunger for in the spiritual realm.

6. How has God sealed Jesus?

7. How is believing in Christ a work? Cite Scriptures to prove your answer.

THE BREAD OF LIFE, I

Text 6:30-40

30 They said therefore unto him, What then doest thou for a sign, that we may see, and believe thee? what workest thou?

31 Our fathers ate the manna in the wilderness; as it is written, He gave them bread out of heaven to eat.

32 Jesus therefore said unto them, Verily, verily, I say unto you, It was not Moses that gave you the bread out of heaven; but my Father giveth you the true bread out of heaven.

33 For the bread of God is that which cometh down out of heaven, and giveth life unto the world.

34 They said therefore unto him, Lord, evermore give us this bread.

35 Jesus said unto them, I am the bread of life: he that cometh to me shall not hunger, and he that believeth on me shall never thirst.

36 But I said unto you, that ye have seen me, and yet believe not.

37 All that which the Father giveth me shall come unto me; and him that cometh to me I will in no wise cast out.

38 For I am come down from heaven, not to do mine own will, but the will of him that sent me.

39 And this is the will of him that sent me, that of all that which he hath given me I should lose nothing, but should raise it up at the last day.

40 For this is the will of my Father, that every one that beholdeth the Son, and believeth on him, should have eternal life; and I will raise him up at the last day.

Queries

a. How could they have the audacity to ask Jesus to work a sign?

b. What is the contrast between "manna" and the "true bread out of heaven"?

c. Does verses 37-39 teach "eternal security"?

239

Paraphrase

Therefore they said to Him, What wonder do You perform that we may see it and believe in You? What can You do to compare with what our forefathers saw? They ate the heaven-sent manna, as the Scripture says, He gave them bread out of heaven to eat. Jesus then said to them, I tell you most solemnly, it was not Moses who gave you the bread from heaven, nor was the manna the genuine Bread from heaven. My Father gives you the genuine Bread out of heaven, for the genuine Bread of God is He Who comes down out of heaven and gives Life unto the world. They replied, Lord, give us this Bread forever more! Jesus answered them, I am the Bread of Life. He who surrenders and follows Me will never be hungry for spiritual sustenance, and he who trusts and obeys Me will never thirst for righteousness. But as I told you before, although you have seen me manifest the works of God, still you do not trust and obey Me. All whom My Father draws to Me will come unto Me and I will never refuse nor reject one of them who comes to Me because I have come down from heaven not to do My Own will, but to do the will of Him Who sent me. And this is the will of Him who sent Me, that I should not lose, through inability, any of those whom God has drawn unto Me. For this is also the will of My Father, that every one who continues to behold the Son with a trusting and obedient recognition should have eternal life; and that I should raise him up at the last day.

Summary

Jesus introduces Himself as the Bread of Life. He makes several claims to deity in answer to their misguided requests for a carnal sign. He further promises not to lose, through powerlessness or refusal, anyone drawn unto Him by the Father.

Comment

Why did the crowd ask for a sign? Had He not just given them one in the loaves and fishes? They seem to demand a sign directly from heaven. This is evident from Jesus' answer. The crowd did not mention any comparison with Moses, but Jesus read their thoughts. He had claimed to be greater than Moses, yet He had not caused manna to rain from heaven. His sign had been merely to take bread and fish already supplied and make more bread and more fish. "Moses gave us bread direct from heaven — if You are greater than Moses, show us a sign directly from heaven."

In verses 32 and 33, their evaluation is shown to be faulty. In the first place, it was not Moses who gave them the manna, but God through Moses. Secondly, the manna was perishable bread, feeding only the physical hunger, while the genuine Bread of God is the Son of God. He satisfies the hunger of the soul. He gives Life with a capital *L* to the world. The manna fed only the Jewish nation, and for only a limited time. The Bread of God feeds everyone who comes to Him for all eternity.

Verse 34 betrays these Galileans as being so eager to fulfill their materialistic desires that they do not sense the divine mysteriousness of Jesus' answer, and they hastily interpret Him to mean literal bread.

The multitude is eager to get something from Christ, and He offers them Himself. This (v. 35) is one of the great "I am" claims of Jesus. He has also said:

a. *I am* the Light of the world (Jn. 8:12)
b. *I am* the Door (Jn. 10:7, 9)
c. *I am* the Good Shepherd (Jn. 10:11, 14)
d. *I am* the Resurrection and the Life (Jn. 11:25)
e. *I am* the Way, the Truth and the Life (Jn. 14:6)
f. *I am* the true Vine (Jn. 15:1, 5)

Christ claims to be, as the Bread of Life, the sustainer of all heavenly life. He communicates life to all who partake of Him. Compare all the other life-sustaining elements spoken of in the Scriptures:

a. The Tree of Life (Gen. 2:9; 3:22, 24; Prov. 3:18; Rev. 2:7; 22:2)
b. The Water of Life (Jn. 4:14; 7:38-39; Rev. 21:6; 22:1)
c. Word of Life (I Jn. 1:1; Jn. 6:63, 68)

Notice the parallelism of "coming to me" and "believing on me." To come to Jesus is to follow Him in trust and obedience. Jesus only introduces Himself as the Bread of Life here — the process of assimilation is explained later.

In verse 36 Jesus refers His listeners to His previous soul-searching statement in verse 26. Although they had seen the miracle and its evident sign that He was deity, they would not surrender to His spiritual kingdom and His rule over their hearts. Their spiritual understanding had been darkened by materialism. They had seen Him work many miracles in Galilee, even to the raising of the widow's dead son (cf. Map No. 3, page 170).

But the unbelief of the multitudes, both in Judea and now here in Galilee, will not bring disaster and loss to those few who do trust and obey Him. His cause will not suffer ruin, neither will His followers be defeated. They will conquer through His victory. He and His are not dependent upon public favor or support, but are supplied with divinely eternal Power.

Verse 37 also considers the question, "How does God give anyone to Jesus?"

a. He draws them to Himself and His Son by His love which has been shed abroad in our hearts (cf. Rom. 5:5; Jn. 3:16).

b. He gives them to the Son through His drawing, and their own free choice. That the freedom of choice is man's prerogative is evident from *all other Scripture and this context*. Man exercises this prerogative until the end of his life on earth. Even after having become a member of the body of Christ (the church) he continually chooses to remain in the fold, or is consequently lost. In exercising this choice, man must continually "show his faith by his works" (cf. Jas. 2:18).

Jesus will never refuse or reject any who come to Him and abide in Him (cf. Jn. 15:1-10). Man's rejection by God is caused by man's rejection of God.

The reason Jesus will not cast any out is that He has come to be baptized (immersed) in the will of the Father. Not only so, but He has also sacrificed the glories of heaven, and has come down to earth to accomplish the Father's will.

In verses 39 and 40 Jesus explains the "will of the Father" more fully. God foreknows who will believe and who will reject, in the sense of foreknowing what men will do. He sees all time as present. He foreknows who will be faithful and, by grace, gives the faithful to Jesus. But these verses are far from teaching any such notions as "once in grace, always in grace." Quite to the contrary, the emphasis here is upon Jesus' *ability* and *willingness* to save that soul, which of its own free will continues committed to Him. The emphasis is not upon an "irresistable grace." Jesus is able to save to the uttermost all those that abide in Him of their own volition. There definitely is the possibility of falling from grace and being eternally lost — even after having come into covenant relationship with God through Jesus (cf. Jn. 17:12; Acts 8:14-24; Gal. 5:4). If there is no possibility of the elect ever falling from grace, why were *all* of the epistles of the New Testament written to warn the elect from falling from grace?! Such doctrines as "irresistable salvation" and "eternal security" are not taught in the New Testament!

The true interpretation of this particular passage can only mean that Jesus keeps only those who remain faithful, from being lost. The Greek participles *theoron* and *pisteuon* (beholding and believing) are in the present tense and can only mean continuing action. One must continue to behold and obey in order that Jesus may keep him from being lost.

Quiz

1. Why did the multitudes ask for a sign in order that they might believe? What did they think about the sign He had just given them?
2. Name five "I am" claims of Jesus.
3. What is another way of saying, "he that cometh to me"?
4. How does God "give" men to Jesus?
5. Does John 6:39 teach "once saved, never lost?"

THE BREAD OF LIFE, II

Text 6:41-51

41 The Jews therefore murmured concerning him, because he said, I am the bread which came down out of heaven.

42 And they said, Is not this Jesus, the son of Joseph, whose father and mother we know? how doth he now say, I am come down out of heaven?

43 Jesus answered and said unto them, Murmur not among yourselves.

44 No man can come to me, except the Father that sent me draw him: and I will raise him up in the last day.

45 It is written in the prophets, And they shall all be taught of God. Every one that hath heard from the Father, and hath learned, cometh unto me.

46 Not that any man hath seen the Father, save he that is from God, he hath seen the Father.

47 Verily, verily, I say unto you, He that believeth hath eternal life.

48 I am the bread of life.

49 Your fathers ate the manna in the wilderness, and they died.

50 This is the bread which cometh down out of heaven, that a man may eat thereof, and not die.

51 I am the living bread which came down out of heaven: if any man eat of this bread, he shall live forever: yea and the bread which I will give is my flesh, for the life of the world.

Queries

a. Why did these people call Joseph Jesus' father?

b. If only those whom the Father draws can come to Jesus, how do we know who is drawn?

c. How is it possible for Christ's flesh to be the Bread of Life? How may man eat of it?

Paraphrase

Because Jesus said, I am the Bread which came down out of heaven, the Jews muttered among themselves, saying, Is not this Jesus, the Son of Joseph, Whose father and mother we know? How then can He say, I have come down out of heaven? Jesus answered them, Stop muttering one to another among yourselves. The reason you cannot accept My claims is bcause of your trust in human knowledge and wisdom, for no one is able to come to Me unless the Father Who sent Me draws him; and those drawn to Me by My Father I will raise up in the last day. Men will be drawn to me, as the prophets said, in this manner: And they shall all be taught of God. Everyone who has heard the Word of God and has learned in his heart is coming to Me. This, of course, does not imply that any mortal has ever seen God face to face. He Who comes from the Father has seen Him. I tell you most emphatically, He who is trusting and obeying Me is now possessing eternal life. I am the Bread of Life — I am the source of eternal life. The fathers you so eagerly referred to before, ate the manna in the wilderness; yet they died. But this is the Bread that comes down out of heaven, so that anyone may eat of it and never die. I am this living Bread which came down from heaven. If anyone eats of this Bread, he will live forever. The Bread that I shall give for the life of the world is My flesh.

Summary

Again the Jews display their utter lack of spiritual insight.
The way to spiritual knowledge is to be drawn of God unto His
Son; the way to be drawn is to hear and learn the Word of God.
The heaven-sent Food which gives eternal life is the atoning
death of Christ. Men appropriate this Food by trusting and
obeying the Son of God.

Comment

From the moment Jesus had declared Himself to be sent from
the heavenly presence of God, the Jews began to mutter among
themselves. One after another was saying, "Isn't this Jesus of
Nazareth, Son of Joseph the carpenter? why, we know His
mother and father! How can He be from heaven? Preposterous!" They were judging by human standards; they rejected
Jesus because:
   a. They judged things by human values and external
      standards
   b. They were too eager to express their opinions and argue,
      while they were not at all interested in God's revealed will.
   c. They listened, but would not learn (cf. Jn. 5:39-42).

These Jews sound just like our self-styled "modernists" of
today who still stumble over the claims of Jesus to be heaven-
sent. Today's skeptics also "know" Joseph (or some other mortal)
to be the father of Jesus. The Galileans said this before (cf. Mt.
13:56; Mk. 6:3). Most conservative scholars see strong inference
for the virgin birth here. These Jews were well aware that, when
Jesus claimed to be sent from heaven, He was claiming supernatural birth into this world. When they muttered about "Knowing His father and mother" the inference is strong that Jesus may
even have mentioned His virgin birth — at least He implied it.
The Fourth Gospel complements the Synoptics in the doctrine
of the virgin birth (cf. Introduction, page 14).

In verses 44 and 45 Jesus explains the reason for their failure
to grasp the significance of His teaching. Then He shows them
the way to true spiritual knowledge and wisdom. There can be
no true knowledge of God apart from His revealed Word. Some
may gain partial knowledge of God through nature (cf. Rom.
1:19-20). To know God in the inward man, however, one must
hear His Word and learn of Him. Thousands *hear* God's Word
but never *learn* it! It is as Jesus said, men must will to do God's
will in order to really *learn* of God (cf. Jn. 7:17).

The major discussion of these two verses (44-45) today, however, centers in the *manner* of God's drawing men unto Jesus. There is no excuse for all the abuse and misinterpretation to which these verses have been subjected. Jesus interprets His statement concerning the "drawing" with preciseness and lucidness. Men and women are drawn to Him through God's revealed Word. The drawing power comes from a knowledge of God's purposes culminating in the "lifting up of the Son of man." R. C. Foster's comments on these verses are very appropriate here:

"The coming is man' part; the drawing is God's part; both work together. God draws men to Jesus by the death of Jesus on the cross. 'If I be lifted up, I will draw all men unto me.' No man can come to Jesus as Saviour and King in the full sense until God has by His divine plan provided the mysterious drawing power of the cross. The statement of Jesus seems to be in sympathy for the crowd in their rejection of Him. They do not understand His spiritual message, but when He has been crucified before them and the gospel of the cross proclaimed if they do not come to Him then, there is no hope. The drawing is to be done by hearing 'from the Father,' i.e., hearing the Word of God and learning the Way of Life. The drawing cannot be irresistible, otherwise man would be but a machine and no one could choose whether or not He should come to Jesus. No one could accept and obey for himself, if he could not resist the drawing. No man could 'come' to God if he could not also 'refuse to come.' Jesus cites the teaching of God in the Old Testament as the very thing which should have helped to draw them and to cause them to come to Him."

The quotation from the Old Testament is not specific, but general (cf. Isa. 54:13; 60:2-3; Jer. 31:33-34; Joel 2:28; Mic. 4:2; Zeph. 3:9; Mal. 1:11).

Although we may learn of God through the Son Who has come from the Father's very bosom, we still do not fully comprehend His purposes and actions, for we are limited by finite restraints and physical hindrances (cf. I Jn. 4:12, 20). Someday, however, we shall see God face to face (cf. I Jn. 3:2). But until then we must behold Him by faith and trust in the incarnate Son.

In verses 47-51 Jesus shows further that coming to God is done through faith in the Son. He is the Bread of Life. We are told that we must eat of the Bread of Life. How are we to do this? Verse 51 is the key. The act which truly makes Jesus the Bread of Life is His atoning death upon the cross. This atonement was done willingly (He *gave* His flesh. cf. Gal. 2:20; Eph. 5:2; Mt. 20:28). To believe (trust, adhere to, obey) is man's way to eat the Bread of Life. The Scriptures teach burial in baptism to be the culminating act where man appropriates the blood of Christ and His atoning death to man's sins (Rom. 6:1-11; Gal. 3:26-27; Col. 2:10-13; Titus 3:4-7).

Quiz

1. What is the significance of the statement of the Jews, "Is not this Jesus, the son of Joseph . . . ?" What is implied?
2. How does one learn of God?
3. How may we know the true interpretation of verses 44-45?
4. What is the drawing power of God (cf. Jn. 3:14; 8:28; 12:32; I Cor. 1:23-24)?
5. Is this drawing able to be resisted? Explain.
6. While we are in this world, how do we behold God?
7. How are we to eat the Bread of Life? How do we appropriate Christ's blood to our sins?

THE BREAD OF LIFE, III

Text 6:52-59

52 The Jews therefore strove one with another, saying, How can this man give us his flesh to eat?
53 Jesus therefore said unto them, Verily, verily, I say unto you, Except ye eat the flesh of the Son of man and drink his blood, ye have not life in yourselves.
54 He that eateth my flesh and drinketh my blood hath eternal life; and I will raise him up at the last day.
55 For my flesh is meat indeed, and my blood is drink indeed.
56 He that eateth my flesh and drinketh my blood abideth in me, and I in him.
57 As the living Father sent me, and I live because of the Father; so he that eateth me, he also shall live because of me.
58 This is the bread which came down out of heaven: not as the fathers ate, and died; he that eateth this bread shall live for ever.
59 These things said he in the synagogue, as he taught in Capernaum.

Queries

a. Why did Jesus speak so emphatically of eating His flesh and drinking His blood?

b. Where, besides verse 56, does Jesus tell how we may abide in Him, and He in us?

c. What is a synagogue, and where in Capernaum?

Paraphrase

The Jews argued angrily with one another, saying, How can He give us His flesh to eat? Jesus replied, I assure you, unless you eat the flesh of the Son of Man and drink His blood you have no Life in yourselves. The one trusting wholeheartedly in the saving efficacy of My death is the one eating My flesh and drinking My blood, and he possesses eternal life. This is true, for My body and blood sacrificed for the world's sin is the genuine food and drink for the soul of man. He who feeds on this spiritual food and drink dwells continually in Me and I also dwell in him. Just as the Father of Life sent Me, and I live by abiding in the Father, even so whoever continues to feed on Me shall live through Me. This is the Bread which came down from heaven. It is not like the manna of which your forefathers ate and died. To the contrary, he who eats the Bread from heaven shall live forever. He said these things in a synagogue while He was teaching in Capernaum.

Summary

Westcott summarizes this section in one sentence: "The personal appropriation of the incarnate Son." In verses 41-51 the question of the Jews was the Personage of Jesus, "Is this not the son of Joseph?" Jesus answered that question. Now the question of the Jews (v. 52-59) is, "How does He communicate to us this life which He claims to offer?" Jesus answers in figurative language: men must take His life into the very center and core of their hearts; men must eat the spiritual dynamic which He alone is able to provide.

Comment

The crowd is a little nauseated (cf. v. 60-61) at the literal implication, which they themselves attach to His words. Their objection is open and argumentative. Unbelief always takes offense at the truth. He is demanding that every man who desires eternal life must eat His flesh. Over and over (cf. v. 53, 54, 55, 56, 57, 58) He repeats the demand that men must eat His flesh and drink His blood. Why is Jesus so emphatic? What does He mean? Can it be that He means a literal eating of flesh and blood? Impossible! Yet, ever since Jesus uttered these words men have misinterpreted and wrested them to suit their purposes and schemes. The Transubstantiationists pervert this context to support their absurd doctrine of the actual presence of the flesh and the blood of Christ in the Loaf and the cup. They contend that one must literally partake of the flesh and blood of Jesus, and they, therefore, sacrifice the body of Jesus anew each week at the Mass. The book of Hebrews is plain as to the heretical nature of such a practice (cf. Heb. 10:10, 12). The sacrifice made of Christ's body at Calvary was "once for all."

The Sacramentalists also pervert this passage. According to the Sacramentalists, this passage demands unfailing observance of the Lord's supper. They make the Sacrament the means of life. According to this teaching, the Christian, by absenting himself from the Lord's Table, cuts himself off from any contact with the saving blood of Jesus Christ. Carried to its logical conclusion, this doctrine is equally as heretical as the Roman Catholic's transubstantiation. The Sacramentalist theory comes very near the Roman system of meritorious works.

None of these false doctrines would prevail today if religious leaders would read this context and apply only the very basic rules of Hermeneutics. A first principle in the interpretation of *any* book is: "Let an author's own explanation of his meaning take precedence over any other interpretation." Jesus Himself explains exactly what He means by "eating" His flesh and "drinking" His blood when He says, "It is the *spirit* that giveth life; the *flesh* profiteth nothing: *the words that I have spoken unto you are spirit, and are life.*" (Jn. 6:63) (Italics mine). It would profit us nothing to eat the literal flesh and blood of Jesus, even if it were possible. We appropriate the flesh and blood of Jesus (Life) when we partake of His humanity and His divinity by abiding in all the words of Jesus and His apostles.

The absolute necessity of living by abiding in God's Word is the point of emphasis here, not the literal flesh. The message Jesus seeks to deliver here is that He is the Word of God manifest in the flesh, and that this multitude must divorce their minds from seeking only the physical bread, and turn to the heavenly Bread of Life (cf. Mt. 4:4). The great apostle Paul says it so clearly, "I have been crucified with Christ; and it is no longer I that live, but Christ liveth in me: and that life which ı now live in the flesh I live in faith, the faith which is in the Son of God, who loved me and gave himself up for me." (Gal. 2:20).

To eat and to drink is to assimilate something external to oneself, digest it and make it a part of one's very being. That is what Paul does by living in faith. There is much more to eating and drinking the flesh and blood of the Son of man than partaking of the Lord's Supper, for even that observance, regardless of how often, may be done unto condemnation unless accompanied with proper attitudes of faith and love and obedience. *"Besides,"* as Barnes says, *"there is no evidence that he (Jesus) had any reference in this passage to the Lord's Supper."*

By assimilating His sacrificed body to our spiritual life, we abide in Him (v. 56). To abide in Him is to continue in His commandments, to participate in the benefits of His death, and to bear fruit. Check all the following references to abiding in Him:

a. Love and obey (Jn. 14:15-17; 14:21; 14:23; 15:10).
b. Bear fruit (Jn. 15:1-6).
c. Dwell in unity (Jn. 17:21-23).
d. Walk as Jesus walked (I Jn. 2:6).
e. Love one another (I Jn. 2:10; 3:17-18; 4:12-13).
f. Let the apostle's words abide in us (I Jn. 2:24).
g. Refrain from continuing in sin (I Jn. 3:6-9).
h. Keep His commandments (I Jn. 3:24).
i. Confess Jesus as the Son of God (I Jn. 4:15).
j. Abide (continue, dwell) in love (I Jn. 4:16).

A very few early manuscripts add, at the end of verse 56, this gloss: "even as the Father is in me and I in the Father. Verily, verily, I say unto you, unless ye receive the body of the Son of man as the bread of life ye have not life in him." Most of our earliest and best manuscripts (Aleph, B, etc.), however, omit this gloss, It is very interesting to note that the latest great manuscript on the Fourth Gospel (Bodmer Papyrus, P. 66) also omits this gloss: more evidence for the purity of our present text.

Verse 57 reads much the same as 5:26. The Son, being One with the Father, "has life in Himself." Because He has life we may be partakers of that life, if we eat Him. The food which Christ gives is His Incarnation. The "bread which came

down out of heaven" is the humanity of Christ. The best explanation for the reason behind Jesus' taking the form of flesh and
blood is found in Hebrews 2:14-18. Christ's participation in our
nature was necessary in order that He might conquer death.
His Incarnation is not only the means of our salvation, but an
example for our daily profession (cf. Phil. 2:5-8). It is well to
note here that the word *trogon* (the one eating) is in the present
tense and must be translated "the one continuing to eat me
. . ." etc. Assimilation of the Bread of Life must be continuous.

In verses 33 and 35 Jesus stated that He was the genuine
Bread from heaven, as contrasted with the transistory manna
which was only the type. The temporal nature of the manna is
emphasized again here in verse 58.

Among the ruins of Tell-Hum, one of the given sites of
Capernaum, an explorer found what remains of a once elegant
synagogue. Upon one of the stone blocks of the former synagogue he found an engraving of a pot of manna. Westcott
remarks, "This very symbol may have been before the eyes of
those who heard the Lord's words." Jesus taught in other synagogues in other villages and cities (cf. Lk. 4:16; Mt. 12:9).

Quiz

1. Give some Scriptural reasons why Transubstantiation is a
false doctrine.
2. Why is the theory of the Sacramentalists wrong?
3. How should Jesus' words be interpreted?
4. What do you think Jesus means by eating and drinking?
5. Is there any evidence that Jesus is speaking of the Lord's
Supper in this passage?
6. Name at least five ways of abiding in Christ.
7. Why, according to Hebrews 2:14-18, did Jesus take upon
Himself the form of flesh and blood?

THE BREAD OF LIFE, EXPLAINED

Text 6:60-65

**60 Many therefore of his disciples, when they heard this, said,
This is a hard saying; who can hear it?**
**61 But Jesus knowing in himself that his disciples murmured
at this, said unto them, Doth this cause you to stumble?**
**62 What then if ye should behold the Son of man ascending
where he was before?**

251

63 It is the spirit that giveth life; the flesh profiteth nothing: the words that I have spoken unto you are spirit, and are life. **64** But there are some of you that believe not. For Jesus knew from the beginning who they were that believed not, and who it was that should betray him.
65 And he said, For this cause have I said unto you, that no man can come unto me, except it be given unto him of the Father.

Queries

   a. What was hard about Jesus' saying?
   b. Why did Jesus mention His future ascension?
   c. How do words give life?

Paraphrase

Now when the great crowds of Galilean followers heard this, many of them said, This saying is offensive and hard to tolerate. Who can be expected to accept such teaching? But Jesus, knowing within Himself that these disciples were protesting concerning His teaching, said to them, Are you stumbling and entrapping yourselves over my teaching? What then will be your reaction should you see the Son of man ascending to heaven where He was before? Eating My flesh would gain you nothing; the Spirit is that which makes alive. The words that I have spoken unto you, they are Spirit and they are Life. But some of you still refuse to trust and obey Me, for Jesus knew from the beginning who they were that did not believe and who it was that should betray Him. And He said, On account of this have I told you that no one can come to Me unless he is drawn unto Me by the Father.

Summary

The Jews openly express their repugnance to Jesus' teaching. He, in turn, explains the real meaning behind His figurative discourse of eating His flesh. The *words* of Jesus are to be assimilated unto life — not His literal flesh. All of this serves to emphasize the fact that only the spiritually-minded (those drawn by the Father) can come to Jesus.

Comment

The Greek word translated "hard" is *skleros,* and does not mean "hard to understand," but "hard to accept, intolerable, exacting." It was not that this multitude of Galilean disciples had failed to understand the implications of Jesus' words. They were murmuring and protesting because they *did* understand Him to a certain degree. They understood Him to be saying, throughout the discourse, that He was the Messiah, and His kingdom was one of the Spirit, of self surrender and obedience to God's Word. They were disgusted with Him because He said, in essence, "the kingdom of God is not eating and drinking, but righteousness and peace and joy in the Holy Spirit" (cf. Rom. 14:17).

We quote here some excellent comments by Barclay in his *Daily Study Bible, The Gospel of John,* Volume 1, page 234.

"Here we come upon a truth that re-emerges in every age. Time and again it is not the intellectual difficulty of accepting Christ which keeps men from becoming Christians; it is the height of Christ's moral demand . . . The real difficulty of Christianity is two-fold. It demands an act of surrender to Christ, an acceptance of Him as the final authority; and it demands a moral standard wherein only the pure in heart may see God . . . The disciples were well aware that Jesus had claimed to be the very life and mind of God come down to earth; their difficulty was to accept that that was true, with all the implications which are in it. And to this day many a man's refusal of Christ comes, not because Christ puzzles and baffles his intellect, but because Christ challenges and condemns his life."

Some commentators find in verse 62 a promise of Jesus intended to clarify His claims and teachings. In other words, when He is resurrected and ascended, then these disciples will have a guarantee of all His claims to be the Bread out of Heaven, and an explanation of all His teachings concerning eating and drinking His flesh and blood. The context, however, seems to indicate otherwise. They have taken offence at His presentation of Himself as having descended out of Heaven, and that He is the Bread of life which must be eaten. "What then will be your reaction," says Jesus, "if you see and be taught that the Son of man ascends to heaven where He was before?" We know very well what their reaction was. They stumbled, took offence and hardened their hearts (cf. Acts 7:55-58).

Verse 63 is the *key* to this entire discourse on the Bread of Life. We present here two great commentators' paraphrases of this passage:

Albert Barnes: "My doctrine is spiritual; it is fitted to quicken and nourish the soul. It is from heaven. Your doctrine or your views are earthly, and may be called flesh, or fleshly, as pertaining only to the support of the body. You place a great value on the doctrine that Moses fed the body; yet that did not permanently profit, for your fathers are dead. You seek also food from me, but your views are gross and earthly."

William Hendriksen: "My flesh as such cannot benefit you; stop thinking that I was asking you literally to eat my body or literally to drink my blood. It is my spirit, my person, in the act of giving my body to be broken and my blood to be shed, that bestows and sustains life, even everlasting life."

The more one reads this entire passage, the more he begins to see that these disciples said one thing and thought another. It seems almost certain that they did not really believe Jesus to mean literal eating and drinking flesh and blood. This was a Hebrew way of saying "abiding in the words and commands of another" long before Christ said it here. They knew what Jesus meant. When they expressed horror (v. 52) at eating His flesh, it probably was a clever dodge of the real issue.

One thing is certain. Jesus makes the meaning of His entire discourse plain enough in verse 63 that "he who runs may read." The entire body of doctrine of Christ is the source of life eternal.

     a. His words shall judge us (Jn. 12:48).
     b. His commandment is life eternal (Jn. 12:50).
     c. His word is able to build up and give an inheritance among the saints (Acts 20:32).
     d. His word is able to save our souls (Jas. 1:21).
     e. His word gives us a new birth (I Pet. 1:22-23).

The passage in Romans 8:1-17 offers itself as an excellent commentary of Jesus' words in verse 63. The summation of this passage in Romans can be made by quoting just two verses: "for if ye live after the flesh, ye must die; but if by the Spirit ye put to death the deeds of the body, ye shall live. For as many as are led by the Spirit of God, these are the sons of God," (Rom. 8:13-14). We are led by the Spirit, of course, when we are led by the words of Christ and the apostles.

For Jesus' power to read the hearts and minds of men, see our comments on 2:23-25. This power is expressed again here in verse 64.

254

And in verse 65 Jesus again expresses the fact, as He has before in this same discourse (v. 37, 44) that men cannot come to Him unless they are spiritually drawn by the Father and by submission of their own wills (cf. our comments on vs. 37, and 44).

Quiz

1. What did the disciples mean by saying, "This is a *hard* saying, Who can hear it?"
2. What is the major barrier for most people to overcome before accepting Christ? Is it intellectual?
3. Did the Jews take offence at the teaching of the Ascension of Christ? Give a Scriptural example.
4. What is so outstanding about verse 63 in this discourse?
5. Give at least three Scriptural references to show that the Word of God is the way to Life.
6. What connection does Romans 8:1-17 have with John 6:63?
7. Does verse 63 show the falseness of Transubstantiation and Sacramentalism? How?

THE TWELVE — THEIR FINEST HOUR

Text 6:66-71

66 Upon this many of his disciples went back, and walked no more with him.

67 Jesus said therefore unto the twelve, Would ye also go away?

68 Simon Peter answered him, Lord, to whom shall we go? thou has the words of eternal life.

69 And we have believed and know that thou art the Holy One of God.

70 Jesus answered them, Did not I choose you the twelve, and one of you is a devil?

71 Now he spake of Judas the son of Simon Iscariot, for he it was that should betray him, being one of the twelve.

Queries

   a. Why did Jesus question the twelve?
   b. What is the significance of Peter's answer?
   c. Why does Jesus mention the betrayer?

Paraphrase

On account of this, many of His disciples left Him and returned to their former way of living and thinking. Then Jesus said to the twelve, You do not also wish to leave Me, do you? But Simon Peter, answering for the group, said, Lord, to whom shall we go? You alone have the words which lead unto eternal life. And we have learned to believe and have come to know that You are the Holy One of God. And Jesus answered them, Did I not expressly choose you as the Twelve? And yet, I know that one of you is a minister of the devil. He was speaking of Judas, son of Simon Iscariot, for this Judas was about to betray Him, even though he was one of the Twelve.

Summary

This is the "moment of truth" for the Twelve. The superficial disciples have been tried, and have judged themselves unfit for His kingdom. However, for the Twelve (excluding Judas), this is their "finest hour."

Comment

Most of the scholars agree that the phrase "After this" introducing verse 66, is a phrase which shows result as well as passage of time. The preceding discourse was not easily tolerated by the multitudes, and a further result of the sermon on the Bread of Life was the defection of many of His Galilean disciples. These "many disciples" were both "fair-weather friends," and disciples of Jesus. They followed Him as long as they thought He was going to give them bread on their tables. But at the first intimation of the spiritual and moral food — the cross and self-surrender on their part — they turned their backs on Jesus. The inference of the original language here helps us to interpret their actions even more fully. They not only ceased following Jesus, but they "gave up what they had gained with Him, and . . . reoccupied their old places." Before, they had called Him Rabbi and Lord (cf. 6:25, 34), but now they disclaimed Him even as unfit to listen to. They had attached themselves to His "bandwagon" — they had put their hands to the plow without first counting the cost. Now, having turned back, they judged themselves unfit for the kingdom of God (cf. Lk. 6:62). The very same attitude prevails today. There are far too many today who, having started with Jesus, have failed to count the cost and are now inactive church-members. (cf. Lk. 14:25-35).

Then the Lord challenges His chosen Twelve in a most direct
manner. What a test this must have been for them! Up to this
moment Jesus was the "Man of the hour" in Galilee. To be one
of His personally-chosen inner-circle was to enjoy a certain
amount of prestige in Galilee. To be one of the Twelve, and to
see the great popularity of its leader was to have great expectations. But now the Man of Galilee is losing His following and
His prestige at one crucial moment when thousands are turning
disgustedly away.

What were the emotions of the Twelve — fear, hate, disgust
and shame? Were they also on the verge of deserting the Lord?
Indeed not! Peter, probably because of his age and personality,
speaks for the Twelve a classic confession full of faith and
devotion to Jesus. Although undoubtedly puzzled and distressed
by the mysterious words of Jesus, Peter is convinced that Jesus
alone has the words leading unto eternal life. We quote here
Professor R. C. Foster's comments on verses 68 and 69:

"When we meet things in Scripture irreconcilable with
our reason, what should be our conclusion? Peter has sum-
med up the true attitude of the Christian. God has not promised to satisfy our curiosity or all our intellectual problems, but
He rather demands that we walk by faith when we cannot
see the way. We should use our reason and all intellectual
gifts in endeavoring to understand, but we should not desert
Christ because we find difficulties. If we cast aside the Bible
just where is the Book of God to be found that will lead us
to eternal life?"

The perfect tenses of the verbs "have believed" and "have
come to know" show that Peter's answer was one of an understanding born of a clear perception . . . through progressive
experience. We must know the Lord before we can believe Him.
Faith is not born of emotion. We must have knowledge of His
life, His claims, and the evidence by which He establishes the
validity of His claims. We must then weigh this evidence and
make a decision as to whether we shall trust Him or reject Him.
This does not mean, however, that we are to reject Jesus and
His words when we cannot understand every thing He says. As
with the Twelve, we have more than sufficient evidence to prove
Jesus' identity as the Son of God. The confession of Peter as
compared with the rejection by the multitude emphasizes further
the axiom that rejection of Christ is generally on moral grounds
and not intellectual.

Peter's impulsiveness and over-confidence, shown by his instantaneous confession on behalf of the whole company, receives a check by Jesus as it does at other times. The Lord cautions him here, as in Matt. 16:23, John 20:15-22; Mark 14:29-30, not to be too confident, for one of the Twelve did not share his faith and trust.

The question is always raised, in connection with verses 70 and 71: "If Jesus knew Judas would betray Him, why did He choose him?" We can only answer, "It was within God's Infinite wisdom, will and plan for the redemption of the world." More than that, we can only speculate. One thing is certain: God did not compel Judas to betray Christ. Jesus tried repeatedly to turn Judas from his evil scheme by warning him that He was aware of his intentions.

Judas is carefully described here as the son of Simon, called Iscariot (a man of Kerioth) probably an area of Judah (cf. Josh. 15:25). This distinguishes him from the other Judas, also one of the Twelve.

Thus this Sixth Chapter has been fitly called "The Great Galilean Crisis" for here the great multitudes of Galilean disciples come to the moment of truth, and fail the test. On the other hand, for the chosen apostles (except Judas), this is their finest hour. They are also put into the crucible, but come out purified. This is the turning point in Jesus' public ministry. Henceforth He will (except for occasional emotional outbursts such as at the Triumphal Entry) be unpopular, criticized, and hunted like an animal throughout all Judea.

Quiz

1. What caused the many disciples to desert Jesus?
2. Why would this be such a big test for the Twelve?
3. How should we react to sayings of Jesus which are difficult to understand?
4. What brought Peter to say, "we have come to know"?
5. How was Peter's display of overconfidence checked by Jesus here?
6. Why is John 6 entitled, "The Great Galilean Crisis"?

258

EXPOSITORY SERMON NO. 6

THE BREAD OF LIFE

Introduction

I PERIOD OF GREAT POPULARITY
  A. Climax of Great Galilean ministry
    1. Great multitudes followed Him.
      a. Visualize the great excitement to catch full meaning of this chapter.
II JESUS' COMPASSION
  A. His compassion not because of their hunger, but because "they were as sheep not having a shepherd."

Discussion

I THE MIRACLE
  A. Describe.
  B. Teaching aspect of the miracle
    1. Passover near — God's sacrificial lambs would be eaten.
    2. What the bread of the miracle was to their bodies, His atoning death (His flesh and blood) would be to their souls.
    3. The spiritually minded would learn of His deity and Messiahship.
    4. The carnally minded would be satisfied with having been filled with the physical food.
  C. The miracle was used by Jesus to sift His disciples.
    1. Could not allow this multitude to continue to follow Him without their knowing the real nature of His Kingdom . . . this would be under false pretenses.
    2. Gospel still sifts today!
      a. It is still a spiritual kingdom.
      b. It still costs, and demands that members count the cost.
      c. There is no promise of physical peace or prosperity for men merely because they become Christians.
  D. Result of the Miracle
    1. They seek to force Him to be their physical king.
    2. Jesus expected certain results:

259

THE GOSPEL OF JOHN

          a. Thoughts of their own hearts needed revealing.
          b. They sought Him, not because of the signs of His Messiahship and deity, but because they had eaten of the loaves and were filled.
   3. Application:
     WE NEED TO ASK OURSELVES THIS QUESTION: WHY DO I FOLLOW CHRIST? It is because of family tradition, because it is the line of least resistance, because of reputation, because of worldly advantage?

II THE SERMON
  A. Jesus introduces by saying:
    1. "You are seeking the wrong things — set your hearts on the spiritual things."
    2. The multitudes say, "How . . . What must we do that we may work the works of God?"
    3. Jesus answers, "Believe on Me."
      a. Jesus Himself taught that faith and works are one and the same . . . we are saved by works as well as by faith
      b. Believing is working
  B. The true Bread of Life is:
    1. Jesus . . . the Person
    2. His atoning death and justifying resurrection is the food for our spiritual life.
    3. The Jews may have thought Jesus spoke of His literal flesh
    BUT JESUS INTERPRETS HIS WHOLE DISCOURSE BY SAYING . . . "THE WORDS THAT I HAVE SPOKEN UNTO YOU, THEY ARE SPIRIT AND THEY ARE LIFE . . ."
    LET US ALLOW JESUS TO INTERPRET HIS OWN SERMON!
  C. The True Bread of Life:
    1. Gives life to the souls of men.
  D. How do we eat this Bread?
    1. Believe — trust — obey Jesus
    2. There are too many "runt" Christians, stunted because they have stopped eating . . . "faith cometh by hearing and hearing by the Word of God."
    THOUSANDS OF BABES IN CHRIST ARE DYING OF SPIRITUAL MALNUTRITION

3. Then there are thousands more dying because they have been fed POISONED BREAD OF LIFE!

    a. A MAN WHO FEEDS POISONED FOOD TO PEOPLE IS A CRIMINAL . . . SO FALSE PREACHERS AND TEACHERS ARE GUILTY OF SPIRITUAL MURDER

    b. Pharisees compassed land and sea to make one proselyte . . . but then they made him twofold more a son of Hell by their false doctrines.

II THE SIFTING

A. Multitudes really knew what Jesus meant when He said, "Except ye eat my flesh and drink my blood . . ."

    1. Their rejection of Him was moral . . . not intellectual.

    2. They wanted to dodge the issue by saying "How can we eat this Man's flesh?"

        a. THE SAYING WAS NOT HARD TO UNDERSTAND, BUT INTOLERABLE TO THEIR CARNAL MINDS.

        b. JESUS WOULD NOT BEND TO THEIR WISHES TO BE MADE A TEMPORAL KING, AND THEY LEFT HIM TO GO BACK TO THEIR OLD WAYS . . .

    3. Most of the rejection of Christ today is MORAL, and not INTELLECTUAL.

        a. It is not that men and women of America do not know about Christ and what they ought to do.

        b. THEY JUST DO NOT WANT TO FORSAKE THE WAYS OF SIN!

B. THIS WAS A GREAT TEST FOR THE TWELVE.

    1. This is their finest hour

    2. Even though confused about the kingdom, their basic desire was to know the words leading to eternal life.

    3. They passed this test of sifting because:

        a. They were sincere in their conviction that only Jesus had the words of Life

        b. They saw clearly that there were only two alternatives . . . accept Jesus and have the words of life, or reject Him and die spiritually.

C. Their confidence in Jesus was:

   1. Possible because of their intimate association with Him and hearing and obeying His teaching.

   2. One cannot trust a stranger with such confidence

   3. Their confession was a result of "having come to know . . ."
WE CANNOT TRUST JESUS TODAY UNLESS WE HAVE AN INTIMATE ASSOCIATION WITH HIM BY STUDY, OBEDIENCE PRAYER AND LABOR IN THE KINGDOM

Conclusion

I WHOLE MATTER OF ETERNAL LIFE IS IN FEEDING ON THE BREAD OF LIFE.
THIS IS DONE BY "ABIDING IN HIM . . ." CONTINUALLY.

II MUST NOT FEED UPON POISONED BREAD OF LIFE.

   A. THE MESSAGE OF ALL RELIGIOUS SECTS MUST BE TESTED AND ANALYZED.
THEY MUST BE COMPARED WITH THE DIVINE STANDARD AND FORMULA AS REVEALED IN THE NEW TESTAMENT.

III FOOD, UNLESS ASSIMILATED DOES NO GOOD.
WE MAY COME TO CHURCH 50 YEARS WITH PERFECT ATTENDANCE, BUT UNLESS THE GOSPEL GETS DOWN INSIDE AND BECOMES A PART OF OUR SPIRITUAL BLOOD STREAM, WE SHALL DIE OF RITUALISM, HYPOCRISY, ETC.

EXAMINATION — CHAPTERS 4, 5, and 6

Here are the questions — You supply the answers as stated in the Scriptures.

1. Q. "How is it that thou, being a Jew, askest drink of me, who am a Samaritan woman?"
   A.

2. Q. "Hath any man brought him aught to eat?"
   A.

3. Q. "Wouldest thou be made whole?"
   A.

4. Q. "Whence are we to buy bread, that these may eat?"

   A.

5. Q. "What must we do, that we may work the works of God?"

   A.

6. Q. "Would ye also go away?"

   A.

True or False?

1. The Samaritan woman at the well was married.
2. The woman, having come nearly two miles to get water, left her waterpot and returned to the city.
3. The sower is always sure of reaping from his own labors.
4. The nobleman was required to have faith before Jesus would heal his son.
5. The man at the pool of Bethesda was healed on the sabbath.
6. Anyone not worshipping Jesus as the Son of God does not worship God.
7. The Jews never searched the Scriptures.
8. The Sea of Galilee has four other names.
9. Jesus interprets His own discourse on the Bread of Life.
10. Jesus always knew that Judas Iscariot would betray Him.

Can You match these portions of Scripture?

1. "But the hour cometh, and now is, when the true worshippers shall worship the Father in spirit and truth:

2. "Say not ye, There are yet four months, and then cometh the harvest?

3. "The hour cometh, and now is when the dead shall hear the voice of the Son of God;

4. "Marvel not at this: for the hour cometh, in which all that are in the tombs shall hear his voice;

5. "Work not for the food which perisheth,

6. "Except ye eat the flesh of the Son of man and *drink* his blood,

7. "I am come in my Father's name, and ye receive me not:

8. "It is the spirit that giveth life; the flesh profiteth nothing:

9. "No man come to me,

10. "For this cause have I said unto you, that no man can come unto me,

a. but for the food which abideth unto eternal life,"

b. if another shall come in his own name, him ye will receive."

c. and shall come forth; they that have done good; unto the resurrection of life; and they that have done evil, unto the resurrection of judgment."

d. except it be given unto him of the Father."

e. the words that I have spoken unto you are spirit, and are life."

f. ye have not life in yourselves."

g. for such doth the Father seek to be his worshippers."

h. behold, I say unto you, Lift up your eyes, and look on the fields, that they are white already unto harvest."

i. and they that hear shall live."

j. except the Father that sent me draw him: and I will raise him up in the last day."

k. God is a spirit: and they that worship him must worship in spirit and truth."

THE GOSPEL OF JOHN

Multiple Choice

(Choose the answer which is most nearly correct)

1. "When the Lord knew that the Pharisees had heard that He was making and baptizing more disciples than John, He . . ."
   a. left Judea and went into Galilee
   b. left and went into Judea
   c. stopped making and baptizing disciples

2. The mountain upon which the Samaritans worshipped was:
   a. Mt. Gerizim
   b. Mt. Gishon
   c. Mt. Gilgal

3. If Jesus was in Samaria "four months before harvest," He was there in the month of:
   a. April or May
   b. December or January
   c. September or October

4. The man at the pool of Bethesda had been lame for:
   a. Thirty-eight years
   b. Forty-eight years
   c. Thirty-eight months

5. The great sermon in John, the fifth chapter, is called:
   a. The Sermon on the Resurrection
   b. The Sermon on the Bread of Life
   c. The Sermon on Deity

6. The Gospel of Luke tells us that the feeding of the five thousand took place near the city of:
   a. Bethesda
   b. Bethlehem
   c. Bethsaida

7. The lad brought to Jesus by Andrew had with him:
   a. five fishes and two loaves
   b. five loaves and five fishes
   c. five loaves and two fishes

8. The Sermon on the Bread of Life was delivered:
   a. In a synagogue in Capernaum
   b. On the shores of the Sea of Galilee
   c. On a mountain near Bethsaida Julias

9. Jesus interpreted His own Sermon on the Bread of Life as:
   a. His literal flesh and blood
   b. The Lord's Supper (communion service)
   c. Abiding in His words which are spirit and are life

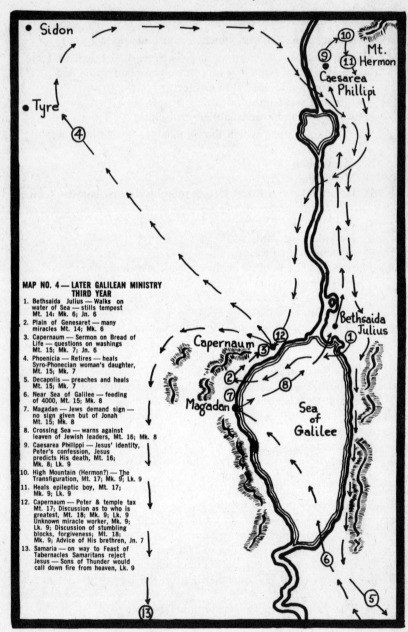

MAP NO. 4 — LATER GALILEAN MINISTRY
THIRD YEAR

1. Bethsaida Julius — Walks on water of Sea — stills tempest Mt. 14; Mk. 6; Jn. 6
2. Plain of Genesaret — many miracles Mt. 14; Mk. 6
3. Capernaum — Sermon on Bread of Life — questions on washings Mt. 15; Mk. 7; Jn. 6
4. Phoenicia — Retires — heals Syro-Phonecian woman's daughter, Mt. 15; Mk. 7
5. Decapolis — preaches and heals Mt. 15; Mk. 7
6. Near Sea of Galilee — feeding of 4000, Mt. 15; Mk. 8
7. Magadan — Jews demand sign — no sign given but of Jonah Mt. 15; Mk. 8
8. Crossing Sea — warns against leaven of Jewish leaders, Mt. 16; Mk. 8
9. Caesarea Philippi — Jesus' identity, Peter's confession, Jesus predicts His death, Mt. 16; Mk. 8; Lk. 9
10. High Mountain (Hermon?) — The Transfiguration, Mt. 17; Mk. 9; Lk. 9
11. Heals epileptic boy, Mt. 17; Mk. 9; Lk. 9
12. Capernaum — Peter & temple tax Mt. 17; Discussion as to who is greatest, Mt. 18; Mk. 9; Lk. 9 Unknown miracle worker, Mk. 9; Lk. 9; Discussion of stumbling blocks, forgiveness; Mt. 18; Mk. 9; Advice of His brethren, Jn. 7
13. Samaria — on way to Feast of Tabernacles Samaritans reject Jesus — Sons of Thunder would call down fire from heaven, Lk. 9

BIBLIOGRAPHY

Commentaries:
1. Andrews, S. J., *The Life of Our Lord Upon the Earth*
2. Barclay, Wm., *The Daily Study Bible, The Gospel of John,* Two Volumes
3. Barnes, Albert, *Barnes Notes on The New Testament, Luke and John*
4. Bernard, J. H., *Critical and Exegetical Commentary on the Gospel According to John (International Critical Commentary)*
5. Bruce, A. B., *Training of the Twelve*
6. Dods, Marcus, The Gospel of St. John *(The Expositor's Greek Testament)*
7. Foster, R. C., *An Introduction to the Life of Christ*
8. Foster, R. C., *Studies in the Life of Christ,* Volume I
9. Foster, R. C., *A Syllabus of the Life of Christ*
10. Godet, F., *Commentary on the Gospel of St. John*
11. Hendriksen, Wm., *New Testament Commentary, John,* Volumes 1 and 2
12. Johnson, B. W., *The People's New Testament with Notes,* Vol. 1
13. Lenski, R. C. H., *Interpretation of St. John's Gospel*
14. McGarvey, J. W., *The Fourfold Gospel*
15. McGarvey, J. W., *Lands of the Bible*
16. Robertson, A. T., *Word Pictures, The Gospel of John*
17. Trench, R. C., *Notes on the Miracles of Our Lord*
18. Westcott, B. F., *The Gospel According to St. John with Greek Text*

Texts, Versions, Lexicons:
1. Nestle, E., Novum Testamentum Grace Text
2. Authorized King James Version
3. American Standard Version
4. New Catholic Edition, Confraternity, Douay Version
5. The Amplified New Testament
6. The Authentic New Testament
7. The New Testament in Plain English
8. *Greek-English Lexicon,* Arndt and Gingrich
9. *Expository Dictionary of New Testament Words,* W. E. Vine